Philip Parker is a writer, consultant and publisher specialising in cartography as well as ancient and medieval history. He studied history at Trinity Hall, Cambridge, and is the author of *History of Britain in Maps* (2016), the *DK Eyewitness Companion Guide to World History* (2010), *The Northmen's Fury* (2014) and *The A-Z History of London* (2019).

He was the general editor of *Himalaya* (2013) and the award-winning *Great Trade Routes* (2010). As a publisher Philip ran The Times books list, including works on ancient civilisations and *The Times History of the World*. He lives in London with his partner and daughter.

THE British History Puzzle Book

THE British History Puzzle Book

Philip Parker

BRITISH LIBRARY

First published in 2021 by
The British Library
96 Euston Road
London NW1 2DB
www.bl.uk

Catalogue-in-Publication Data
A catalogue record for this book is available
from the British Library.

ISBN: 978 0 7123 5440 0

Project Editor: Christopher Westhorp
Design: Blok Graphic, London
Picture Research: Sally Nicholls
Printed and bound in Malta by
Gutenberg Press

Contents

Introduction

History, in its original sense, which derives from the Greek ´ιστορια, meaning an inquiry or investigation into what happened, has kept historians employed and their readers engaged ever since the Greek historian Herodotus wrote his *Histories* in the fifth century BC. In recounting the epic David-and-Goliath struggle between the Greek city states and the previously unbeatable might of the Persian Empire, Herodotus eschewed the tendency of previous writers to ascribe men's deeds, both heroic and vile, to the inspiration or provocation of the gods, in favour of an inquiry into what actually happened, and, where possible, establishing the thoroughly human motives for men's actions.

Inquiry, then, lies at the heart of history, even as the breadth of knowledge and the tools available to historians have increased in scope and sophistication over the ages. We now know, for example, considerably more than Herodotus ever did about the Achaemenid Empire, the would-be destroyers of Greek independence, through archaeology and a sprinkling of Persian sources. Yet it is still as necessary for modern historians – as it was for Herodotus – to ask what happened, who carried out the act, where it was done (and how) and only then to turn to the more difficult – and sometimes, particularly for the ancient period, almost inscrutable – question of why they acted as they did.

It is in this spirit of inquiry that it seems entirely appropriate to present British history through the medium of a puzzle book, setting almost 500 questions both to test reader's knowledge of our national history, from the everyday to the abstruse, each of those 'inquiries' acting as a jumping-off point for a little further exploration of the question's subject matter.

It is inescapable that a puzzle quiz book should deal in facts, the small change of the historian's trade, whose steady accumulation over time grows into a treasure of knowledge to be pored over, hoarded or shared as the mood dictates. History

Penda of Mercia defeats Oswald of Northumbria, the Queen Mary Psalter, 1310-20.

without facts (the who, the what and the where) is like a plot without characters, a paradigm devoid of examples, a charm-bracelet without charms, a spot marked as 'forest' on a map that has no trees.

Yet on their own facts are just shiny golden nuggets – alluring but unsatisfying, a feast without taste. That's where the historian comes in, to weave a story, using those facts as his thread to create a historical tapestry that suddenly makes sense (even though, in other hands, the story might be entirely different, and the 'sense' a different one). The *British History Puzzle Book* uniquely presents both the 'what' of history, through 42 question rounds testing readers' knowledge of both the mainstream and the picturesque alleyways of British history, and something of the 'why', with extended answers that do not present just a monosyllabic morsel to those hungry to know more, but provide background information setting the answer in context (as well as extra material which I happened to find intriguing or engaging as I went along).

Opposite page: Trade card for Cadbury's Cocoa, c.1885.

The question rounds are divided into various streams. The spine, which runs through the book, deals with various eras in British history, from the prehistoric, through the Romans, Anglo-Saxons, the Medieval (or Middle Ages), Tudors, Stuarts, the Victorians, World Wars and the modern day. It is accompanied by a series of thematic sections, posing teasing questions on subjects such as sport, medicine, literature, architecture, film, television and food, as well as dedicated rounds for Scotland, Wales and Ireland. Each round has a picture question, nearly all of which are illustrated with an image from the British Library's unique and rich collection of books and manuscripts. Three rounds are composed entirely of pictures, while the Answers section has further pictures, so readers can enjoy a visual as well as a verbal tour through British history. For those in search of something particularly puzzling, each round has a 'Genius Question', which presents an especially difficult challenge, while for those in need of an even more vigorous historical workout, there is a special anagrams and enigmas round, and three map rounds in which the answers are to be gleaned by poring over some of the British Library's stunning collection of beautiful maps.

Sometimes the answers to questions will be straightforward, at others they will involve an extra layer of complexity, such as linking what historical figures had in common (for example, 'What linked Aethelred the Unready, Henry I and Richard II?' - they all had two wives). Some questions involve solving anagrams: either straightforward ('Flit on, cheering angel, in another direction?' = 'Florence Nightingale' (an anagram of 'Flit on, cheering angel'); or more cryptic 'They castrated a messenger, must be mixed up'= Aethelred the Unread (an anagram of 'They neutered a herald').

In the end the joy of history is the discovery of the surprising and the unexpected, leavened with a reassuring touch of the familiar. I hope that within the pages of this book you will find a measure of both and that you will enjoy as much as I have wandering within the labyrinth of British history, pausing every so often to delight at images from its greatest national collection.

Philip Parker London July 2021

CADBURY'S COCOA

THE TYPICAL COCOA OF ENGLISH
MANUFACTURE ABSOLUTELY PURE-

(THE ANALYST)

NO CHEMICALS USED

(AS IN THE SO CALLED
PURE FOREIGN COCOAS)

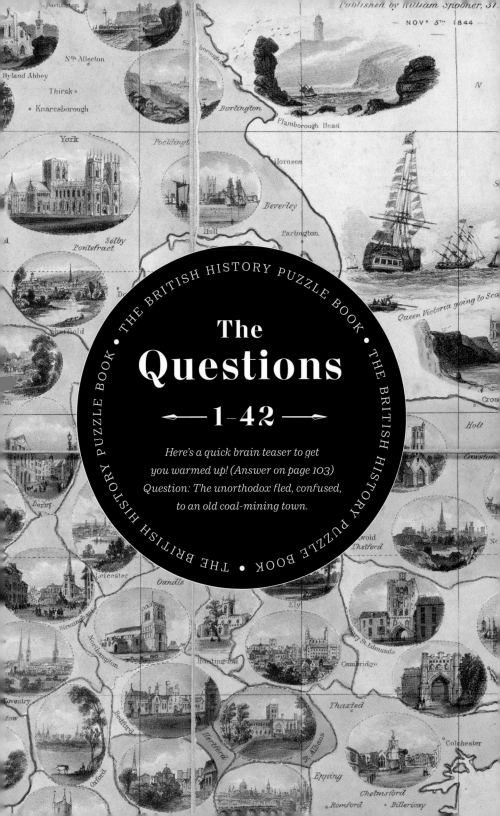

THE BRITISH HISTORY PUZZLE BOOK • THE BRITISH HISTORY PUZZLE BOOK • THE BRITISH HISTORY PUZZLE BOOK

The
Questions
◆—— 1-42 ——◆

Here's a quick brain teaser to get
you warmed up! (Answer on page 103)
Question: The unorthodox fled, confused,
to an old coal-mining town.

Elementals

1 | What is the longest river entirely in Wales?

2 | Which is Britain's wettest city?

3 | When and where was Britain's deadliest landslide?

4 | What knocked down 15 million trees?

5 | When did snow stop play?

6 | Why was July 1911 a good time to be in Eastbourne?

7 | What is the longest river in Scotland?

8 | When was the deadliest recorded storm in British history?

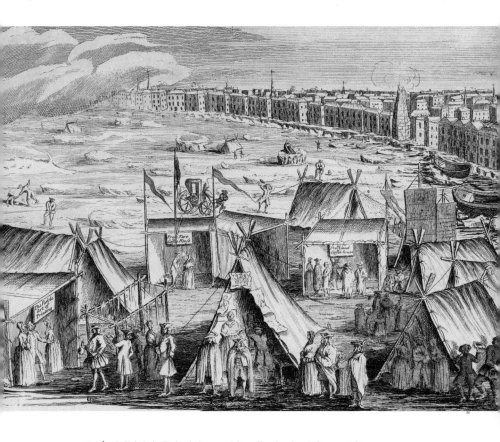

9 | Which is Britain's most landlocked settlement?

10 | What caused the abandonment of a performance of *La Traviata* on 5 December 1952?

11 | Which event is being shown here? (*picture above*)

| GENIUS QUESTION | What do Darcy, Evert, Fleur, Gavin, Julia, Klaas and Lilah have in common? |

Prehistoric & Romans

1   Where was the earliest evidence of habitation by human ancestors found in Britain?

2   What are the two main types of stone used at Stonehenge called?

3   What is particular about the inner chamber at the Newgrange passage tomb in Ireland?

4   Deva is the Roman name of which city?

5   Who said of the Romans: 'They make a desert and they call it peace'?

6   Who was the first Roman governor of Britain?

7   Of which tribe was Caratacus, the main British leader opposing the Roman invasion under Claudius, the ruler?

8   Hadrian's Wall was the main Roman wall in Britain; which was the other, to its north?

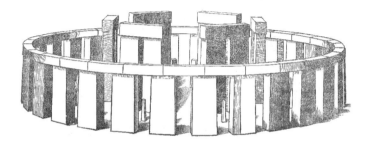

9 | Burgh Castle, Reculver, Pevensey and Portchester formed part of which Roman defence system?

10 | What were the 'Groans of the Britons'?

11 | Who is the deity pictured here? (*picture above*)

| GENIUS QUESTION | Which was the first Roman legion to be based in York? |

auentny

Brimidghan

most Illustrious and High borne PRINCE RUPE
RINCE ELECTOR, Second Son to FREDERI
ING of BOHEMIA, GENERALL of the HO
f His MAJESTIES ARMY, KNIGHT of the N
Order of the GARTER.

Battles in Britain

1 | What evil omen disturbed William of Normandy's retinue before the Battle of Hastings?

2 | At which battle was the dog pictured here the most unusual casualty? (*picture opposite*)

3 | Most defeated commanders flee after a battle. Who hid up an oak tree?

4 | Which British battlefield sounds like paradise?

5 | This place of battle sounds like it's associated with a cake?

6 | At which battle did the last British monarch to die in combat die?

7 | Which battle began the English Civil War?

8 | Which was the bloodiest battle fought on British soil?

9 | In which battle did a kingmaker die?

10 | Known as the 'Butcher', his most famous victory was delayed a day to avoid his birthday. Who was the general?

11 | Which battle received its name even before it was fought?

GENIUS QUESTION	What was the last land battle fought on British soil?

Kings & Queens *(part one)*

1 | What do the following kings have in common: Edmund of East Anglia, William II and Edward II?

2 | Who is the longest-reigning English king?

3 | What was unique about the coronation of Queen Elizabeth II?

4 | At whose coronation was the anthem 'Zadok the Priest' first performed?

5 | Which ruler was nicknamed 'the Peaceable'?

6 | Two English monarchs in succession were deposed and then restored to the throne. Who were they?

7 | How many English monarchs since the Norman Conquest have been unmarried?

8 | Who was the last sovereign who could not speak English?

9 | Which monarch was the oldest to accede to the throne?

10 | Who was the last British sovereign to be poisoned?

11 | Who are these two monarchs and what is the relationship between them? *(pictures opposite)*

GENIUS QUESTION	What do the following have in common: Eustace, Alphonso and Arthur?

Scotland *(part one)*

1 According to legend, the last Pictish king chose to die rather than reveal what secret?

2 Which famous Scot wrote: 'No society can surely be flourishing and happy, of which the far greater part of the members are poor and miserable.'?

3 Who was the first Scottish National Party (SNP) candidate to be elected MP to Westminster?

4 What is the most westerly point in Scotland (and the United Kingdom)?

5 What is the name of the personal tartan of Queen Elizabeth II?

GENIUS QUESTION	Where became part of Scotland as a result of a defaulted debt?

6 | Who was the first woman to matriculate at a Scottish university and which one?

7 | Who was nicknamed the 'Flying Scot'?

8 | Who were nicknamed the 'Flying Squadron'?

9 | Which Scot was buried in Westminster Abbey minus his heart?

10 | Which Scottish city has a cake named for it?

11 | After whom is this cathedral named? (*picture below*)

Wales

1 How many cathedrals are there of the Church in Wales?

2 When was the medieval Welsh independence leader Owain Glyndŵr captured by the English?

3 Near what town was the Roman legionary fort of Isca Augusta?

4 Which Welsh parliamentary constituency did Keir Hardie, Labour's first parliamentary leader, represent from 1900?

5 Where is Beatrix Potter's *Tale of the Flopsy Bunnies* set?

6 What is the name of the traditional historic barrier between England and Wales?

7 What is traditionally awarded to the winner of the two most prestigious competitions at the National Eisteddfodd?

8 Who was Twm Shon Cati?

9 Where did Amelia Earhart land when she became the first woman to fly across the Atlantic in 1928?

10 What proportion of people reported being able to speak Welsh in the 2011 census?

11 Identify the Welsh castles. (*pictures opposite*)

GENIUS QUESTION	What is Edgar Evans's main claim to fame?

A British Miscellany *(part one)*

1 | Which was the smallest 'rotten borough'?

2 | In which year was the English East India Company founded?

3 | What links William Wallace, King Charles I and Simon Fraser, 11th Lord Lovat?

4 | Who was the first person to die in a railway accident, and when?

5 | Where was the first place in Britain to suffer an air raid?

6 | Which king of England was crowned in France?

7 | A principal grandmother all mixed up digs up old bones?

8 | Which English defeat was said to have been foretold by Halley's Comet?

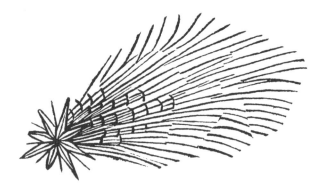

9 | During which war was the photo taken? (*picture above*)

10 | What did the Bishop of Nidaros in Norway apologise for in 1993?

11 | Which of the following is - or perhaps is not - an English invention: fish and chips; cricket; brewing beer with hops?

GENIUS QUESTION	The most common names of ruling kings in Britain have been Edward and Henry, with eight each. Which is the next most common monarch's name?

Britain in Pictures *(part one)*

1 | What do these three buildings have in common?

2 | Where is this bridge and what is unusual about it?

3 | Who was the original owner of this building?

4 | What was unusual about this Wimbledon final?

5 | The construction of which famous British landmark is shown opposite?

Cils vint as portes arpes
Deres deuent et de tranuers
Bien ont enpointe et bu bote
E bien petit dit e bu trole
Ue par force a la mehoni
E purrent fair pendre pu tou

Bialhez vous dit ceslui en sus
Qa par force ne serez plus
E serrez engine e demon
Euls qe serchi de corps vallen
Inic alast auant si seduiet
Tdur gardast le seue uint
Iui lide qe sist qreisin
E qan sil list ourisoun
Nut ad les spiritus rapele

Laws & Liberties

1   How many Tolpuddle Martyrs were deported to Australia?

2   Who cannot vote in United Kingdom national elections?

3   Which of the following is *not* illegal: wearing armour in Parliament; eating mince pies on Christmas Day; being drunk in a pub; riding on a bus while suffering from the plague?

4   Who and when was the last person imprisoned under the Witchcraft Act?

5   What percentage of adults could vote after the Great Reform Bill of 1832?

6   Who was the last person to be hanged for treason in the UK?

7   What is the age of criminal responsibility in England and Wales?

8   Who was the first person of African origin to vote in a British General Election?

9   When did divorce become legal in Northern Ireland?

10   What was the value of goods that triggered a death penalty for theft in the early nineteenth century?

11   What first for women did the person pictured here achieve? (*picture opposite*)

GENIUS QUESTION	How many clauses of Magna Carta are still in operation?

Sport

1. The only man to have captained England at both cricket and football, he was also the first English batsman to score a double century in a test. Who was he?

2. Which sport's founding rule 58 forbade the use of 'projecting nails' and 'iron plates'?

3. At what sport was Britain's first ever Olympic Gold Medal won?

4. Who was the youngest ever Wimbledon Ladies Singles champion?

5. On which course was the first golf Open Championship played?

6. At which sport has Britain been the unbeaten Olympic champions since 1900?

"WELL TAKEN SIR!"

THE HON. A. F. KINNAIRD

CAPTAIN OF THE OLD ETONIANS

THE ENCLOSURE

S. A. WARBURTON

CAPTAIN OF THE BLACKBURN OLYMPIC

CROSSLEY KICKING THE DECISIVE GOAL

THE PRESIDENT PRESENTING THE CUP

7	What did Edward II try to ban in 1314, and Edward IV in 1477?
8	What sport are these terms used in: biter, house and hog line?
9	Which is the only horse to have won the Grand National three times?
10	Which British Formula 1 driver has the most career victories?
11	What 'first' happened at this FA Cup Final? (*picture above*)

| GENIUS QUESTION | Which is the oldest football stadium in Britain? |

Anglo-Saxons & Vikings

1   What was the Anglo-Saxon unit of land measurement?

2   The death of which Anglo-Saxon king is depicted here? (*picture opposite*)

3   To what does Aethelred II's nickname 'the Unready' refer?

4   Of which kingdom was Offa, after whom Offa's Dyke is named, the ruler?

5   At which battle did Alfred the Great defeat the Danes in 878?

6   Which Scandinavian ruler invaded England in 1066?

7   Which pair of warriors were traditionally said to have led the first Anglo-Saxon settlement in England?

8   Which king, who called himself 'King of all Britain', defeated a Viking-Scottish coalition at Brunanburh in 937?

9   By what name is the Viking army that conquered Northumbria and East Anglia and invaded Wessex in the 860s usually known?

10   Which was the first Anglo-Saxon kingdom to convert to Christianity?

11   Who was the last Viking king of York?

GENIUS QUESTION	Cnut, the Danish king who ruled England from 1016 to 1035, married his predecessor's wife. Who was she?

The noble story, to putte in remembrance
Off seynt Edmond, mayde, martir, & kyng,
With his support, my style I wyl avaunce,
First to compyle affter my connyng
His glorious lyff, his birthe, & his crownyng,
And by dyscent how he that was so good,
Was in Saxonye born of the royal blood.

In rethoryk thoughe I have no flour,
nor no colours his story to enlumyne,
I dar nat faylle to do for socour,
nor to the muses that been in noumbre nyne,
But to this mayen his grace to enclyne,
To forthre my penne of that I wolde wryte,
his glorious lyff to translate, and endite.

For be the sentence of present eloquence
In Stacion, where he doth spreffye,
Grate fforthoryng more, than doth eloquence
Which of al corners, hath the regalye
for mornynge, nouther phylologye
To rethir kyng, and joyned in maryage
With oute grace, may have noon avauntage.

No grace hath power al corners to directe,
With oute whoom a vayleth no prudence,

Ireland

1 | What links Dublin and a popular Lancashire seaside town?

2 | Brian Boru famously won the Battle of Clontarf against the Viking Dubliners, but which Irish king fought (and died) on the other side against him?

3 | What was the nickname of Richard de Clare, Earl of Pembroke, who led the Anglo-Norman invasion of Ireland in 1170?

4 | What common word originates in an 1880 Irish protest against rising land rents and evictions?

5 | Where is the Northern Ireland parliament building and seat of the Northern Irish Assembly?

6 | Which Irish city was nicknamed 'Linenopolis'?

7 | Which famous Irish writer's mother also wrote under the pen-name Speranza?

8 | Where was the Book of Kells written?

9 | For which shipping line did the RMS *Titanic* sail?

10 | What was the nickname of Thomas Fitzgerald, 10th Earl of Kildare, who revolted against Henry VIII in 1534?

11 | Which famous writer is depicted here? (*picture opposite*)

GENIUS QUESTION	In which Olympic discipline has the Republic of Ireland won the most medals?

Faustin

Prime Ministers

1. Who was the longest-serving British prime minister?

2. What was the odd nickname of the Duke of Newcastle?

3. Both his aristocratic title and middle name contain a flower. Which prime minister?

4. Since 1900, only two politicians have held the position of Home Secretary for more than six years. Name the one who went on to become prime minister?

5. Which prime minister said, 'In youth the absence of pleasure is pain, in old age the absence of pain is pleasure'?

6. Who was the last prime minister never to have served as a member of the House of Commons?

7. What was Winston Churchill's first parliamentary seat?

8. Who had the shortest tenure as prime minister?

9. Who is the only prime minister to have been assassinated?

10. Who is the only prime minister to have been born outside Britain or British-controlled territory?

11. Under this prime minister an Act was passed to pay landlords to close down their pubs. Who was he? (*picture opposite*)

GENIUS QUESTION	Who is the only prime minister to have served under three monarchs?

Britain in Pictures *(part two)*

1 | What links the two places and the book?

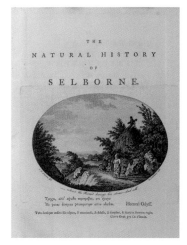

2 | What building is shown under construction here (*opposite*)?

3 | What links the authors of *A Journal of the Plague Year*, *Le Morte d'Arthur* and *The Tragicall History of the Life and Death of Doctor Faustus*?

4 | What links these three images?

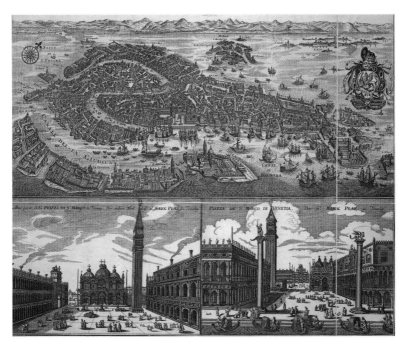

ROUND	SUBJECT	ANSWERS
15	MAPS	Pages 156–157

A Map of Britain

'Totius Britannaie Tabula Chorographica', c.1400

1	On an island and the map's shortest place name.
2	Light Welsh jacket?
3	The only canonised place on the map.
4	Find a place now lost.
5	Light a fire with this place?
6	Historic snack?
7	You might come across a true cross here.
8	The only three place names containing a body part.

Shire to Metropolis

1 | Why is Lincoln green and Coventry blue?

2 | How many Cinque Ports are there?

3 | What is Verulamium better known as?

4 | Which city's emblem is a bee?

5 | What does Cardiff's name mean?

6 | When did Berwick become part of England?

7 | What is the county town of Wiltshire?

8 | Which was the first British town to use full postcodes?

9 | Which town was once known as Eoforwic?

10 | On the outskirts of which city would you find Napoleon's nose?

11 | Can you identify these towns? (*pictures opposite*)

GENIUS QUESTION	Which is the smallest British city by population?

Land of Dreaming Spires

1 | Use a razor to rearrange crime family's grassy hill and draw conclusions about a philosopher?

2 | Where did Karl Marx write *Das Kapital*?

3 | Who said the life of man was 'solitary, poor, nasty, brutish and short'?

4 | What unusual death did the seventeenth-century philosopher and statesman Francis Bacon suffer?

5 | Which is Scotland's oldest university?

6 | The University of Cambridge was founded as a result of what event at the University of Oxford?

7 | At which British university can you study parapsychology?

8 | Who was known as the *Doctor Mirabilis?*

9 | Which famous philosopher donated his body to be put on public display?

10 | Which philosopher devised the 'trolley problem'?

11 | Identify this renowned nineteenth-century philosopher. (*picture opposite*)

GENIUS QUESTION	Who is the only British philosopher to win a Nobel Prize for Literature?

A British Miscellany *(part two)*

1   What was unusual about the election of Edward Legge as MP for Portsmouth in 1747?

2   What is the highest military rank to have been held by a British prime minister, and who held it?

3   In what decade was the first public bus service in Britain?

4   Which was the last prison in Britain to have a gallows?

5   What links the location of a 1217 copy of Magna Carta, an Anglo-Saxon rebel and the last prime minister to lead a majority Liberal government?

6   Who was the first character to speak in the long-running soap *EastEnders*?

7   What was the name of the 1536 popular uprising against Henry VIII's Dissolution of the Monasteries?

8   Where is Britain's most northerly cathedral?

9   How did James Somerset achieve fame?

10   Who wrote *A Vindication of the Rights of Woman*?

11   Place these authors in the order of their date of birth? *(pictures opposite)*

GENIUS QUESTION	What do the following have in common: the islands of Minorca, Corfu and Heligoland?

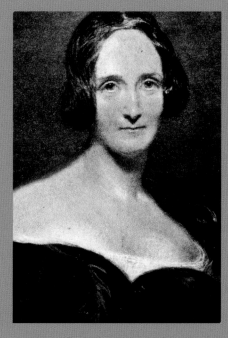

On the Move

1 | Which Roman road linked London and Lincoln?

2 | What was the first legally mandated speed limit on United Kingdom roads?

3 | Mother's gone to the gallows where she made cars?

4 | When was the driving test first introduced?

5 | In what century were locks first installed on a British waterway?

6 | What event is being shown here? (*picture below*)

7	William Robinson Clarke holds which transport 'first'?
8	What was the 'Flying Coach'?
9	Where was London's first airport?
10	In which decade did the first fatal accident involving a car take place?
11	In which years were the first and last passenger flights of Concorde?

GENIUS QUESTION	When was a Bluebird the fastest thing in Britain?

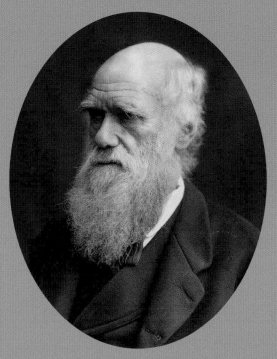

Making Money

1   What coin was nicknamed a 'tanner'?

2   What trading organisation was popularly known as John Company?

3   What is the highest rate of annual inflation officially recorded in the United Kingdom?

4   How many note-issuing banks are there in the United Kingdom?

5   What was the South Sea Bubble?

6   Which British monarch first issued gold coins?

7   Which of these was not a main export of Roman Britain: hoodies, hunting dogs or silver platters?

8   What was the name of the first-ever comprehensive land survey in Britain?

9   When was income tax first introduced?

10   Where was the original home of the London Stock Exchange?

11   What money theme connects these three famous British figures? (*pictures opposite*)

GENIUS QUESTION	What do the following have in common: Barclays Bank, Cadbury's Chocolate and Clarks Shoes?

Medieval, Tudors & Stuarts

1 | Place these kings in ascending order of the length of their reign: Henry II, Henry III, Henry IV.

2 | What position did Thomas Becket hold before becoming Archbishop of Canterbury?

3 | Wat Tyler and John Ball were leaders of which revolt?

4 | Where did Henry Tudor land on his way to defeating Richard III at Bosworth Field?

5 | Which rebel ended up working in the royal kitchens?

6 | Who was the commander of the English fleet against the Spanish Armada?

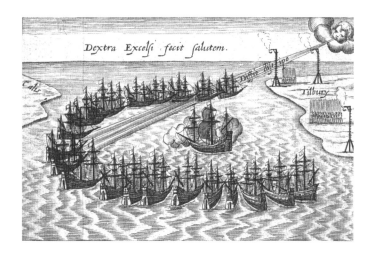

7	What was the 'Spanish match'?
8	Mashed up plant spray, mix up again to get a parliamentary expulsion.
9	What was the main battle of the 1689 Jacobite uprising?
10	When did the Dutch capture a royal Charles?
11	How did these men achieve infamy? (*picture above*)

GENIUS QUESTION	What is the 1549 rebellion in Devon and Cornwall against Henry VIII better known as?

Kings & Queens *(part two)*

1 | Which dynasty in English history has had the highest proportion of female monarchs?

2 | What were the nicknames of George I's mistresses, Ehengard Melusine von der Schulenburg and Sophia Charlotte von Kielsmanegg?

3 | Which British monarch was the youngest on accession to the throne?

4 | Which monarch was the first to style himself king of Britain?

5 | What is a Bretwalda and how many were there?

6 | Whose tomb is inscribed 'Pactum Serva' ('Keep the Promise')?

7 | Which monarch had two coronations in England?

8 | Which monarch had the most children?

9 | Who was Britain's first Christian monarch?

10 | Who was the last British king to succeed his father on the throne?

11 | What is unique about these monarchs? *(pictures opposite)*

GENIUS QUESTION	Which monarch was killed by 'a gentleman in velvet'?

Johannes Rey anglie gemuit

Henricus Rey anglie gemuit

The South Prospect of the Metropolitical Church of S.t Peters in York.

Buildings & Architecture

1 | Which architect designed Battersea Power Station?

2 | Which railway station is named after a Walter Scott novel?

3 | What is unusual about the Lawn building in Harlow?

4 | What is the largest, surviving Anglo-Saxon church in England?

5 | Which architect designed the Mind Zone at the Millennium Dome, the 2012 London Olympics Aquatics Centre and the Heydar Aliyev Centre in Baku, Azerbaijan?

6 | Which cathedral was begun by Bishop Walkelin in 1079?

7 | Who links Hereford Gaol, Buckingham Palace and the Royal Pavilion, Brighton?

8 | Which famous architect's first major building commission was the Sheldonian Theatre in Oxford?

9 | Where is the largest expanse of medieval stained-glass window in Britain?

10 | As part of what event was the Royal Festival Hall built?

11 | Place these cathedrals in the order in which they were built. (*pictures opposite*)

GENIUS QUESTION	Which British building was the first in the world to be air-conditioned?

Britain in Pictures *(part three)*

1 | What links these three images?

3 | One was the first Black Briton to achieve this and the other the first woman – to be a member of what?

R S

N. Littleton   Pebworth   Quenton   Stoure flu.

Middle Lyttleton   Brode marston   Stoke   Ilminton   P

S: Lyttleton   Cawhonyborn   Mickleton

Bradfron

Avon flu.   EVESHOLME   Churchhonyborn

PERSHOKE   Wikenford   Aston   Ebrighton

THE VALE OF EVESHOLME   Weston   CAMPDEN   Stratton

Elmeley   THE Hynton   Childes wican   Willersey   Saenbury   Bur

Bredon hill   Somerffeld aston   Bradwey   Paxford   Hangineafton   Todenham   Wulf

Sedgebarow   Buckland   Northwick   VIGORNIÆ PARS   Lemmyngton

Streufha   Overbury   Aston Underhill   Snowshill   Blockley   Batesford   Bart

Kemmerton   Brkford   Womington   Staunton   Morton   Che thury

Twinnyng   VIGOR. PARS   Dombleton   Stanewey   Toddinoton   henmershe   VIGOR PARS

Ripple   Washborn magna   Washborn pua   Aulfton   Staunton   Burton   fup mont.   o /e 1592

Bufhley   Myton   Teddenton   Alderton   Didbrok   VIGORNIÆ PARS   Longboro   Ewenlode   Caft

Afhburch   Oxendon   Dikfon   Stanley   Cutefdon   Cundecote   Bradwell   Tadfh

TEWKESBVRYE   Wulfton   Gretton   Halley   Farngcote   Templegytyng   Ouerfwell   Oddington   O

Forthhton   The Paffage   Lanale   Kobley   GE   Netherfwell   STOW ON THE

The Vineyard   WINCHCOMBE   Cundecote   WOWLD   Icombe

Chafeley   Tredington   Sudeley caft   Nethergityng   Naunton   Netherflaughter   Bledi

The hau paffage   Cleue   Pachby   Charleton   Ouerflaughter   Weke   Idb

Coffe court   Orchardftoke   pauncye   Hawlyng   Notgroue   Weftcote

Turley   Southin   Prefthurye   Semynton   Burton   Bifynton pua

Norton   Swindon   Reddenton   Coldafton

Hatheri   CHELTENHAM   Whittenton   Saperton   Broder ifyne   BERCERL

Wauelodehill   Sanethroft   Charleton regu   Dowdefwell   Shiptons   Durdene   PARS

Glocefter marfhe   Leckhington   Hafelton   Clapton   Barrington

Badgeworthe   Alefwood   Comptonabdale   Hampnet   Farmenton   Windrufhe   Barrinto   Wr

GLOCESTER   Churfon   Cobherley   Wythenton   N. LECHE   Sherbora

Newwork   Shrynton   Brockworth   Cowley   Set Iohns affhes   Stowell   Eaftenton   Windrufhe   Barrinto

Hemffed   Wytcombe   Churne flu.   Chadworth   Colnedeans   Aulfworthe

Quodfly   Vilonleonard   Cotes   Coulefborne   Comerogers   Colnealyns   Lechi flu.   Eftle

Matfon   Bidlip   Wowlde   Randcombe   Wynfton   Byburye   Bowthorp   Southorp

Waddon   Cranham   Elfton   N. Sirney   Colnealyns

Bruckthorp   Painfwicklodge   Syde   Wynfton   Ouerdantefourne   LECHLAI

Hardwrk   Hardwrk   Muffadyne   Badgende   Barnfley   Quennyton   Hathorp

Hafenton   Cotes-Wowlde   Netherduntefburye   Baunton   Peteramney   Faierford

Standyfh   Pitfcombe   Bufley   Edgeworth   Daglingworth   Holliwoodeamney   WILT

Stonehoufe   Pauntwick   Daglingworth   Stratton   Piefton   Meffhampton

Eaftington   Lypiate   Bufley   Ockelwood   CIRENCESTER al. CICITER   Harnell   Downeamney   Kemfford

L. eonardftanley   PROWDE   Saperton   Cotes   Pulton   Inj   Marfton   Caftleeaton

Woodchefter   Stroude flu.   Siddintons   Dryffeld   WILT

Radwick   Frampton   Torleton   S. Sarney   Laiton

MYNCHINHAMPTON   Rodmerton   Kemble   Sharncote   CREKELADE

Hilley   Auaning   Cheryton   Pole   Somerfordeanes

Bigfley   Cuckefton   Thamefis flu.

Viey   Afhley

Kingefcoit   Beuerftonenfe   Longnewton

The Newwork   Newmeton hagpath   TETBVRY

A Map of Gloucestershire

by Christopher Saxton, 1579

1 | Where did heaven fall to Earth in 2021?

2 | Where did a prince die and a rose emerge triumphant?

3 | Where sounds like an up and down murder?

4 | Where might be the most secret place on the map?

5 | The first was murdered, the second poisoned while under arrest, the third lost a crown. What place's duchy links this unfortunate trio?

6 | Old west town who, when mixed up, has a link with the band?

7 | Can you find the longest place name on the map?

8 | The opposite of sea? It's the only place you'll find this on the map.

Heroes & Heroines

1 | What is the inscription on the Victoria Cross?

2 | Where and when was this picture taken? (*picture opposite*)

3 | In what year was the George Cross first awarded?

4 | Who risked her life to save the crew of the SS *Forfarshire*?

5 | Who rescued his crew from Elephant Island?

6 | 'Come Quick, Engine Room Nearly Full' was whose last message?

7 | Who scored England's first goal in their 1966 World Cup Final victory?

8 | Which organisation was founded by Chad Varah in 1953?

9 | What did the author of *The Interesting Narrative of the Life of Olaudah Equiano* campaign to abolish?

10 | Whose life was immortalised in the 1955 film *Reach for the Sky*?

11 | Which British nurse was shot by the Germans in Brussels in 1915?

| GENIUS QUESTION | At which battle did Admiral Horatio Nelson lose the sight in his right eye? |

Food & Drink

1. Which cake did the UK government unsuccessfully try to class as a biscuit?

2. Excessive desire shriek makes breakfast dish?

3. When did the first Chinese restaurant open in Britain?

4. Which popular cake is named for a German principality?

5. When was the foodstuff being sold here first served in England? (*picture opposite*)

6. In what era of British history would you have been most likely to eat a dormouse?

7. What dessert sounds like a boy with measles?

8. Which of the following was not introduced to Britain as a foodstuff by the Romans: cherries, cucumber, almonds, lentils and rabbit?

9. What are the national dishes of Scotland, Wales and England?

10. What do the following have in common: lampreys and peaches?

11. When was Cheddar cheese first recorded?

GENIUS QUESTION	Which drink was described in 1674 as a 'little base, black, thick, nasty stinking nauseous puddle'?

Industry to Empire

1. Who was the prime minister at the time of the American Declaration of Independence?

2. What did the Black Act of 1723 try to stamp out?

3. What was *Catch Me Who Can*, showed off by Cornish mining engineer Richard Trevithick in London in 1808?

4. Who taught Charles Darwin taxidermy?

5. From whom did Empress Catherine the Great of Russia order a dinner service decorated with frogs in 1770?

6. Where was London's original Chinatown?

7. Whom did Edmund Burke call a 'captain-general of iniquity', 'spider of Hell' and 'a ravenous vulture devouring the carcasses of the dead'?

8. What was the name of Robert Owen's experimental mill intended to provide improved working conditions for labourers?

9. What are the defensive forts called that were built along the English coast to guard against an invasion from Napoleon's France?

10. What were the 'Captain Swing' riots?

11. What event is being depicted here? (*picture opposite*)

GENIUS QUESTION	What was first published on 1 January 1785?

London

1 Which is London's largest park?

2 Who first donated the pelicans in St James's Park?

3 Suite 212 in Claridge's was briefly the sovereign territory of which other country?

4 In what century was the White Tower of the Tower of London built?

5 Which famous novelist lived at 48 Doughty Street?

6	Which London street is named after a version of croquet?
7	How many London boroughs are there?
8	Who conducts the annual census of swans on the River Thames?
9	Which is the only London borough on both sides of the Thames?
10	What did the Greek entrepreneur Pasqua Rosée bring to London in 1652?
11	Which famous literary figure is buried in this church? (*picture below*)

GENIUS QUESTION	After which sovereign is King's Cross named?

Scotland *(part two)*

1   Where is the oldest building in Britain?

2   Who was the first woman elected to the Royal Astronomical Society?

3   Which Scottish mythological creature is half-seal, half-human?

4   Which Scottish foodstuff is famous for being square?

5   Which colonial venture almost bankrupted Scotland?

6   How many Scottish monarchs were from the House of Stewart?

7   Which song was inspired by the escape of Bonnie Prince Charlie?

8   Who is the only Scottish writer to have won the Commonwealth Writer's Prize Best Book Award?

9   Where was the most northerly Roman legionary fortress in Britain?

10   What unit of measurement is named for a Scot?

11   What significant position was this man the first to hold? (*picture opposite*)

GENIUS QUESTION	Which Scottish king died at Lumphanan?

A Map of Scotland & Islands

by James Dorret, 1750

1	Where is a dyke not a dyke?
2	Where might you find a cattle market?
3	Two infant Scottish monarchs were born at a palace here. Where is it?
4	Scotland's ratification of the 'Auld Alliance' took place here.
5	The only place name with just three vowels and one consonant.
6	One letter away from a currency?
7	Not any of two Norsemen mixed up?
8	Hill with a pub?

Art & Music

1 | Who is the only musician to have been given a state funeral at Westminster Abbey?

2 | During the reign of which English monarch was the Wilton Diptych painted?

3 | Which Flemish painter became principal painter to Charles I and his court?

4 | Which British painter produced a series of works known as *A Rake's Progress*?

5 | *Mr and Mrs Andrews* is one of the most famous portraits by which painter?

6 | *Rain, Steam and Speed* is one of the first British artistic evocations of the age of the train. Who painted it?

7   Of which artistic movement were William Holman Hunt and John Everett Millais leading members?

8   Part of which composer's *Coronation Ode* for King Edward VII has since become a regular feature of the Last Night of the Proms?

9   What links John Lennon and a Black circus composer?

10   Which famous composer was director of music at St Paul's Girls School in London?

11   The première of which piece of music is shown here? (*picture above*)

GENIUS QUESTION	Who was the first British artist to paint a zebra?

The Victorians

1 | When did 'Mr Peaceful' almost become the cause of a war?

2 | To where was the first Thomas Cook excursion in 1845?

3 | Who was the 'Window of Windsor'?

4 | Which intrepid Victorian traveller wrote *Unbeaten Tracks in Japan*?

5 | For what did the Chartists campaign in the 1840s?

6 | When were the Corn Laws repealed?

7 | Where did the Zulus inflict a devastating defeat on a British force in 1879?

8 | What organisation did William Booth found in 1865?

9 | Which famous children's tale originally took place 'Under Ground'?

10 | In what year did Queen Victoria become Empress of India?

11 | This Victorian invention remained in use for over 125 years: what is it and who was the inventor? (*picture opposite*)

GENIUS QUESTION	Which famous Victorian poet wrote 'In the Bleak Midwinter'?

Symposium Gastronomicum
of all Nations.

Crème à la
Jenny Lind

eman
as been
om acute
body and
utterly
attend to
ficial
s" for the
weeks

Maladies & Medicine

1 | What was the 'sweating sickness'?

2 | Where was Britain's first successful heart transplant carried out?

3 | What did the Anatomy Act of 1832 make legal?

4 | What was unusual about Jane Sharp's 1671 work *The Midwives Book*?

5 | Where, traditionally, did the Black Death first arrive in England?

6 | Snow and water pump: what is the connection?

7 | During which war did Mary Seacole achieve fame as a nurse?

8 | Who gave the first vaccination for smallpox?

9 | What antiseptic did pioneer James Lister first use?

10 | What notable contribution did Joseph Bazalgette make to London's public health?

11 | From which book is this illustration taken? (*picture opposite*)

GENIUS QUESTION	What disease did James Lind find a cure for in 1757?

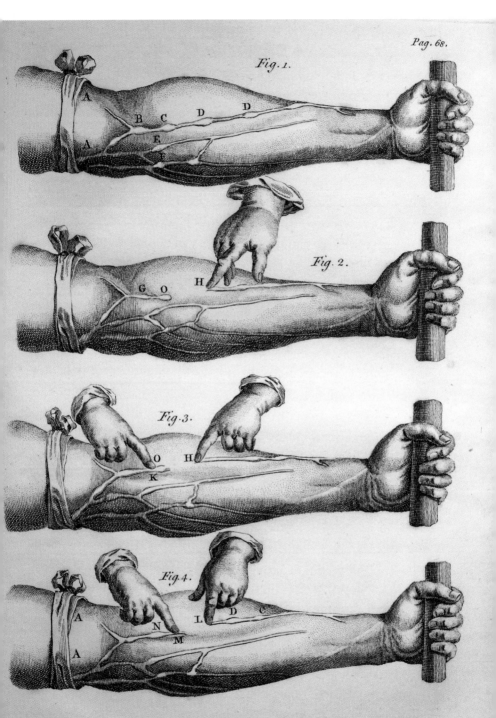

Fig. 1.

Fig. 2.

Fig. 3.

Fig. 4.

I. Mynde Sc.

A British Miscellany *(part three)*

1 | What is attainder and who was the last person to be attainted?

2 | Which composer directed a long-running music festival at Aldeburgh in Suffolk?

3 | Whom did Adolf Hitler call 'the most dangerous woman in Europe'?

4 | Which monarch has an animal named after them?

5 | What is the longest road in the United Kingdom?

6 | Which seventeenth-century philosopher wrote *Two Treatises on Government*?

CARIBBEAN CARNIVAL SOUVENIR

Televised by B.B.C. Television
Organised by the West Indian Gazette

SEYMOUR HALL — PRICE TWO SHILLINGS

FEBRUARY SIXTH

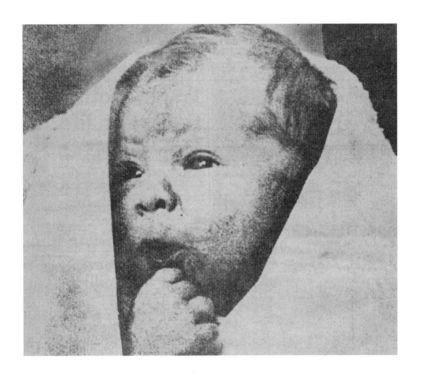

7	When was the first Notting Hill Carnival held?
8	Who was the first winner of the Booker Prize?
9	When did the Isle of Man become part of the United Kingdom?
10	Who was Britain's first MP of South Asian origin?
11	What first did this baby achieve in 1978? (*picture above*)

| GENIUS QUESTION | What did eighteenth-century clergyman Edward Stone discover? |

War & Peace, Britain 1901–45

1 In which year was universal female suffrage established in the United Kingdom?

2 Which was the first 'garden city' in Britain?

3 What was the purpose of the 1931 statute of Westminster?

4 'April is the cruellest month' is the first line of which poem?

5 Enliven Herbal Claim mixed up and waving a piece of paper?

6 What, during World War Two, was Pluto?

YOUR COUNTRY NEEDS "YOU"

7 What was the maiden name of Mrs Simpson, whom Edward VIII abdicated to marry in 1936?

8 How did Dorando Pietri achieve fame at the 1908 London Olympics?

9 What was unusual about the arrest of the poisoner Dr Crippen in 1910?

10 In World War One, what was the Shell Crisis?

11 Where is this and what special role does it play in Britain's recreational history? (*picture above*)

| GENIUS QUESTION | Which was the first British battleship sunk in World War Two? |

Ways with Words

1. On which day is Geoffrey Chaucer's *The Parlement of Foules* set?

2. Under what pseudonym did Charlotte Bronte first publish *Jane Eyre*?

3. What was remarkable about *The Travels of Dean Mahomet*, published in 1794?

4. Breaking his spectacles all scrambled up leads to great expectations?

5. Who was the first English woman to earn her living from writing?

6. Which author dedicated his novel about a demon writing to his nephew to the novelist J.R.R. Tolkien?

7 Which novelist set his stories in a fictional 'Wessex' based on southwestern England?

8 Which novelist's last words were, 'Go Away, I'm alright!'?

9 The adventures of which character is the author of the play *Wurzel-Flummery* better known for?

10 The epitaph 'Blessed be the man that spares these stones, And cursed be he that moves my bones' appears on the grave of which British writer?

11 What do these two authors have in common? (*pictures below*)

<table>
<tr><td>GENIUS QUESTION</td><td>Which Nobel Prize-winning author wrote Savrola: A Tale of the Revolution in Laurania?</td></tr>
</table>

112

For the Benefit of Mr. SIDDONS.

This prɛfent FRIDAY, October 2d. 1778,
Will be prefented a TRAGEDY, call'd

HAMLET.

(With ALTERATIONS.)

Hamlet (for this night, by Defire) Mrs. SIDDONS,
King by Mr. PLATT,
Horatio by Mr. SIDDONS,
Polonius by Mr. CONNOR,
Laertes by Mr. KEMBLE,
Marcellus by Mr. WHYTE,
Rofencraus by Mr. HAMMERTON,
Guildenftern by Mr. PHILLIPS, Player King by Mr. LEWIS,
Lucianus by Mr. BATES, Bernardo by Mr. BANKS,
GRAVEDIGGERS,
By Mr. POWELL, and Mr. LAKE,
Ghoft by Mr. RUNDELL,
Queen by Mrs MONTAGUE,
Player Queen by Mifs DILLON,
Ophelia by Mrs. VINCENT.

With SONGS between the Acts,
By Mr. TANNETT:

To which will be added a Farce [never perform'd here] call'd, THE

FEMALE OFFICER.

[Written by Mr. KEMBLE.]

Timothy Tamarind Mr. CONNOR, Frederic Mr. POWELL,
Sir Anthony Ancient Mr. PLATT, Jack Finikim Mr. BATES,
Spencer Mr. SIDDONS, Servant Mr. BANKS,
Fanny Mrs. KNIVETON, Charlotte Mrs. MONTAGUE.

Tickets to be had of Mr. Siddons, No. 11, Dawfon Street; at Mr. Smith's Navigation
Shop, Pool Lane; and at the Theatre, where Places for the Boxes may be taken.

Stage & Screen

1 | Where was the first home of the BBC?

2 | Where was the first purpose-built cinema in Britain?

3 | In which theatre does *The Mousetrap*, Britain's longest-running theatrical production, play?

4 | What is said to have caused Shakespeare's first Globe Theatre to burn down in 1613?

5 | Who was the first British actor to win an Oscar?

6 | In what year was the long-running science fiction TV series *Doctor Who* first broadcast?

7 | Which eighteenth-century actor also became famous as the manager of the Drury Lane Theatre?

8 | What was Scotland's first public theatre?

9 | In which year did the radio soap opera *The Archers* begin transmission?

10 | Who is the only singer to have performed more than one James Bond title theme?

11 | What is the unique relationship between Hamlet and Läertes in this production? (*picture opposite*)

GENIUS QUESTION	In the Ealing comedy *Passport to Pimlico*, which European state did the London suburb declare itself a part of?

Modern Britain

1   How many Old Etonian prime ministers have there been since 1945?

2   At which port did the HMT *Empire Windrush*, carrying the first Caribbean migrants, dock in 1948?

3   Who is the only British Asian football player to have represented his country at international level?

4   In which year did General de Gaulle veto British membership of the European Economic Community (EEC) for the second time?

5   What was the Skylon?

6	Who gave the 'Winds of Change' speech?
7	'That Great Charmer?' – some may think you're getting mixed up with a ferrous dame.
8	In what year did The Beatles break up?
9	Who is the only woman to have served as Speaker of the House of Commons?
10	In what year was the Good Friday Agreement signed?
11	What parliamentary first does this MP hold? (*picture above*)

GENIUS QUESTION	Which was the first British city to be a European Capital of Culture?

Inventions & Technology

1 What invention appeared for the first time in 1868 outside the Houses of Parliament?

2 Who invented the algorithm?

3 What was first demonstrated in a Soho attic in 1926?

4 What navigation conundrum did John Harrison solve in 1769?

5 What useful construction material is named for its inventor, John Loudon McAdam?

6 What problem was Humphry Davy's Davy Lamp designed to solve?

7 | Who invented the collapsible baby buggy?

8 | Who invented the 'world wide web' in 1989?

9 | What did Peter Higgs theorise in 1964, but whose existence was only proved in 2012?

10 | Who invented the Anglepoise lamp in 1932?

11 | Why might this cause a scientist to reflect? (*picture above*)

| GENIUS QUESTION | What useful mathematical innovation did Robert Recorde invent in 1557? |

A British Miscellany (*part four*)

1 | When was the anthem 'God Save the King' first sung in public?

2 | What was the *White Ship*?

3 | What was the name of the body that organised forces' entertainment during World War Two?

4 | Which ballistic missile system preceded Polaris and Trident as Britain's main nuclear deterrent system?

5 | Why was the Battle of Waterloo not front-page news on *The Times*?

6 | Which king of Norway led the last Viking/Scandinavian raid against Britain?

7 | Until when was it illegal for a Catholic to succeed to the British throne?

8 | Confused Peruvian beasts of burden gunned it down, was it a composer?

9 | Name the first British writer to win the Nobel Prize for Literature?

10 | What links a royal estate, a military academy and a place that gave its name to a popular snack?

11 | From match girl's strike to Indian independence, who was this radical nineteenth-century activist? (*picture opposite*)

GENIUS QUESTION	Which war involving Britain was named after a body part?

Anagrams & Enigmas

1   Add the number of steps in a Hitchcock thriller to the number of nights in a translation by Richard Burton and divide by the number of King Edwards there have been since 1066.

2   If Henry VIII was his father's son, why did he claim that the wife of his father's son could not be his wife?

3   Take the number of Dodie Smith's dogs, add the number in Jerome K. Jerome's boat, and divide by the number of cities in a Dickens' tale.

4   Take the number of years between Bannockburn and Flodden Field and subtract the number of years in the title of a Walter Scott novel.

5   Rough metal patch in a ten-event competition gives a first in another sport.

6   Get mixed up by turning up at a Caribbean island uninvited, but you'll be used to solving mysteries.

7   It is five minutes to midnight on 2 September, in ten minutes it will be five minutes after midnight on 14 September. How is this possible?

8   Woodwind instrument throws a rider, but its arrangement makes a residence fit for a queen.

9   Wellington's consonants and the vowels of Napoleon make a settlement for which ship?

| GENIUS QUESTION | Cracking 1, 12, 1, 14, 20, 21, 18, 9, 14, 7 will solve an enigma. |

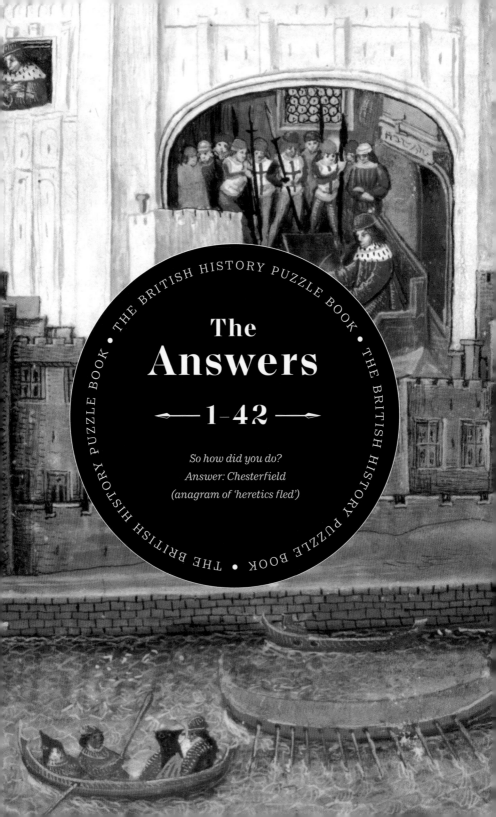

The
Answers
←— 1-42 —→

So how did you do?
Answer: Chesterfield
(anagram of 'heretics fled')

Elementals

1

The River Tywi (or Towy). At around 75 miles (121km) in length, and famed for its salmon and the sea trout which breed in its many tributaries, the Tywi is the longest river whose course is wholly within Wales. Four other Welsh rivers – the Severn, Wye, Teme and Dee – are longer, but run partly through England. Rising in the Cambrian hills, the Tywi runs southwest through Carmarthenshire before it reaches the sea at Carmarthen Bay, where its estuary is guarded by the brooding bulk of the twelfth-century Norman Llansteffan Castle.

2

Cardiff. The Welsh capital endures an average of 1,152 millimetres (45.3in) of rain each year, roughly twice the level of London (at 557 millimetres/22in). It is not quite the rainiest region in the United Kingdom, however, which is Argyllshire in Scotland, where a soaking 2,219 millimetres (87.4in) of rain falls annually. The wettest places tend to be in the west, because mountains there cause the prevailing westerly winds to rise, which precipitates rainfall. The rainiest year on record was 2000, when the level in the UK reached 1,337.3 millimetres (52.6in), around 15 per cent above the long-term average.

3

Aberfan, near Merthyr Tydfil, on 21 October 1966. In the days before the landslide heavy rain saturated large slag heaps of mining waste near the village of Aberfan. Early that morning one of them began to slip, sending a cascade of 140,000 cubic yards (107,000 cubic metres) of slurry down onto the Pantglas Junior School just as lessons were beginning. Of the 144 dead, 116 were children at the school, and five of the 28 adults their teachers. The worst landslide in England

was in Lewes, Sussex, after an appalling blizzard and high winds caused a massive snowdrift to form on the edge of the town's Cliffe Hill on Christmas Eve 1836. Further snow over the next two days destabilised the drift and in the mid-morning of 27 December the drift collapsed onto a row of workers' cottage beneath the cliff, killing eight people. In 1840 a pub was built on the site of the ruined cottages, called the Snowdrop Inn.

4

The Great Storm of 1987. The weather forecast for 16 October 1987 had been for winds and heavy rain, but the BBC's weather presenter Michael Fish famously reassured a viewer worried about rumours of a hurricane on the way, 'Don't worry, there isn't'. In the event, winds of up to 115mph (185kmph) were recorded at Shoreham as the south of England received a battering that killed 18 people, caused around £2 billion of damage and knocked down 15 million trees, including six of the famous 'Coronation Oaks' of Sevenoaks.

5

2 June 1975. At the start of June 1975, as heavy rain fell, temperatures dropped, causing the downpour to turn into sleet, and then heavy snow. The freak summer snowstorm interrupted the Essex vs Kent County Cricket match underway at Colchester, and the match between Derbyshire and Lancashire at Buxton was abandoned after an inch of snow carpeted the outfield. Snow fell as far south as London, the first time it had been recorded in June since 1888, causing havoc on public transport. Arguably, things were worse in the last Ice Age, which ended 11,000 years ago, but Britain was hardly inhabited then and cricket was some millennia short of being invented.

6

The town enjoyed the sunniest month in British weather history. Eastbourne in Sussex basked in nearly 384 hours of sunshine in July 1911. The month was in general a bright one over the south of England, with many locations recording an average of ten hours of sunshine each day as part of a heatwave that lasted four months, seeing temperatures rise as high as 36 degrees C and making the coronation of George V on 22 June a distinctly sticky affair. Eastbourne continues to vie with its south coast neighbours for the title of Britain's sunniest town, with an average of 1,888 hours annually over the last 30 years, as against 1,920 for Bognor Regis and 1,871 for Hastings.

7

The River Tay. At 115 miles (185km) in length from its source near Oban to its mouth on the North Sea between Broughty Ferry and Tayport, the Tay is also the seventh-longest river in the United Kingdom. An important habitat for salmon, otters, lampreys and the freshwater pearl mussel, the largest settlement along the river's course is Dundee with a population of 148,000. The most historic is Dunkeld, which was a centre of early Scottish Christianity in the eighth century and in the ninth century became the capital of Kenneth McAlpin, the King of

Dal Ríada, who conquered the Picts in 850 to form the kingdom of Alba, the forerunner of the united Scottish kingdom.

8

The Great Storm of 1703. The autumn of 1703 had seen weeks of high winds and rain, and then on the night of 7 December 1703 a cyclone smashed through the country from the coast of Wales to the Midlands and southern England. It was memorably described by the novelist Daniel Defoe in his 1704 book *The Storm*, in which he calls it 'the Greatest and the Longest Storm that ever the World Saw'. Although it may not have been as severe as some others in purely meteorological terms, the damage it caused was devastating. It was said that the winds had been so strong that a cow was even blown into a tree, it rained fish in St James's Park in London as they were swept out of the ponds there, and somewhere between 8,000 and 15,000 people were killed, including 6,000 sailors.

9

Coton in the Elms, Derbyshire. The village, of 896 people, is 70 miles (113km) from the coast at Fosdyke Wash in Lincolnshire, White Sands in Cheshire and Westbury-on-Severn in Gloucestershire. The precise geographical centre of England, calculated in 2002 by the Ordnance

View of Dunkeld on the River Tay, 1813.

Survey, is at Lindley Hall Farm in Fenny Drayton in Leicestershire.

10

Smog. Britain's cities, hosting heavy industry and populations that burned wood and coal for fuel, had long suffered from severe air pollution and periodic smogs. On 5 December 1952 an anticyclone led to a blanket of cold air settling over London in which sulphur dioxide, carbon dioxide and smoke particles coagulated to form a choking, swirling green soup of smog – 12,000 people died in its suffocating embrace. That evening the smog tendrils infiltrated a showing of *La Traviata* at Sadler's Wells, and as the audience choked and the stage became obscured, the performance was abandoned. In the aftermath of the Great Smog, a Clean Air Act was passed in 1956 that abolished the most polluting practices and made such 'peasoupers' a thing of the distant (and hazy) past.

11

The Frost Fair of 1739. Before the demolition in 1831 of the medieval London Bridge, its piers tended to retard the flow of the Thames. This and the comparatively cold climatic conditions in the seventeenth and eighteenth century (known as the 'Little Ice Age') meant that the river periodically froze over in its central reaches. This allowed the holding of Frost Fairs, with sales booths, spectacles and skating on the ice-bound sections. Between 1607 and 1814 there were seven major Frost Fairs, one of the greatest of which was in 1739, when the river was frozen for nearly two months, towards the end of which a section of ice gave way, and tents and several people were sucked into the icy waters. The very last Frost Fair was in 1814, during which an elephant actually walked on the frozen river.

Genius Question

They are the UK storm names for the 2020-21 season. Since 2015, the UK Met Office (in partnership with Met Éireann in Ireland and KNMI of the Netherlands) has followed the practice across the other side of the Atlantic since the 1950s in pre-naming storms for a given year. The storm names are allocated in alphabetical order (with the exception of Q, U, X, Y and Z), alternating male and female names picked from a list of the most popular submitted by the public the previous year. Previously used names are discounted, as are those not regarded as authentic names (thus there will be no Storm Baldrick for the *Blackadder* character), and where a storm begins its journey in the United States it retains its American designation.

'Evening Scene on Vauxhall Bridge', an illustration by Yoshio Markino of London smog, from *The Colour of London*, 1907.

Prehistoric & Romans

1

Happisburgh in Norfolk. A scattering of a few dozen flint tools on an eroding Norfolk beach at Happisburgh are evidence of the earliest hominin (or human ancestral) settlement in Britain. Those who discarded the tools, who were probably members of a species called *Homo anteccessor*, lived around 800,000 years ago, at a time when the climate, which had been a little warmer than today, was beginning to cool – making food scarcer, and predators such as sabre-toothed tigers hungrier. Four years after the tools were found in 2010, archaeologists identified a set of footprints found at low tide as dating from the same era. They were left by at least five individuals, including one adult male and several children, the first direct evidence of the earliest inhabitants of the British Isles.

2

Bluestones and Sarsen stones. The complex stone circle at Stonehenge, whose origins lie around 3000 BC, but whose main stone settings date from about 2500 BC is composed of rings of massive sarsen stones, around 25 tons in weight, and smaller bluestones, each weighing about 2-3 tons. There were originally about 80 sarsens, which were probably quarried in the Marlborough Downs, around 19 miles (30km) away, and a roughly equal number of bluestones, whose origins lie in the Preseli Hills in southwest Wales, some ten times that distance. The effort required to move them must have been prodigious and it is still unclear to archaeologists quite how Neolithic peoples managed the feat.

3

The rays of the rising sun light it up on the Winter Solstice. Built around 3200 BC, the chamber-

passage tomb at Newgrange in County Meath is one of Ireland's most important prehistoric monuments. Composed of a mound surrounded by kerbstones within which a 62-foot-long (19-m) stone-lined passage leads into several chambers, which may originally have been tombs, Newgrange's alignment was carefully chosen by its builders, such that at dawn on the Winter Solstice a ray of light penetrates through a 'roof-box' opening, illuminating the innermost chamber for just over a quarter of an hour. This phenomenon clearly originally had a religious significance, and it now draws tens of thousands of applicants for the 60 places available each year to witness it. There are no refunds, however, in the case of cloudy weather, a not-uncommon problem on a late-December Irish morning.

4

Chester. With its position at the highest navigable point on the River Dee, the site of Chester was one of considerable strategic importance and around AD 70 the Romans built a legionary fortress there, garrisoned by the II Adiutrix Victrix Legion. Around AD 90 the II Adiutrix was moved away and replaced with the XX Valeria Victrix, which had previously garrisoned Viroconum (Wroxeter). A settlement grew up on the outskirts of the fort, in part made up of families of the legionaries (who, in theory, were not allowed to be married, and so could not have their wives and children inside the fort itself). By now the fort had acquired the name Deva Victrix (or 'Victorious Deva') and the normal trappings of Roman urban life, such as baths and an amphitheatre, and probably remained a military base until the late fourth century. The modern city owes its name to a corruption of the Latin word *castrum*, meaning 'fort'.

5

Calgacus, leader of the Caledonii. By the early
AD 80s, Julius Agricola, the Roman governor of
Britain, had crushed the last opposition to Roman
rule in North Wales, and then sent his legions
into what is now Scotland, establishing a series
of forts along the line of the Forth of Tay. Hard
fighting in AD 82, as native resistance stiffened,
was led by Calgacus, chieftain of the Caledonii,
who assembled a formidable coalition against
the Romans. The following year Calgacus was
pushed back into the Highlands and made a last
stand at a place called Mons Graupius (which
has not been identified). Before the battle he
made a speech – or, rather, the Roman historian
Tacitus put a speech into his mouth – declaring
that the Roman strategy was to 'make a desert
and they call it peace'. The next day his host was
defeated; Agricola, unusually, put the non-citizen
auxiliaries into the front line instead of the
better-trained legionaries. British resistance was
broken, and the Romans marched even further
north, possibly as far as Inverness, while their
commander sent a fleet that sailed around the
Orkneys, the furthest point north ever reached by
Roman forces.

6

Aulus Plautius. Although Julius Caesar had led
two Roman invasions of Britain, in 55 and 54
BC, his legions withdrew on both occasions after
short campaigns. The successful invasion in AD
43 was the work of the Emperor Claudius who,
as a non-military man, was in need of a success
to boost his reputation. He appointed Aulus
Plautius, who had been legate of Pannonia,
to lead it and the four legions which made up
the expedition (numbering over 20,000 men)
landed somewhere near Richborough in Kent,
fought their way across the Medway and then
stormed what is now Colchester, chief centre of
the anti-Roman resistance. Claudius, who did
not accompany the initial invasion, found time
to reach Colchester just before it fell, so that
he could bask in Plautius's reflected glory. He
rewarded his general with the first governorship
of the new Roman province. By the time he was

recalled to Rome three years later, possibly to
avoid his star rising too high and threatening the
emperor, Plautius had pushed Roman control as
far as a line from Exeter to the Humber.

7

The Catuvellauni. Caratacus succeeded his father
Cunobelinus – the 'Cymbeline' of Shakespeare's
play – as king of the Catuvellauni around AD 40 at
a time the tribe had expanded from its heartlands
around its capital at St Albans to dominate
neighbouring tribes such as the Trinovantes
of Suffolk and Essex and the Dobunni of
Gloucestershire. With such sway in the south of
England, Caratacus was the obvious choice as
leader to oppose the Roman invasion in AD 43
and he fought long and ably, but after the loss of
Colchester he was forced to flee. Taking refuge in
North Wales, he was accepted as chieftain by the
Ordovices and Silures, leading their resistance to
Roman encroachment until his final defeat in AD
50. He escaped to the territory of the Brigantes,
in what is now Yorkshire, but Cartimandua, their
queen, betrayed him and he was captured, taken
to Rome and paraded in a triumph celebrating
Claudius's conquest of Britain. His demeanour
impressed the emperor so much he did not suffer
the expected fate of execution and was allowed to
live the rest of his life in obscurity in Italy.

8

The Antonine Wall. Hadrian's Wall, the
impressive barrier of stone and turf, studded
with forts, which stretched the 80 Roman miles
(73 miles/117km) from Wallsend on the Tyne
in the east to Bowness-on-Solway in the west
looked set, when built in AD 122, to mark the
definitive frontier of Roman Britain. Yet, after
Hadrian's death in 138, his successor Antoninus
Pius decommissioned the wall and sent the
legions north to build a new turf barrier along the
narrower Clyde-Forth isthmus. It is unclear why
he did so – although at 37 miles (60km) it was a
shorter length to defend than Hadrian's Wall – and
it may simply have been the need to gain an easy
military victory by the short advance northwards.
By the early 160s, however, the Antonine Wall

and its new complement of forts had themselves been abandoned and the frontier line returned to Hadrian's Wall, to remain there until the end of the Roman province some 250 years later.

9

The Forts of the Saxon Shore. Although the Roman provinces in Britain (two after Septimius Severus divided it in 211, and later four) remained relatively untroubled, save for occasional raids from unconquered Scotland, as the third century proceeded the situation darkened. Raids by Picts, Irish pirates and from across the North Sea in what is now the northern Netherlands, Germany and Denmark became more common. To face them the Romans built a series of forts along what had been the hitherto undefended southeastern coast. Beginning with the early third-century forts at Brancaster, Caister and Reculver, further strongpoints were added at Lympne, Pevensey, Portchester, Walton, Burgh Castle, Bradwell-on-Sea and within the earlier Claudian-era fort at Richborough, until the system was complete by around 300. They were then progressively

abandoned, until by 380 most were deserted, with Pevensey and Portchester surviving the longest (being still in use in the early fifth century). Both also later housed medieval castles, and Pevensey was used as a prisoner-of-war camp in the early nineteenth century for French soldiers captured during the Napoleonic Wars.

10

An appeal to the Romans to reoccupy Britain. The last Roman troops had left Britain in 407, following the usurper Constantine III to France (where he was ultimately defeated), and they never returned. Three years later, British leaders expelled the Roman civilian administration. Then, as Anglo-Saxon raids began to mount and the post-Roman landscape proved more lethal than liberating, the British leaders sent a final desperate appeal to 'Agidius' (probably Aetius, the *magister militum*, or senior Roman military commander). Penned around 446 to 454 the

View of Portchester Castle, engraving by Samuel Buck, 1733.

letter, which became known as the Gemitus Britannorum ('Groans of the Britons'), laments that: 'The barbarians drive us to the sea, the sea drives us to the barbarians.' It was in vain. No help came. Rome itself fell to the barbarians less than 30 years later, and England, now left to its own devices, was gradually conquered by Anglo-Saxon invaders.

11

Mithras. Mithras became the subject of one of a number of mystery cults in the early Roman Empire; the cult's secrets were only open to adherents and knowledge of its rites was generally subject to advancement through a cult hierarchy. The central deity of Mithraism may have been imported from Persia, where he was a solar god, and the god of oaths and loyalty in the Zoroastrian pantheon. In his Roman incarnation, which began to spread in the early second century AD, he became tied to a cult of imperial loyalty and was especially popular in the army. The central ritual seems to have been the sacrifice of a bull, from whose blood the moon and the stars were reborn. This altar stone, showing Mithras in a Phrygian cap, was unearthed in York's Micklegate district in 1776. The *mithraeum*, or Mithras temple, was normally an underground cavern, where acts of worship were held by the seven grades of adherent: *corax* (raven), *nymphus* (groom), *miles* (soldier),

leo (lion), *perses* (Persian), *heliodromus* (sun courier) and *pater* (father). Because Mithraism was especially popular in the army, *mithraea* have often been found associated with military sites. Once Christianity became tolerated in the Roman Empire, Mithraism began to fade. With its secrecy and being open only to men, it was simply outcompeted by the new religion.

Genius Question

Legio VI, Valeria Victrix (Sixth Legion). When the Roman legionary fortress at Eboracum (the forerunner of York) was established in AD 71, its initial garrison was the Legio IX Hispana (Ninth Legion), which had been part of the initial invasion force in AD 43. It remained there until AD 108, after which there is no more evidence of the legion in Britain. This led to long-standing suggestions that it had perished en masse on campaign in Scotland and the 'missing legion' gave rise to a host of literary speculations such as Rosemary Sutcliffe's novel *The Eagle of the Night*. In fact, there is evidence it was based at Noviomagus (Nijmegen in the Netherlands) until 120 and although there are no traces of it thereafter, whatever happened, disbandment or defeat in battle, it did not disappear in Scotland. The Legio IX was replaced in York by the Legio VI Valeria Victrix, which remained the garrison there until the end of Roman rule in the fifth century.

Battles in Britain

1

His mail armour was put on the wrong way round. As William of Normandy prepared to face the English host led by King Harold II in the early morning of 14 October 1066, he had much on his mind. It had been a big risk to carry his invasion fleet bearing 7,000 knights and men-at-arms over the English Channel late in the campaigning season, risking storms and becoming isolated in a foreign land with no possibility of resupply or reinforcement. When it turned out that his squires had put on his coat of mail armour, made of finely interlinked metal circles, the wrong way round, it was regarded as a terrible omen. William shrugged it off and went on to win a hard-fought encounter through a series of faked retreats that drew the English army down from the hilltop ridge they occupied, and Harold's death from an arrow wound in the eye capped the victory and won him the throne of England.

2

Marston Moor, 1644. When the English Civil War broke out in 1642, among those who rallied to the cause of Charles I was his nephew Prince Rupert of the Rhine. A year earlier he had been gifted a white hunting poodle, which (despite its being female) he called 'Boy'. It became his inseparable companion, but soon propaganda on the parliamentary side of the war claimed that the hound had supernatural powers and was a shapeshifter. At the Battle of Marston Moor in July 1644, Boy was left safely in camp but broke free and loyally chased after her master in battle. The fight, although initially going well for Rupert, turned into a rout as Oliver Cromwell's horsemen decimated the royalist cavalry – and among the casualties was Boy. Perhaps it was true that the poodle gave Rupert's cause magical support,

because after Marston Moor the royalist cause went into a decline, which ended in total defeat the following year.

3

King Charles II, after the Battle of Worcester in 1651. After his father's execution in 1649, Charles II allied with Scotland's Presbyterian Covenanters and two years later ordered an invasion of England, hoping that a march through traditionally royalist areas such as Lancashire and the West Country would rally support to his cause. Harried all the way by

Engraving from *The History of his Sacred Majesties most Wonderfull Preservation, after the Battle of Worcester*, 1660.

parliamentary detachments, Charles finally found at Worcester that the way forward to London was blocked. The parliamentarians outnumbered his 16,000 men roughly two-to-one when the two sides clashed on 3 September 1651 and the royalist army was crushed. Fleeing with the remains of his force, Charles hid in the branches of an oak tree in the grounds of Boscobel House to elude his pursuers. Once the coast was clear, Charles took a circuitous route to the coast and six weeks later was on a ship to Normandy. The oak-tree escapade is commemorated by the name 'The Royal Oak' given to many English pubs and in Oak Apple Day, a public holiday which was celebrated on 29 May, Charles's birthday, until the 1850s and is still remembered by an annual parade at the Chelsea Hospital, established by the king for British Army veterans.

4

Heavenfield, 634. In 633 Penda, the pagan ruler of the Anglo-Saxon kingdom of Mercia, which occupied most of the Midlands, made common cause with Cadwallon, the Christian ruler of Gwynedd. As a native Briton, Cadwallon should have been implacably opposed to Penda, whose kingdom's borders threatened to encroach on his own Welsh domain. But their common enemy was Northumbria, which dominated the northeast. In 633 the allies invaded, killed King Edwin of Northumbria and retired south. In the ensuing chaos, Oswald, from a different branch of the Northumbrian royal house, returned from Scotland to claim the throne of Bernicia, one of the two kingdoms into which Northumbria had dissolved. Cadwallon reacted by launching a new invasion (this time without Penda). Faced with superior forces, Oswald positioned himself beside the old Roman wall, close to Hexham. That night, while praying, he had a vision of St Columba, who prophesied that he would be victorious. The next day Oswald raised a great cross and announced the saint's prediction to his troops who duly routed Cadwallon's army. In honour of the saint's appearance, the battlefield was ever after known as the Heavenfield.

5

Bannockburn, 1314. The place where Robert the Bruce's schiltrons, an offensive phalanx of infantrymen, ground down their English opponents and won a signal victory that re-established Scottish independence, sounds as though the name is related to 'bannock', a flat barley or oatmeal cake cooked on a griddle, but in fact they are unrelated. The battlefield takes its name from the Gaelic *bannog* or 'peaks', referring to the hilly land in the nearby Carron Valley (the 'burn' part is from the stream that runs through the battlefield).

6

Flodden Field, 1514. In 1502 James IV of Scotland signed a Treaty of Perpetual Peace with Henry VII of England. In this case, perpetuity turned out to mean just 11 years, for in 1513 James declared war on England in support of his French allies. On 9 September his army encountered the main English force at Flodden Edge, near Branxton, just south of the River Tweed. James made the mistake of positioning himself too close to the front line. As the Scottish units on his flanks were pushed back by the English, James found himself surrounded by the Earl of Surrey's men, and was killed by two arrow wounds. James thus became the last British monarch to die in battle (along with 10,000 of his men), leaving Scotland with a 13-month-old infant, James V, as king.

7

Edgehill, 1642. Charles I's fractious relations with Parliament, which he did not summon at all between 1629 and 1640, broke down completely when he reconvened it in 1640 in a desperate bid to raise funds to suppress a revolt in Scotland. With opposition mounting, the king fled London and proceeded to raise an army, as Parliament in turn assembled militias to defend its cause. On 22 August the king raised the Royal Standard at Nottingham, in effect a declaration of war. After a series of preliminary manoeuvres, Charles's army struck out from Shrewsbury towards the capital. The two sides met at Edgehill on 23 October, an encounter in which, not for the last time, a royalist cavalry charge almost won a victory, only to lose it by an ill-disciplined pursuit of the enemy infantry. The battle ended inconclusively, beginning a bitterly contested three-year war.

8

Towton, 1461. By 1460, the Wars of the Roses between the Lancastrian and Yorkist claimants to the English throne had reached its climax. Although Richard, Duke of York, died at the Battle of Wakefield in December that year, his son Edward took up the Yorkist standard and marched north from London with a large force to meet the main Lancastrian army. They met at Towton in Yorkshire on 29 March, Palm Sunday, 1461 in the middle of a driving snowstorm .The wind favoured the Yorkist archers, whose arrows were carried far into the Lancastrian ranks. Then, after prolonged hand-to-hand fighting, the Lancastrians fled, with many trampled to death in the rout or drowned in rivers that ran through the battlefield. Contemporary chroniclers claimed 36,000 died, although modern estimates are closer to 9,000, making it Britain's bloodiest battle, as well as probably its chilliest.

9

Barnet, 1471. In 1470, it seemed the Yorkists had won the Wars of the Roses, with a Yorkist, Edward IV, on the throne. But then the king's relations with his chief supporter, Richard Neville, Earl of Warwick (nicknamed 'the Kingmaker'), broke down irretrievably, and Warwick defected to the Lancastrian cause, engineering the release of Henry VI from the Tower. It took a little time for Edward IV, who himself was forced into exile, to return, but he did so in March 1471, rapidly gathering forces and seducing waverers from the Lancastrian side. In a chaotic fight at Barnet to the north of London on 14 April, made more disordered by a heavy blanket of fog, Warwick, who was fighting on foot and could not make his escape, was cut down and killed. With 'the Kingmaker' dead, the Lancastrian cause was all but doomed, and collapsed completely after a final defeat at Tewkesbury three weeks later.

10

William Augustus, Duke of Cumberland. By April 1746, the Jacobite Highlanders were at

Plan of the Battle of Culloden, 1746.

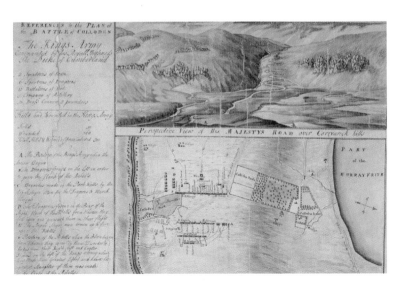

bay after having followed 'Bonnie Prince Charlie', the Stuart claimant to the English throne, on a march in 1745 as far south as Derby in England only then to endure a morale-fraying retreat back to Scotland. Finally, at Culloden Moor, near Inverness, the better-supplied redcoats of the Duke of Cumberland (a younger son of George III) closed on the Jacobites. It happened to be 15 April, the duke's birthday, and rather than force a battle that day, he held back and issued his troops with an extra ration of brandy. It almost proved a fatal mistake as the Jacobites tried to launch a surprise night attack, but in the dark they lost the track and arrived too close to dawn to risk an assault. The next day on Culloden Moor the Highlanders charged across boggy ground as the redcoats' muskets cut them down in their hundreds, and the survivors struggled in the mire to reach the duke's lines. The Jacobite army was routed and their cause was ruined.

11

The Battle of Britain, 1940. On 18 June 1940 Prime Minister Winston Churchill gave a speech in the House of Commons in which he warned: 'I expect that the Battle of Britain is about to begin. Upon this battle depends the survival of Christian civilization. Upon it depends our own British life, and the long continuity of our institutions and our Empire. The whole fury and might of the enemy must very soon be turned on us.' Churchill was right – and three weeks later, on 10 July, the first major attacks by the Luftwaffe on British soil began. The battle hung in the balance for the next three months, until the high rate of attrition of their aircrews forced the German High Command to turn to the bombing of Britain's cities rather than destroying its air force as a means of forcing surrender, and on 13 October the invasion of Britain was in effect called off.

Genius Question

Fishguard, 1797. After the outbreak of the French Revolutionary wars, the Directory, the French revolutionary government of the time, came up with a scheme to bypass the problem of the English Channel and land a force in the West Country. Short of first-line generals, the Directory entrusted the task to Colonel William Tate, a septuagenarian American soldier of fortune, and equipped him with a force of 1,400 assorted ne'er-do-wells, including a large complement of released convicts. His motley armada missed the appointed landing place near Bristol, and instead came ashore near the village of Llandwna in Fishguard Bay. There, Tate's men broke into a store of wine looted by locals from a recently grounded ship and became drunk. Next morning, while sleeping it off, they were accosted by what Tate later described as 'several thousand' British troops, but which in reality was a group of local women led by the redoubtable Jemima Nichols, the wife of a local cobbler. The terrified French 'army' surrendered to Jemima 'Fawr' ('the Great') and so the last battle on British soil – and the last foreign invasion of Britain – ended in total ignominy.

Kings & Queens *(part one)*

1

They were all murdered. Edmund was captured by invading Danish Vikings from the Great Army in 869. According to one account, when he refused to recant his Christianity, he was flayed alive, tied to a tree, then shot to death with arrows. Just to make sure, the Vikings then beheaded him. William II (nicknamed 'Rufus', probably on account of his red beard) went hunting on 2 August 1100 in the New Forest, then a royal preserve. At some point during the hunt a stray arrow struck the king, who died soon after. Fingers pointed to Walter Tyrel, a royal huntsman, and there has long been a lingering suspicion that William's brother Henry, who just happened to be in the same hunting party and inherited the throne, may have been responsible. Edward II, who had roused baronial hostility

over his favouritism towards the Despenser family, was deposed by his own queen, Isabella, in alliance with Roger Mortimer the Earl of March. After fleeing to Wales, Edward was captured and then incarcerated in Berkeley Castle. There, in September 1327, he was murdered, allegedly by having a red-hot poker thrust upwards into his intestines.

2

George III, who reigned 59 years, three months and five days from 1760 to 1820. Both Victoria (63 years, seven months and three days, 1837-1901) and Elizabeth II (currently more than 69 years, from 6 February 1952) are queens. George III was the third king of the Hanoverian dynasty and the first to speak English fluently. Suffering a gradual decline into insanity from the 1780s,

William II on his throne wounded by an arrow, from 'The Chronicle of England 1307-1327'.

finally, in 1811, the king, popularly known as 'Farmer George' because of his fascination with agricultural 'improvement', was declared unfit to rule and the Prince of Wales became regent for the last nine years of his father's reign.

3

It was the first coronation of a British monarch to be televised. An estimated 27 million people in Britain alone watched the three-hour-long service on June 1953, many of them having bought a television set for the first time. The dish Coronation Chicken was devised by Constance Spry and Rosemary Hulme of Le Cordon Bleu cookery school to serve the thousands of guests at the post-coronation banquet (although it was referred to on the menu as 'Poulet Reine Elizabeth').

4

George II. The coronation of George II and Caroline of Brandenburg-Ansbach took place at Westminster Abbey on 11 October 1727. Among the four anthems composed by George Frideric Handel for the coronation, the most enduringly popular has proved to be 'Zadok the Priest', based on the first chapter in the Bible's 1 Kings in which Zadok and the prophet Nathan anoint Solomon as King of Israel, which has been used for every British coronation since.

5

Edgar. Edgar, who reigned as King of Wessex from 959 to 975 (and because Wessex was the last remaining of the Anglo-Saxon kingdoms after the Viking invasions, he was in effect king of England, or at least of the English). Only 12 at the time of his accession, he was fortunate enough to become king during an interval in the Viking raids against Britain. His reign was characterised by a monastic reform spearheaded by the redoubtable Dunstan, the Archbishop of Canterbury, giving Edgar's memory a rosy glow in ecclesiastical chronicles, and a showy ceremony in which eight kings of 'Wales and the north' submitted to him and rowed Edgar down the River Dee, while the king steered.

6

Henry VI and Edward IV. Henry VI came to the throne in September 1422, aged just nine months. When the victorious Yorkists marched into London during the Wars of the Roses in March 1461, he was deposed and incarcerated in the Tower of London, and Richard of York's son Edward was declared king as Edward IV. Unfortunately, after crushing the last Lancastrian hold-outs, Edward lost popularity because of his marriage to Elizabeth Woodville, whose family were Lancastrian sympathisers, and he also alienated his chief supporter, Richard Neville, the Earl of Warwick. Warwick earned his soubriquet 'the Kingmaker' by rebelling, landing with an invasion fleet at Dartmouth in September 1470, and releasing Henry VI from captivity to resume the throne. However, once Edward had regained his equilibrium his forces proved too strong; he defeated and killed Warwick at Barnet in April 1471. Henry was captured and his convenient death two weeks later – the Yorkists claimed he had died of natural causes – allowed Edward IV to rule unchallenged for the last 12 years of his reign.

7

Four. Unusually for an aristocratic male of the time, William II (r. 1087–1100) had never married at the time of his death, aged 43, although there were rumours – never confirmed – that he had an illegitimate son. Edward V (r. 1483) was only 12 years old and two months into his reign when he was deposed by his uncle Richard, the Duke of Gloucester, and incarcerated, with his younger brother Richard, in the Tower of London. There, they disappeared, presumed murdered. Edward VI, who was only nine when he became king in 1547, suffered from persistent bad health and was finished off by a bout of measles followed by tuberculosis in 1553, when he was still too young to contract a marriage. Elizabeth I (r. 1558–1603) spent much of her reign avoiding getting married, despite occasional rumours hinting at a series of royal marriages (including to Archduke Charles of Austria and the Duke of Anjou).

Elizabeth I, from the *Atlas of England and Wales* by Christopher Saxton, 1579.

Clemens et Regni moderatrix iusta Britānī
Hac forma insigni conspicienda nitet.

An. Dñi.

Tristia dum gentes circum omnes bella fatigant,
Cæciq; errores toto grassantur in orbe:
pace beas longa, vera et pietate Britannos:
Iustitia moderans miti sapienter habenas.
Chara domi, celebriq; foris, longæuaq; regni
Hic teneas, regno tandem fruitura perenni.

1 5 7 9

8

George I. George was the Elector of Hanover and only inherited the throne because none of the many children of his predecessor, Anne, survived childhood. He settled down well to his new realm, largely keeping out of the limelight. Only his new subjects' failure to appreciate him rankled – he was jeered when he arrived in London – and his lack of grasp of English meant that he was reliant on his son, also George, to translate the proceedings of Cabinet meetings. He died in 1727 while visiting his beloved Hanover, and became the first reigning British monarch since Richard I to be buried abroad.

9

William IV. William was 64 when he became king in 1830. He never expected to succeed to the throne, only doing so after his brother George IV's last child, Caroline, died in 1817, and his other brother, Frederick of York, died ten years later. Despite a string of liaisons that produced numerous illegitimate offspring, his only legitimate children died as infants, as a result of which, when William died in 1837 his niece Victoria became queen.

10

George V. In declining health, the king suffered a debilitating bout of septicaemia in 1928 and then a serious lung disorder in 1936. As he lay

William IV, from *Political Sketches*, 1829-43.

dying on the night of 20 January 1936, the royal physician Lord Dawson gave him two injections of a mixture of morphine and cocaine, in part to ease his pain and in part to accelerate his death so that, it seems, it could be announced in *The Times* newspaper the next day. The truth that the king had not exactly died of natural causes was kept a strict secret until its revelation 50 years later.

11

Queen Anne and George I: second cousins. George I was already Elector of Hanover (his title making him one of the eight German princes and archbishops who had the right to elect a new Holy Roman Emperor) when he became king of England in 1714, succeeding his second cousin Anne. Both were great-grandchildren of James I (who himself had been monarch of another state, Scotland, before acquiring the English throne).

Genius Question

They are the names of heirs to the throne who died before they could be king (so depriving England of a King Arthur, not to mention a King Eustace and King Alphonso). Eustace of Boulogne, born in 1130, became heir to the English throne after his father Stephen took – some say usurped – the throne after the death of his uncle Henry I, but died shortly after an agreement that ended the civil war between Stephen and Henry's daughter Matilda, which would have excluded Eustace from the throne. Alphonso was the son of Edward I and his wife Eleanor of Castile. Born in 1273, he was named for his mother's brother, King Alfonso of Castile. He fell ill and died in August 1284, leaving his six-month-old younger brother Edward eventually to succeed to the throne in 1307 as Edward II. England's almost King Arthur was the eldest son of Henry VII. He was everything that his younger brother Henry was not: chivalrous, measured, handsome and wildly popular. Married in 1501 to Catherine of Aragon, Arthur succumbed less than a year later to 'sweating sickness', a peculiarly Tudor affliction, whose precise nature is unknown. The grieving widow remained in England and when Arthur's brother Henry became king eight years later, he took her as his wife.

05 Scotland *(part one)*

1

The recipe for heather ale. The Picts, the original inhabitants of northern and eastern Scotland, were the guardians of the secret of how to brew ale from heather, which grew in copious quantities in their territory. When the Scots overcame the Picts in the ninth century, their last king hurled himself off a cliff rather than let slip the recipe for a drink that, according to Robert Louis Stevenson's poetic account, 'Was sweeter far than honey, Was stronger far than wine'. In reality, the Picts (from *picti*, the Latin for 'painted people'), who spoke a Celtic language which has not been deciphered, dominated their region from at least the third century, creating a united kingdom and beating off all comers, including the invading Northumbrians from England in 685. A complex struggle ensued with the Gaels of Dal Riata, with monarchs of Pictish descent coming to rule in Dal Riata also. The last to hold the title 'King of the Picts' was Domnall (charmingly nicknamed 'the Madman'), but his death in 900 was not at the hands of invaders, nor is there any evidence of any association with heather ale.

2

Adam Smith. Born in Kirkcaldy in Fife in 1723, Smith was the founder of modern economic thought, laying out clear principles of political economy in his 1776 work *An Inquiry into the Nature and Causes of the Wealth of Nations*, from which the quote is taken. Its injunction to ensure fair distribution is characteristic of his practical approach to the subject, which also established the principle of comparative advantage, by which countries grow rich in trade by producing only what they are best at, rather than seeking self-sufficiency. A professor of moral philosophy at Glasgow University for 11 years from 1752 to 1763, he obtained much material for his work from his subsequent travels in Europe as the tutor for the Duke of Buccleuch, and he also devised the theory of the 'invisible hand' that guides individuals to act in their best economic interest even if they are not aware of it.

3

Robert McIntyre in 1945. Founded before World War Two, the SNP made little immediate progress because there were no general elections between 1935 and 1945. When James Walker, the Labour MP for Motherwell, died in January 1945, the subsequent fiercely contested by-election on 12 April was won by the SNP's Robert McIntyre with a narrow majority of 617. An Edinburgh University Medical School graduate, 'Doc Mac' lost the seat just three months later in the July 1945 general election and, despite standing at every subsequent election until 1974, never won another. It was the start of a fallow period for the SNP until Winnie Ewing's victory at another by-election, this time in Hamilton in 1967, finally gave them another Westminster seat. This resurgence ultimately resulted in the SNP winning 48 out of Scotland's 59 seats in 2019.

4

Rockall. Just over 187 miles (301km) west of the nearest point of Scotland at Soay on the St Kilda archipelago and around 250 miles (400km) northwest of County Donegal in Ireland, possession of the granite islet of Rockall brings a handy claim to a large slice of Atlantic waters (and the accompanying mineral and fishing wealth). Uninhabited (and only a handful of people are known to have set foot on it), a British naval expedition managed to scramble ashore in 1810, gaining a precarious foothold on the 82-foot by

100-foot (25-m by 30-m) speck of land. The Royal Navy returned in 1955 and raised the Union Jack, formally claiming Rockall, which was then declared by the 1972 Island of Rockall Act to be part of Invernesshire. In the event Scotland should become independent, the most westerly part of the United Kingdom would then become Belleek in County Fermanagh, Northern Ireland.

5

The Royal Stewart. The wearing of distinctive patterns by the various Scottish clans was suppressed by the Dress Act of 1746, passed in the wake of the Jacobite defeat at Culloden. The law was repealed in 1782 and the influence of Sir Walter Scott's highland settings for his novels and a visit by George IV in 1822 led to an upsurge in interest in Scottish traditions, and tartans in particular. The fashion was cemented under Queen Victoria, whose husband Prince Albert designed a special Balmoral Tartan. However, the tartan most associated with the monarch is the Royal Stewart, in view of the current royal family being direct descendants of the Scottish Stewart royal house, which ruled the country from 1371 until the personal union with England in 1603 (when the spelling became Stuart).

6

Elizabeth Garrett Anderson, St Andrews. Although English-born, Elizabeth Garrett Anderson was forced north to Scotland to find a medical school prepared to let her study. She matriculated from St Andrews, before returning to England to take the examination of the Worshipful Society of Apothecaries and become the first female registered practitioner in British history in 1865. Garrett Anderson had no successors at St Andrews until the university introduced the LLA (Lady Literate in Arts) diploma in 1876, which was open to women only. The first woman actually to graduate from St Andrews, once women were admitted to full degrees, was Agnes Forbes Blackadder in March 1895.

7

Racing driver Jackie Stewart. Dumbartonshire-born Stewart was one of the most successful Formula 1 drivers of all time, beginning his career with BRM in 1965. He went on to win 27 Formula 1 races and three world championships and campaigned tirelessly for improved driver safety. Well known for his helmet blazoned with the Royal Stewart tartan, the 'Flying Scot' went on to establish his own Formula 1 team in the late 1990s.

8

A grouping of MPs in the Scottish parliament from 1704 to 1707. More commonly known at the time as the *Squadrone Volante*, the Italian term that translates as the 'Flying Squadron', was a grouping of around 30, mostly young Presbyterian aristocrats who acted as a middle ground between the pro-English Court Party (such as the Duke of Queensberry) and the Country Party, led by the Duke of Hamilton, which was opposed to English involvement. The leading lights of the 'Flying Squadron' included John Hay, the Marquess of Tweeddale, John Ker, the Earl of Roxburghe, and John Leslie, the Earl of Rothes, whose role in persuading Queen Anne that the opposition in Scotland was not riddled with Jacobites helped smooth the way to the passing of the Act of Union in 1707.

9

David Livingstone. Born in Lanarkshire in 1813, Livingstone joined the London Missionary Society and arrived in southern Africa in 1841. His missionary travels and journeys of exploration took him deep into the African interior, including becoming the first European to see the mighty waterfall on the Zambezi he named Victoria Falls in 1855. After brief returns to Britain, he embarked on a final expedition in 1866, but contact with him was lost and he was believed dead until the *New York Herald* correspondent Henry Stanley found him at Ujiji on the shores of Lake Tanganyika (famously remarking, 'Dr Livingstone, I presume?'). Worn out and sick from

David Livingstone, from *Missionary Travels*, 1857.

Wm Holl.

David Livingstone

From a Portrait by Henry Phillips,

in the possession of Mr Murray.

his travels, Livingstone died at Chitambo, now in northern Zambia, in May 1873. His loyal servants embalmed his body, a process that involved the removal of the heart, which they buried under a mpundu tree. The preserved corpse was taken to the coast, put on a steamship to Southampton and interred in Westminster Abbey, London, on 18 April 1874.

10

Dundee. Legend had it that the Dundee cake, a fruit cake made with orange, currants and a concentric pattern of almonds on top, was developed because Mary Queen of Scots did not like cherries on her cakes and so her patissier used almonds instead. In fact, it seems to have been first sold commercially in the 1790s in the Dundee shop of Janet Keiller, who also developed the first modern recipe for marmalade.

11

St Magnus. Magnus Erlendsson became Viking Earl of Orkney in 1105, sharing the islands with his cousin Haakon. Relations between the two men were poisonous, a rivalry dating back to the struggle between their fathers for the earldom and not helped by Magnus's reputation for piety in contrast to his cousin's preference for action. In 1107 a truce was brokered, with the two contesting earls agreeing to meet on the island of Egilsay with just a small retinue. Haakon broke the terms, brought a large group of followers,

captured Magnus and had his cook Lifolf strike his cousin's head off with an axe. At first buried where he lay, Magnus's remains were later transferred in 1137 to the new cathedral built in the islands' capital Kirkwall by his nephew (the son of his sister Gunnhild). Over time, the interment site was forgotten until in 1919, during restoration work on the cathedral, a box was found secreted in a column. The skull showed signs of crushing injuries consistent with being struck with an axe, indicating it was, in all likelihood, that of St Magnus.

Genius Question

Orkney. Inhabited for at least the past 8,000 years, Orkney was invaded by Scandinavian Viking settlers in the eighth century, who established a jarldom that dominated the islands and the mainland opposite in Caithness. The Orkney jarls seem to have driven out the indigenous Pictish population and owed allegiance - sometimes nominal - to the kings of Norway (and Denmark after the unification of the two crowns in 1368), until in 1468 both Orkney and Shetland were pledged by Christian I of Denmark as surety for the payment of the dowry due on the marriage of his daughter Margaret to James III. Although the marriage took place the following year at Holyrood Abbey, Christian struggled to find the 60,000 guilders due and in 1472 the Scottish parliament declared him in default and annexed both Orkney and Shetland to Scotland.

1

Six. The Church in Wales's cathedrals are at Bangor, Brecon, Llandaff, Newport, St Asaph and St Davids. Bangor is both the oldest cathedral in Wales, and also the oldest in Britain, founded in around 525. Although Christianity largely disappeared in England as the Anglo-Saxons advanced north and westwards from the mid-fifth century, in what would become Wales the native population preserved the religion. They held fast to specific Celtic rites, such as a particular way of calculating Easter and a tonsure for monks different to their European equivalent, which would lead to clashes with missionaries sent out from Rome to re-evangelise England in the sixth and seventh century. Bangor began as Deiniol, a monastic foundation named for its first bishop, a contemporary of St David. It is said to have been given to the monks by Maeglwn, king of Gwynedd, and may have taken its name from a Welsh term meaning 'wattle', referring to the fence the monks put up around their property.

2

He was never captured. Glyndŵr was, through his mother, a descendant of Llewelyn the Great, king of Gwynedd, the thirteenth-century unifier of the Welsh kingdoms. He served in the English army in campaigns in Scotland in the 1390s, but a decade later had turned against the English over disputed landholdings. In 1400 he raised the standard of revolt, declared himself Prince of Wales and won a string of victories that led to his calling a Welsh parliament at Machynlleth. Thereafter the tide turned and the castles he had captured fell one by one. By 1410 he was a fugitive, taking refuge in mountain fastnesses. After 1412 all trace of him disappeared and his fate is unknown. Tradition states that if Wales is threatened, Glyndŵr will return to save it.

3

Newport. Established in around AD 75, the legionary fortress of Isca Augusta, now in fields near the village of Caerleon, was the base

The Cathedral Church of Bangor by Johannes Kip, 1708.

of the II Augusta legion for over 200 years. Replacing an early fortress nine miles (15km) to the northeast at Burrium (now Usk), Isca was one of only three permanent legionary fortresses in Britain – the others being at Deva (Chester) and Eboracum (York). Despite the hard-fought conquest, with the Romans taking 30 years to complete it in bitter fighting against the Silures and Ordovices and culminating in an assault on Anglesey in AD 77-78, the Roman era in Wales was relatively tranquil, with few revolts. Isca was abandoned in the 380s as part of a general retraction of the Roman presence in Britain.

4

Merthyr Tydfil. Born in Lanarkshire in Scotland, Hardie was a union organiser in the 1880s, and then helped form the Independent Labour Party and sat for it as MP for the English constituency of West Ham from 1892 to 1895. After defeat in the 1895 general election, he worked on the Labour Representation Committee (which would in 1906 become the Labour Party) and in 1900 won the South Wales seat of Merthyr Tydfil for it. He held the seat until his death in 1915, devoting himself after he stepped down as Labour leader in 1908 to campaigning for votes for women and Indian self-rule, and against Britain's involvement in World War One.

5

Gwaenynog Hall, Denbigh. Beatrix Potter's tale of the adventures of the six children of Benjamin Bunny and his cousin Flopsy after their capture by Mr McGregor, a gardener with a penchant for rabbit pie, was first published in 1909 and has remained in print ever since. Potter made many of the sketches for the book's illustrations, in particular the garden setting at Gwaenynyog, the home of Harriet and Fred Burton, her aunt and uncle. Now restored by the author's great-great-great-niece, the garden is a regular pilgrimage site for Potter devotees.

6

Offa's Dyke. At roughly 80 miles (130km) in length (but with gaps stretching along a 150-mile/240-km area of the Welsh-English border), Offa's Dyke is one of the most imposing earthworks in Europe. Around ten feet (3m) in height and flanked by a ditch, it is associated with Offa, king of Mercia from 757 to 796, who elevated his kingdom to be the most powerful in Anglo-Saxon England. The ninth-century Welsh chronicler-monk Asser relates that Offa raised his barrier 'from sea to sea', although it does not quite stretch from the estuary of the Dee in the north to the Wye in the south. Exactly why Offa built the Dyke is unclear: it was not a strong enough obstacle to deter full-scale invasions and there is no evidence of forts or other installations needed to defend it in depth. Although it probably could hinder cattle rustling and other small-scale incursions it was most likely simply a statement of Offa's power: only a mighty king could undertake such a project.

7

The Crown and the Chair. Now held annually in August, the National Eisteddfod has its origins in medieval bardic competitions, and is the premier showcase for Welsh language oral literature. Periodic revivals culminated in an event in 1861 that marks the birth of the modern Eisteddfod. The winner of the competition for the *pryddest*, or 'free verse', is awarded the Crown, while that for the *awdl,* a far stricter metric form, is seated in a ceremonial Chair. Only three people have won both prizes in a single Eisteddfod (T.H. Parry-Williams, Alan Llwyd and Donald Evans), but perhaps the most dramatic award ceremony of all was in September 1917 when the winner of the Chair was announced to be Hedd Wyn. Traditionally, the winner, whose identity has been kept a secret, is then conducted to the Chair, but the adjudicators had to announce that he had died six weeks earlier at the Battle of Passchendaele and the Chair was instead draped in black cloth in his memory.

8

The Welsh equivalent of Robin Hood. Otherwise known as Thomas Jones, Twm Sion Catti was probably born around 1530 in Tregaron. His true identity has been muddled over time in a skein of tall tales about a kind-hearted brigand who tricked the wealthy into parting with their goods and distributed them to the poor. In one story, a farmer comes looking for a stolen bullock and Twm offers to hold his horse while he looks for it, but then he makes off with the man's steed. Just like Robin Hood, Twm's arch-enemy was a sheriff, this time the Sheriff of Carmarthen. Twm died a more tranquil death than his English counterpart; after becoming a landowner and Justice of the Peace, he died of old age at 79. His adventures were first collected in a book in 1763 and most recently immortalised in the 1978 television series *Hawkmoor*.

9

Pwll or Burry Port. On 17 June 1928 pioneer female aviator Amelia Earhart set out from Trepassey Harbour, Newfoundland, as a passenger on *Friendship*, a Fokker VII Tri-Motor, which was piloted by Wilmer Stultz and Louis Gordon. Twenty hours and 40 minutes later (a title Earhart later gave her book about the crossing) their seaplane came down at Pwll Inlet, and was then towed into the village of Burry Port, where the aviators set foot on land. The celebrity Amelia gained by becoming the first woman to cross the Atlantic in a plane helped her subsequent ventures, including the first solo flight and the final attempt to fly solo to Australia, which ended in her disappearance and presumed death in 1937.

10

Around 19 per cent. Under pressure since the conquest of Wales by Edward I in the 1280s, and especially after the formal annexation to England in 1536, the Welsh language gradually retreated. A revivalist movement in the nineteenth century and intense pressure from nationalists culminated in the Welsh Language Act in 1967, which restored the language's legal status. In the 2011 census, 18.6 per cent of respondents reported they could speak Welsh, a proportion that ranged from 64.3 per cent in Gwynedd to 7.6% in Blaenau Gwent.

11

Caernarvon, Conwy and Harlech. Although English influence along the Welsh borders had steadily grown in the twelfth century, a progression reversed by the campaigns of Llewelyn Fawr ('the Great') of Gwynedd between 1200 and 1240, the accession of Edward I to the English throne in 1272 presaged trouble for the Welsh. In two invasions in 1277 and 1282 he overran North Wales, killing Llewelyn's namesake grandson (who thus acquired the nickname 'the Last'), and extinguished the last embers of Welsh resistance the following year. To keep his new possession subdued, Edward ordered the building of a string of large castles: Caernarvon, completed in 1285; Conwy, on whose fortifications and town walls 1,500 craftsmen and labourers toiled between 1283 and 1287; and Harlech Castle, with its 108-step 'way to the sea', which allowed for resupply from ships. Together with Beaumaris and a number of smaller forts, these acted as a focal point for English influence in Wales and largely kept the peace until the revolt of Owain Glyndŵr in the fifteenth century.

Genius Question

The first Welshman to reach the South Pole. Born at Middleton on the Gower Peninsula, Evans joined the Royal Navy and served Robert Scott on a previous Antarctic expedition from 1901 to 1904, before signing up for Scott's final *Terra Nova* expedition in 1910. Tall and enormously strong, 'Taff' Evans was picked by Scott to be part of the five-man party making the final push to the South Pole, in which his strength would prove invaluable in man-hauling the heavy sleds. Evans cut his hand badly on the approach to the Pole and on the return march, after they found on 17 January that the Norwegian Roald Amundsen had beaten them by five weeks, the cut became infected, he suffered frostbite on the hands and face, and his condition steadily deteriorated after he suffered concussion as a result of a fall into a crevasse. On 17 February he became the first of the polar party to die, expiring of hypothermia in a tent on the Beardmore Glacier.

A British Miscellany (part one)

1

Old Sarum in Wiltshire. The 'rotten boroughs' were relics of the original development of the English parliament in the Middle Ages, each having had the right to return two members (MPs). Over time, many of them decayed as their population declined or, as in the case of Dunwich in Suffolk, they literally disappeared (the East Anglian village was washed away by the sea). Most 'rotten boroughs' fell into the clutch of landowners who, in the absence of secret ballots, were able to force their choice of MPs on their tenants, or at least to pay bribes to entice the few electors to pick the right man. By 1832, when it was abolished by the Great Reform Act, Old Sarum had just three voters. Up until then, Old Sarum had retained its right to return two MPs, the most famous of whom was William Pitt the Elder, who represented the borough from 1735 to 1747.

2

1600. Informally known as 'John Company' and officially as the 'Governor and Company of Merchants Trading into the East Indies', the East India Company (EIC) was established to obtain a share of the fabulously lucrative spice trade in the East Indies (modern-day Indonesia), where commodities such as nutmeg and cloves, obtainable only on a few small islands, yielded fabulous profits. Squeezed out by its far more aggressive Dutch equivalent, the Vereenigde Oostindische Compagnie (VOC), the EIC focused its efforts on India, where it inveigled itself into the good books of the Mughal emperors, obtaining the rights to operate from Surat in 1629 and then expanding by trade, trickery and naked force until by the mid-nineteenth century it dominated almost the entire Indian subcontinent.

3

They were all executed by being beheaded. The Scottish leader during the First Scots War of Independence, who famously defeated the invading English at Stirling Bridge in 1297, William Wallace suffered a particularly brutal death after his capture in 1305, being hanged, having part of his bowels cut out while still alive and burned in front of him before, finally, being beheaded. Charles I was executed in front of Whitehall Palace's Banqueting House on a chilly late January day in 1649. After a speech declaring himself 'a martyr of the people', Charles submitted to his executioner without a struggle, although the crowd, in search of gruesome relics, afterwards cut off locks of his hair as souvenirs. Lord Lovat became the last person to be publicly beheaded in Britain, at Tower Hill, London, on 9 April 1747 after having been convicted of High

Arms of the East India Company, cast from a ceiling boss in St Matthias Church, Poplar.

Execution of Charles I, German engraving, 1649.

Treason for his part in the Jacobite uprising in support of 'Bonnie Prince Charlie'.

4

William Huskisson on 15 September 1830. The MP for Chichester, Huskisson had enjoyed a successful political career, including stints as the Secretary for the Colonies and President of the Board of Trade, but he had resigned his position over a disagreement on the abolition of 'rotten boroughs'. Huskisson attended the opening of the new Liverpool and Manchester Railway, and when the train carrying the invited guests stopped, he went over to try to speak to the prime minister, the Duke of Wellington. Unfortunately, he stepped onto a second line carrying trains in the opposition direction. Aged 60 and recovering from recent surgery on his liver, Huskisson was too slow to move; he grabbed the door of the

VIP train, which then swung open, propelling him directly into the path of the other oncoming engine. The badly injured Huskisson was taken to a nearby village, where he died several hours later.

5

Great Yarmouth. In World War One, Germany soon put the new technology of aviation to military use, deploying zeppelins – airships with lighter-than-air balloons – to attack Britain. On 19 January 1915, three zeppelins set out to attack the docks on Humberside, but bad weather and night-time conditions diverted them to King's Lynn and Great Yarmouth. Zeppelin *L3* reached Great Yarmouth first, offloading ten small bombs on the St Peters' Plain area of the town, killing two people, including Samuel Smith, a shoemaker, who was decapitated by shrapnel. In total, these raids had killed 557 people by 1917, when the zeppelins were replaced by the more effective Gotha heavy bombers.

Historiated initial 'A' with Henry VI, 1488-89.

6

Henry VI, in the church of Notre-Dame in Paris on 16 December 1431. The Treaty of Troyes (1426), which marked the high point of King Henry V's successes in France after the Battle of Agincourt, agreed that on the death of King Charles VI, the then French monarch, Henry or his heirs would succeed to the throne. Charles, who suffered from a psychosis that made him believe he was made of glass and liable to shatter, finally died in 1422 and the English went to war to press their claim. To reinforce it, the ten-year old Henry was crowned king of France in Paris, then under English occupation. After the shortest of stays, Henry was whisked back to England. He remained titular king of France until his own deposition in 1461, while Paris continued as an 'English' city for only a further 15 years, falling back into the hands of the French in 1436.

7

Mary Anning (anagram of 'main granny'). Anning's father was a cabinetmaker who collected fossils along Lyme Regis's beach in his spare time.

Zeppelin raid damage, 1915.

When he died in 1810, Mary raised money for the family by finding further fossils and selling them to collectors. Her fame rose when, the next year, aged just 12, she dug out the first ichthyosaur (an aquatic dinosaur) ever found from a cliff face. In 1823 she was the first to find a plesiosaurus and then, five years later, a pterodactyl. Unlike those male geologists whom she helped through her fossil finds, Anning was never admitted to the Geological Society (which admitted its first female fellow in 1904). Recognition of a sort came with the composition of a song in 1908 containing the tongue-twister 'She sells seashells on the seashore', which was alleged to have been inspired by her life. In 2021 the society belatedly sought to make amends, when it joined a campaign to have a statue of Anning erected as part of the wider debate about 'the forgotten women of history'.

8

The Battle of Hastings in 1066. Although they didn't know it as Halley's Comet, the Anglo-Saxons were perturbed by the appearance of a fiery star travelling through the sky early in 1066. A monk named Eilmer of Malmesbury is said to have lamented of it that 'I see you brandishing the downfall of my country'. Eilmer knew a thing or two about disaster: in his youth he had devised a means of flying by attaching feathered wings to a harness, on which he launched himself from a tall tower. He is said to have travelled 600 feet (five times the distance of the Wright Brothers' first flight in 1903) before crashing to the ground and suffering such terrible injuries that he never walked again. The comet may indeed have been an omen – for that autumn Duke William of Normandy invaded England and took the throne for himself.

9

The Crimean War. Pioneering war photographer Roger Fenton took the picture on 15 April 1855 and it shows Frances Isabella Duberly and her husband Captain Henry Duberly of the 8th Royal Irish Hussars. Fenton, the founder of the Royal Photographic Society, got himself appointed as official photographer of the British army in the Crimean War. Both the technology available at the time, which required several minutes exposure per shot, and his official capacity, mean that action shots and shots of the gory aftermath of battles, were out of the question and so most of Fenton's work consists of shots of soldiers in camp, or rarities such as Mrs Duberly.

10

The Viking raid on the abbey of Lindisfarne in 793. In 1993 Finn Wagle, Bishop of Nidaros, and his dean, Sven Oppegaard, wrote a letter to the Church of St Mary's on Lindisfarne apologising for the Viking raid launched on the island on 8 June 793. Although possibly not the first Viking raid on England (which might have been a few years beforehand), it is the earliest whose date we know and it began a century in which the Scandinavian raiders terrorised the coastal communities of Britain, culminating in the conquest of much of the north of England, where they established a kingdom in York in 866 and finally, under King Cnut of Denmark, established Scandinavian rule over all of England from 1016 to 1042.

11

None of them. The practice of frying fish and coating it with batter is said to have been introduced in the mid-seventeenth century by Jewish refugees from Spain and Portugal. Most had been expelled from Spain in 1492, and increasing persecution in Portugal, including the establishment of the Inquisition in 1536, had led many to migrate to France and the Netherlands, from where they made their way to Britain.

Brewing beer with hops was a Dutch tradition and hops began to be imported into England around 1400. The resulting drink wasn't popular with some and a tract in 1519 condemned hops as a 'wicked and pernicious weed'. Even so it caught on and from 1524 hops began to be grown in Kent, in time establishing hop-brewed beer as a drink that became quintessentially English.

Cricket originated not in England, but in Flanders, where shepherds and weavers played it in their spare time, some of whom brought the game to England with them after the revolt of the Netherlands against Spain in 1568 generated waves of refugees. An English poem in 1533, complaining about the numbers of immigrants coming to the south, called on them to 'Now shut upp your wickets', linking cricket to foreigners in a way that seems distinctly strange today.

Genius Question

James. Although there have only been two kings of England with that name (James I and James II), they were both also kings of Scotland and had five predecessors with the same name, beginning with James I, who came to the Scottish throne in 1406. James VII (or James II as he was known in England) was deposed in 1688, his pro-Catholic and pro-French tendencies worrying the stauncher Protestants in Parliament and among the nobility. The Jacobites, who continued to support James as legitimate king after his deposition, then also acclaimed his son, James Francis Edward Stuart (the 'Old Pretender'), as king in 1701, so arguably he is the eighth king James.

James I enthroned, from the Letters Patent of James I, 1610.

Britain in Pictures (part one)

1

They all hold original versions of Magna Carta - the buildings are the British Library, Lincoln Cathedral and Salisbury Cathedral. The document signed in 1215 by King John (or to which, to be more precise, he appended his Great Seal) was in origin a way to buy him time in the quarrel with his leading barons that threatened to turn into an unstoppable rebellion. Since then it has become seen as a cornerstone of Britain's unwritten constitution, assuring fundamental rights (although most protected the barons' position and not that of humbler folk). Still, it guaranteed that 'No free man shall be seized or imprisoned ... except by the lawful judgement of his equals', a clause that has stood the test of time, despite the king's almost instant abjuration of the charter. For such a surprisingly important

document, few copies have survived, in part because it was revised or reissued periodically under John's successors (for the first time in 1216 under his son Henry III). Of the four that remain, two are held by the British Library, one by Lincoln Cathedral and one by Salisbury Cathedral. The Lincoln copy seems to have been in the cathedral archive right from the beginning, the Salisbury copy arrived not long after the church's construction began in 1220, while the British Library's two versions formed part of the collection of the bibliophile and antiquarian Sir Robert Cotton (1571-1631), which was bequeathed to the nation by his grandson John in 1753. All four manuscripts were united

The British Library's copy of the original 1215 edition of Magna Carta, Cotton MS Augustus II 106.

together for the first time in February 2015 at the British Library as part of the 800th anniversary commemoration of Magna Carta's signature.

2

Coalbrookdale Iron Bridge. Erected over the River Severn by Abraham Darby III in 1779, it was the first major bridge made of cast iron. Coalbrookdale's position in a region richly endowed with coal made it one of the heartlands of Britain's earliest industry and a pioneer in both railways (wooden rail tracks were used to run wagons with coals from the pits to the Severn) and in the smelting of iron. In 1709 the Quaker industrialist Abraham Darby used coke instead of charcoal in his blast furnaces, hugely increasing their capacity. As Coalbrookdale pits and furnaces continued to innovate, including the production of cast iron, the problem became

A view of the cast iron bridge over the Severn at Coalbrookdale, Shropshire, 1782.

increasingly pressing that there were few convenient crossings of the Severn in the region. The task fell to Abraham Darby III, grandson of the pioneer. Following a design for a high single arch – to avoid impeding river traffic – drawn up by local architect Thomas Pritchard, Abraham cast 384 tons of iron in his own foundries and took three months to complete the revolutionary structure, at the princely cost of £6,000.

3

Cardinal Thomas Wolsey. Hampton Court is today one of the most famous royal palaces in England, but it began its life as the seat of Cardinal Thomas Wolsey, the Archbishop of York. Wolsey himself had come far. Born around 1475 the son of an Ipswich butcher, he obtained an education at Oxford University and entered the Church. His rise was meteoric. His shrewdness and intelligence won him patronage that secured him a place as Henry VII's personal chaplain, dean of Lincoln, and then under Henry

VIII a dizzying series of promotions to Bishop of Lincoln and Archbishop of York (both in 1514) and cardinal (1515). By then he had acquired the site of Hampton Court in southwest London from the Order of St John of Jerusalem and begun building a palace fit for a cardinal. Chief minister to the king and confidant of popes, Wolsey's attempt to straddle the secular and ecclesiastical worlds came crashing down when he failed to persuade Clement VII to allow his royal master a divorce from Catherine of Aragon. Angered, Henry struck out at Wolsey, stripping him of his offices and then summoning him from York on 4 November 1530 to face charges of treason. He died during the journey south, at Leicester on 29 November, so sparing both sides the embarrassment of a formal trial. A useful side-effect of Wolsey's fall, from Henry's point of view, was that he acquired control of the dead cardinal's estate, most notably the grand palace at Hampton Court, which he had long coveted.

4

It was the first Wimbledon Singles Final to be played between twins. The 1882 Wimbledon Singles Final, played on 8 July, was very much a family affair, played between Warwickshire twin brothers Willie and Ernest Renshaw. Willie won 6-1 2-6 4-6 6-2 6-2, the first of three times he would best his younger brother in the final (the others being 1883 and 1889). Willie Renshaw dominated the tennis world for over a decade, still holding the record for the most consecutive Wimbledon Men's singles titles (six between

1881 and 1886). Ernest won his sole, consolation, singles title at Wimbledon in 1888, while his brother was taking a break (because of a case of tennis elbow), before Willie resumed his crown the following year for a final, seventh, title. It would take until 2017 for Roger Federer to surpass this tally when he won his eighth Wimbledon title. It took less time for a new pair of twins to fight it out in Wimbledon: in 1898 Reginald Doherty beat his younger twin brother Laurence, once more over five sets.

5

Stonehenge. The image is from a fourteenth-century copy of the twelfth-century chronicler Wace's *Roman de Brut* (a barely historical account of Britain's history from its legendary foundations by Brutus, an alleged refugee from Troy's sacking by the Greeks), and it shows Merlin helping to build Stonehenge. This is the earliest known image of the great stone circle and it relates to the part of Wace's narrative recounting how the British king Aurelius was advised by the wizard to erect a stone circle in honour of his warriors killed in battle against the Saxons. An expedition was mounted to Ireland in search of suitably large stones, but the craftsmen found them too heavy to move. At that point, Merlin intervened and cast a spell that made them light enough to be moved easily to the ships, which then bore them to England. Archaeologists now know that Neolithic Britons moved the five-ton bluestones of the monument from Wales and erected it around 2400 BC.

Laws & Liberties

1

Six. In the aftermath of the Napoleonic Wars, harsh measures were passed to prevent the organisation of workers into unions. These Combination Acts were repealed in 1824, but their replacement still carried penalties for swearing membership oaths. Nonetheless, unions began to gather strength, among the most important of them the Grand National Consolidated Union. In 1834 the authorities clamped down, arresting six agricultural labourers in the Dorset village of Tolpuddle. The men, including the alleged ringleader George Loveless, were tried, found guilty of administering illegal oaths and sentenced to transportation to Australia. The reaction was far stronger than the government expected, with a petition gathering 250,000 signatures and a mass march down Whitehall demanding the commutation of the sentences. In March 1836 the six were granted a full and free pardon and given a free passage from Tasmania and New South Wales.

2

Any adult 18 or over, whether a UK, Irish or Commonwealth citizen, who is a peer in the House of Lords, a prisoner serving a prison sentence or has been convicted within the previous five years of electoral crimes. In principle, any adult British, Irish or Commonwealth citizen can vote in UK general elections (as long as they register to do so). Prisoners have been barred from voting since the 1870 Forfeiture Act, which denied them most civil rights, including that of voting. Peers cannot vote because the House of Commons is precisely that, a body elected by the 'commons',

THE DORCHESTER UNIONISTS IMPLORING MERCY !!! OF THEIR KING.

and the Lords, being ennobled, are not part of that group. Currently, people who have resided outside the United Kingdom for a period exceeding 15 years are also barred from voting.

3

Eating mince pies on Christmas Day. Technically, eating mince pies was only illegal in 1644 when the Puritan-minded Long Parliament voted Christmas Day a mandatory day of fasting. Parliament then went one further by its Ordinance for the Abolishing of Festivals of 1647, which banned all Christmas celebrations (yes, they really cancelled Christmas!). After the Restoration brought the monarchy back in the shape of Charles II in 1661, all such measures were expunged, making mince pies on Christmas Day entirely legal again. The 1313 Statute Forbidding Bearing Armour, which outlaws entering the parliamentary chambers clad in armour, is still in force; the 1872 Licensing Act says 'every person found drunk' on any licensed premises, such as pubs, is liable to a penalty; and the 1984 Public Health (Control of Disease) Act lays down that anyone suffering from a notifiable disease must notify the driver of a public conveyance (such as a bus) of their condition.

4

Helen Duncan, 1944. Sentenced to nine months in Holloway Prison after a seven-day trial, Scottish spiritualist Duncan was not actually convicted of witchcraft, but of claiming the power of a witch. The latter had been illegal under the 1735 Witchcraft Act, whereas before that the law had recognised the existence of witches (and the unfortunate accused, most often women, frequently suffered the death penalty). Duncan had conducted seances with dead servicemen, which brought her to the attention of the authorities, and was released in September 1944. The Witchcraft Act was finally repealed in 1951, although those claiming supernatural powers could still be prosecuted for fraud. Duncan was not quite the last person to be prosecuted under the 1735 Act, as Jane Rebecca Yorke, a medium who lived in Forest Gate in Essex, was convicted in September 1944, but was given a non-custodial sentence, being fined £5 on condition that she ceased her activities.

5

Roughly 9 per cent. Although hailed as the dawn of modern democracy in Britain, the Great Reform Act of 1832 extended the franchise only

(Left) 'The Dorchester Unionists imploring mercy!!! of their king', a cartoon by G. Drake, 1834–35.

(Right) 'True Reform of Parliament,-i.e.- Patriots lighting a revolutionary bonfire in New Palace Yard', by James Gillray, 1809.

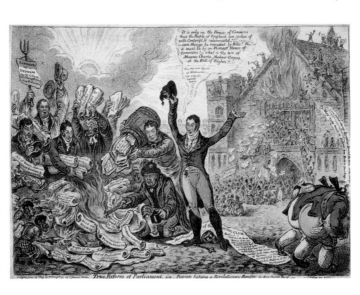

in a relatively modest way, mainly to property-owning adult males in towns. Before 1832 the situation had been even worse, with only around 214,000 out of eight million adults in England and Wales having the vote (or around 3 per cent), and even fewer in Scotland. After the Great Reform Act, the total increased to 650,000 votes or about 18 per cent of adult males (and 9 per cent of the total). Universal adult male suffrage only became a reality in 1918, when women over 30 were also given the vote. Universal suffrage, including all adult women, only became the law in Britain in 1928.

6

William Joyce in 1946. Nicknamed 'Lord Haw-Haw', the American-born fascist sympathiser William Brooke Joyce had worked as a courier for the British Army during the early 1920s, but afterwards joined a series of fascist organisations, including Sir Oswald Mosley's British Union of Fascists. In 1939 Joyce travelled to Germany, took German citizenship and began broadcasting pro-Nazi propaganda back to Britain. At the end of the war he was captured by British forces in Hamburg on 28 May 1945, transported back to London and put on trial for treason. Sentenced to death, he was hanged at Wandsworth Prison on 3 January 1946.

7

Ten. Children below the age of ten cannot be arrested or charged with crimes (although those between ten and 17 can be). In Scotland, the age of criminal responsibility is 12. The debate over the age at which children should be treated as adult in criminal cases is centuries old. In early Anglo-Saxon times, free children could take oaths at the age of 12 and were as responsible as their elders for keeping the peace. In the 930s, King Aethelstan considered that far too many children were being executed for capital crimes and raised the age at which the death penalty could be levied to 15 years. Later ages were less lenient, and in 1629 a certain John Dean, aged eight or nine, was sentenced to death for the arson of two houses in Windsor.

8

Ignatius Sancho. Taken into slavery shortly after his birth in West Africa, around 1729, Sancho lived most of his life in London, first as the servant of three sisters in Greenwich and then in the household of the Duke and Duchess of Montagu who took him under their wing, encouraged him to learn to read and gave him employment as a butler. He used the annuity of £30 the duke left him in his will to buy a grocery store, which he operated with his wife for many years. As a property owner he was eligible to vote in general elections and did so in 1774 and 1780. A well-known figure in Georgian London, he corresponded with Lawrence Sterne, sat for a portrait by Thomas Gainsborough, advocated for the abolition of slavery, wrote an autobiography, several musical compositions and a *Treatise on Music* and appeared in several stage performances.

9

1939. Although divorce had become legal in England and Wales in 1857 on grounds of adultery, previously it had been necessary to obtain an Act of Parliament to get a divorce, and this continued to be the case in Northern Ireland. Between 1924 and 1939 Northern Ireland's Stormont Parliament passed 63 such acts, at a rate of just four a year. The expense and disparity with the rest of the United Kingdom led to calls for reform, and under the Matrimonial Causes (Northern Ireland) Act, divorce was allowed for the first time on the grounds of adultery, cruelty or desertion.

10

Five shillings (or 25p). By the early nineteenth century around 200 crimes carried the death penalty, perhaps the harshest of which was for the theft of goods worth five shillings of more (equivalent to around £25 today when adjusted for inflation). It caused the system of justice to be referred to as the 'Bloody Code' and led to the practice of 'pious perjury', by which juries deliberately underestimated the value of stolen goods so that they would not have to impose the death penalty. As the nineteenth century progressed, increasing numbers of those convicted of capital crimes were instead transported, largely to the new penal colonies in Australia. Finally, between 1832 and 1837 Sir Robert Peel had most capital crimes (save murder) removed from the statute book, although as late as 1834 an accused could, in theory, be hanged for sacrilege or letter-stealing.

11

The first woman to be elected as an MP. An activist for woman's suffrage, Sligo-raised Countess Constance Markievicz turned her political energy to Irish nationalism after moving to Dublin in 1903, becoming a member of Sinn Féin and helping establish the *Na Fianna Éireann*, a republican youth movement. Jailed several times for her activities, including participation in the 1916 Easter Uprising, she was in prison when she stood in the December 1918 general election for the St Patrick's constituency in Dublin and was elected with twice the votes of her nearest rival. She never took up her seat, in line with Sinn Féin's abstentionist policy (although she was subsequently elected to the Irish Dáil). The first female MP to take up her seat was Nancy Astor, who was elected in a by-election in Plymouth Sutton in November 1919, taking the place of her husband, who had been elevated to the House of Lords.

Genius Question

Four. The price of peace between King John and his rebellious barons, Magna Carta largely answered noble concerns about royal overreach, including the charging of excessive fees for allowing aristocratic heirs to come into their inheritances and the onerous levying of *scutage*, a feudal charge payable in lieu of providing an actual man-at-arms for royal campaigns, as well as some seemingly trivial gripes (such as the removal of all fish weirs from the River Thames). In subsequent centuries Magna Carta has come to be seen as the foundation of British national liberty, largely through some rosy-tinted reinterpretation of its provisions, but in particular because of the clauses forbidding the selling of justice and that no person could be held indefinitely without trial, and that all had the right to trial by jury. Of the 63 clauses, only four still survive on the statue books: clause 1 guarantees the freedom of the English Church; clause 13 guarantees the ancient privileges of the City of London and other cities with charters; clause 39 states 'No free man shall be seized or imprisoned, or stripped of his rights or possessions, or outlawed or exiled, or deprived of his standing in any way, nor will we proceed with force against him, or send others to do so, except by the lawful judgment of his equals or by the law of the land'; and clause 40 reads 'To no one will we sell, to no one deny or delay right or justice'.

1

Reginald Erskine Foster. Nicknamed 'Tip', Foster really came to notice when he smashed 171 for Oxford in the 1900 Varsity Match. In an era when long-distance travel was prohibitively time-consuming, he declined to join the England Test team in Australia in 1902, and he played little cricket before joining the 1903 Ashes tour. There, at the First Test at the Sydney Cricket Ground on 11–17 December, he scored 287 in the first innings, the driving force behind his team's five-wicket victory and the first English test cricketer to score a double century (and he held the world test batting record until Andy Sandham surpassed him with the first triple century in 1930). Thereafter, Foster's record was patchy as he played little cricket until 1907 when he captained against South Africa, and following that played only two first-class matches.

Earlier, he had been torn between cricket and football; having played for the Old Malvernians, he appeared five times for England between 1900 and 1902, and, in the final match, against Wales in March 1902, was awarded the captaincy. Tragically, he died of complications from diabetes in 1914, aged just 36.

2

Rugby Union. Although legend has it that rugby was born when William Webb Ellis picked up the ball and ran with it during a football match at Rugby School in 1823, there is no firm evidence to support the story. But by the 1850s a version of the game was well entrenched at the school and had begun to spill out, both into other public schools and to outside clubs (such as Blackheath in 1858). Disputes over the rules (and confusion with those of football, themselves

'Oxford v Cambridge – A Run by Baker', from *The Illustrated Sporting and Dramatic News*, 19 December 1896, by C.M. Padday.

being codified at the time) led to a meeting of
the representatives of 21 rugby clubs at the Pall
Mall restaurant on London's Regent Street on 26
January 1871. After two hours of debate (and no
doubt of fine dining), the Rugby Football Union
was born and a code of rules agreed, of which
law 58 forbade the use of 'projecting nails, iron
plates or gutta percha' on the players' boots.

3

Weightlifting (one-handed lift). The 1896
Athens Olympics, the first of the modern era,
were a much more modest affair than today's
multi-billion-dollar events. Of the roughly 240
athletes representing 14 nations, just ten were
British. From an aristocratic Scottish family,
India-born Launceston Elliot was pipped for a
gold by Dane Viggo Jensen in the two-handed
lift, but immediately after got his revenge by
raising 71.0kg in the one-handed lift, whereas
Jensen could only manage 57.2kg. As if winning
Britain's first Olympic gold was not enough,
Elliot then found time to compete in the 100
metres, wrestling and the gymnastics rope-
climbing event (although in none of them did he
win a medal). There wasn't any weightlifting at
the 1900 Paris Olympics, so Elliot was denied
the chance to defend his title and competed in
the discus instead, where he came 11th.

4

Lottie Dod. Born in Bebington in Cheshire in
1871, Dod learnt tennis on the courts at her
cotton magnate father's estate and soon proved
herself a prodigy, winning regional titles by 1886,
before entering Wimbledon in July the following
year, where she beat the reigning champion
Blanche Bingley 6-2 6-0. Aged just 15, her record
as the youngest Ladies Single's winner has stood
ever since, and she went on to beat Bingley in
four further finals (in 1888, 1891, 1892 and 1893).
A multi-talented sportswoman, Dod also tried
her hand at figure skating, mountaineering and
archery, captained the England hockey teams
in two matches in 1899 and 1900, and won the
British Ladies Amateur golf championship at
Troon in 1904.

5

Prestwick Golf Club. The Open Championship
was first held after a group of golfers at
Prestwick decided to hold a challenge event to
find a worthy to successor to Allan Robertson,
who died in 1850 and had dominated the
Scottish golf scene since the 1840s. Invitations
were sent out to four other Scottish clubs and
Blackheath in England to send their best golfers.
In the end, eight competitors took part, teeing
off for the first time on 17 October 1860, with
the prize on offer a belt of red Morocco leather
with a silver buckle, which was secured by
Willie Park of Musselburgh, who won by two
strokes. The famous 'claret jug' was only first
competed for in 1872.

6

Cricket. There had been plans to have a cricket
tournament at the 1896 Athens Olympics, but
they collapsed, and it looked as though Paris,
in 1900, would go the same way, when two (the
Netherlands and Belgium) out of the original
four teams (the others being Britain and France)
pulled out. The sole match, therefore, was the
final, played on the Vélodrome des Vincennes
on 19 August between an England team made
up of the Devon and Somerset Wanderers club,
and a scratch 'All Paris' team made up of British
émigrés. In a low-scoring match, 'All Paris' fell far
short of its 185 target in the fourth innings, being
bowled out for 26 (with just five minutes to
spare). Cricket never made it onto the Olympic
programme again, leaving Britain technically
Olympic champions for over 120 years.

7

Football. The earliest versions of football
resembled a riot more than an organised
sport, being played between village teams of
indeterminate size on pitches that could even
be miles long. Understandably nervous about
public disorder, medieval monarchs made
periodic attempts to ban the pastime, including
a law of Edward II which lamented the 'certain
tumults, arising from great footballs in the fields
of the public, from which many evils may arise'.

Clearly it didn't work, because in 1477 Edward IV passed a new law stating that 'No person shall practise any unlawful games such as dice, quoits, football', instead being enjoined to practise archery (although it isn't clear what threat to national security was posed by quoits players).

8

Curling. Played in Scotland since at least the sixteenth century, in curling two teams of four players slide granite stones across an ice pitch (called a sheet) towards target areas called houses. The hog line is the line before which players must release the stones for them to be considered in play. A biter is a stone that is just barely on the edge of the outer ring of the house. The world's oldest club is Kilsyth Curling Club, founded in 1716.

9

Red Rum. Astonishingly, Red Rum overcame a chronic bone inflammation to win the Aintree Grand National, one of Britain's premier steeplechase events, in 1973, beating Crisp by three-quarters of a length, and repeating the feat in 1974 with an even more convincing seven-length win against L'Escargot. Placing second in 1975 and 1976, Red Rum won a never-equalled third Grand National victory by 25 lengths in 1977. The horse, which retired in 1978, continued to lead the pre-Grand National parade for many years before its death in 1995, aged 30.

10

Lewis Hamilton. Stevenage-born Hamilton joined the McLaren young drivers' programme in 1996, but only got a Formula 1 start at the Malaysian Grand Prix in April 2007, becoming the first Black driver in the sport's history. A second place in that race was a sign of great things to come. By the end of the 2020 season he had racked up 98 F1 wins, a record, and seven world titles (making him the joint record-holder with Michael Schumacher), including four in a row from 2017 to 2020. Hamilton has campaigned against child poverty, including work for UNICEF, the UN Children's Fund and Save the Children.

11

It was won by a team from the north of England (Blackburn Olympic). For a decade after the FA Cup was first contested in 1871, the competition was dominated by teams associated with public schools (such as Old Etonians). Gradually, more professional, working-class teams began to make their mark and the 1882 final was a hotly contested one between Blackburn Olympic, the north of England's most successful outfit, and Old Etonians, which the latter won 1-0. Olympic came back the following year, seeking revenge and having overturned Ruabon Druids, the leading Welsh side, 4-1, they then overcame Old Carthusians in the semis in a match delayed when nobody could find a ball. In the final, played at Kennington Oval, the Old Etonians' traditional rugby-like tactics of scrimmages and rushes gave them an early lead, but Olympic's more fluid passing game – just coming into vogue – earned them extra time and a late winner. Afterwards, the Old Etonians complained that the match wasn't fair because Blackburn had prepared for it, but that didn't detract from the celebrations of England's first northern FA Cup winners.

Genius Question

Mansfield's One Call Stadium. In the mid-Victorian era a number of varieties of football were emerging, some from public schools (such as Rugby Union), others from among working class communities. While many early football clubs (and the original Football Association) were London-based, there was also a particular concentration in the north of England, and Sheffield clubs produced the first football rule book in October 1858 (although the goalposts were set so narrowly apart that at first most games were goalless draws). Although Sheffield United's Bramall Lane is the oldest top-flight ground (hosting its first game on 29 December 1862 against Hallam FC), the very oldest professional ground is Mansfield Town's One Call Stadium (previously known as the Field Mill), where the Greenhalgh's XI (drawn from workers in Herbert Greenhalgh's local cotton business) played their first match in 1861.

Anglo-Saxons & Vikings

1

The hide. The hide was an ancient Anglo-Saxon measure that traditionally denoted the amount of land necessary to support one family. This varied depending on the quality of the land (more pastoral than arable land was needed), but the average was about 120 acres (just less than 50 hectares). It later became a unit of tax assessment, and a seventh-century document known as the Tribal Hidage lists the various Anglo-Saxon kingdoms with the number of hides they were assessed at (with Wessex being the leviathan at 100,000 hides, East Anglia a more modest 30,000, now largely forgotten kingdoms such as the Hwicce in the West Midlands at 7,000, and tiddlers such as the West Willa in Cambridgeshire and the North Gyrwe in Lincolnshire at just 600 hides). Under Alfred the Great, the hide became a unit of military assessment, and a document called the Burghal Hidage (dating from around 910) suggests each hide was expected to provide one man to garrison the fortified 'burhs' Alfred had established, with each man patrolling some 16 feet (5m) of wall, and Winchester having a garrison of around 2,400.

2

King Edmund of East Anglia, killed by tying him to a tree and shooting arrows at him. The Viking host that invaded East Anglia in 869 soon overwhelmed the forces of its ruler Edmund. As the Anglo-Saxon chronicler Asser wrote, 'he was killed there with a large number of his men, and the heathen rejoiced triumphantly'. Later, stories circulated claiming that the Vikings had demanded Edmund renounce his Christian faith, and when the king refused they tied him to a tree and used him for archery practice before beheading him. When his followers came to recover the body they could not find the head until a helpful wolf (who just happened to speak Latin) growled out 'Hic hic!' ('Here, here!') on the spot where it lay. Edmund's body parts were reunited and he soon came to be venerated as a saint.

3

His lack of good advice. Aethelred's nickname 'Unready' does not mean that he was unprepared for the (many) challenges of his long reign from 978 to 1016, but that he was *unraed,* which in Old English means 'lacking in advice' or badly advised. He was a king sorely in need of good advice; the early part of his reign was overshadowed by rumours that his faction at court had orchestrated the murder of his elder brother Edmund in order to gain the throne; and then in the late 980s he had to face renewed Viking invasions. The dam broke in 991 when the Norsemen won a signal victory at Maldon in Essex. In the aftermath of the defeat, Aethelred chose to bribe the Viking leaders to leave, which simply encouraged other warbands to come in the hope of a similar pay-off. Ransacking the treasury, extorting ever-greater levies from his subjects and even campaigns of prayer availed him little, and finally in 1014 he was forced out, caught between a massive Viking invasion by King Sweyn Forkbeard of Norway and his own rebellious and exasperated son Edmund Ironside. A brief restoration in 1014 proved an illusory coda to a little-lamented reign as Sweyn's son Cnut conquered the north of England and was poised to overwhelm the south when Aethelred passed away in April 1016.

4

Mercia. Meaning 'people of the march (or borderlands)', Mercia emerged in the Midlands in the early seventh century, where its central

Reis Audebert qe Kent teneit
De lignage Hengist eit esteit
Sil ad seint Austin baptizet
Et en le seint fontice regeneret

Aupres le Rey fu la meisne
regenerez et baptize
Par la terre alont sermonant
Musters fesant clers ordenant
Fist li Rey et li barony
Primes li englesf et li baroy
Kent air receit baptesme
Enfauz levez et oint de creme
Reis sey est repaire
Melk esteit ioiouse et lie
Lapostoill ad tot oie
Kui out le people regenere
Arthkalein un gentil bier

position allowed it to expand in all directions but also made it vulnerable to coalitions against it. Mercia first rose to real prominence under the pagan king Penda (d. 655), who invaded Northumbria several times and exercised an overlordship over Wessex. Under Aethelbald (r. 716-757) the Mercians took control of London, but the zenith of its power was reached in the reign of Offa (757-796), who dominated the other Anglo-Saxon kingdoms, treated on equal terms with the great Frankish ruler Charlemagne and built the defensive dyke on the western border of his kingdom that bears his name. Mercia suffered badly in the Viking invasions: the eastern part of it fell under Danish rulers after the 870s (becoming part of the Danelaw) and its western portion briefly retained a form of independence, but after 918 came under the rule of ealdormen appointed by the kings of Wessex.

5

Battle of Edington. Alfred had never expected to become King of Wessex, being the fourth son of Aethelwulf, but between 855 and 871 his brothers Aethelbald, Aethelbert and Aethelred died, the last in battle against the Vikings. Alfred managed to hold off the Danes and then bought peace, only for a new invasion in 878 to catch him unawares while celebrating the New Year at the royal estate at Chippenham. Forced to flee, he spent several months biding his time in the marshes at Athelney in the Somerset Levels - a sojourn during which the almost certainly apocryphal story of his burning of the cakes is set - before emerging and joining up with the forces his surviving ealdormen had recruited. Alfred's army then marched towards Chippenham, where it met the Viking host at a place called Ethandun (or Edington). A long struggle ensued, but finally the Anglo-Saxons, arrayed in a shield-wall bristling with spears, forced the Vikings to flee back to Chippenham. After a brief siege, their leader, Guthrum,

Aethelbert baptised by Augustine, from a manuscript by Wace of Bayeux, around 1450.

surrendered, accepted a Christian baptism with Alfred as his godfather, promised to keep the peace and retired back to East Anglia.

6

Harald Hardrada. Harald Hardrada's career - his nickname means 'harsh ruler' - included a long spell of exile in Russia after his half-brother King Olaf II was killed by a pro-Danish army in 1014, service in the Varangian Guard (an elite force of imperial bodyguards) in Constantinople, and finally the winning of the Norwegian crown in 1047. Harald believed he had a right to the throne of England through an agreement Magnus, his predecessor as Norwegian king, had made with Harthacnut of Denmark that whoever predeceased the other would cede all their territories to the other. Because Harthacnut, who died first, had become king of England, Harald Hardrada reckoned this gave him a right to the English throne. As a result, when Edward the Confessor died in 1066 and Harold Godwinson was chosen as king by the Anglo-Saxon nobility, Harald, encouraged by Harold's renegade brother Tostig, assembled an invasion fleet and made for England. Despite early success in defeating an army of northern earls near York, on 25 September 1066 Hardrada was defeated and killed at Stamford Bridge by an army that Harold had hastily marched north. The battle is often regarded as the end of the Viking era in British history.

7

Hengist and Horsa. The end of the Roman period in British history and the invasion by Anglo-Saxons that followed it is shrouded in uncertainty. The much later *Anglo-Saxon Chronicle* says that the leaders of the first invaders were two brothers named Hengist and Horsa who landed at Ebbsfleet in Kent in 455. The eighth-century monastic historian Bede enlarges on the story, saying that a king of the Britons named Vortigern invited in a force of Saxons to defend his kingdom against the depredations of Scottish and Pictish pirates, but that these mercenaries, led by Hengist and

Horsa, demanded more and more payment before they finally revolted and took over the kingdom, causing so much destruction that 'there was no one left to bury those who had died a cruel death'. In reality, there were probably no real individuals called Hengist and Horsa (the names mean 'gelding' and 'horse'), although their story may well represent something like what actually happened around the 440s, when the first wave of Anglo-Saxon invaders is thought to have arrived in Britain.

8

Aethelstan. The grandson of Alfred the Great, Aethelstan became king of Wessex in 924. Three years later he conquered the Viking kingdom of York, effectively making himself the master of all England. As a result of this, and the recognition of his overlordship by rulers including Constantine II of Alba (the forerunner of Scotland), Hywel Dda of Deheubarth in Wales and Owain of Strathclyde,

Aethelstan's claims on his coins to be *Rex totius Britanniae* ('king of all Britain') had a certain ring of truth. His success, however, caused a reaction and in 937 a coalition of Constantine II, Owain and Olaf Guthfrithson, the Viking king of Dublin, assembled against him. Marching south they met Aethelstan's host at a placed called Brunanburh. Exactly where the battle took place is unknown, and possible candidates have been put forward in Yorkshire, Lincolnshire, Northamptonshire and Northumbria. Recent work indicates that it was very likely on the Wirral, not far from a village that bears the similar name of Bromborough. After hard fighting, the Anglo-Saxons were victorious. Five Viking kings and a number of jarls were killed and the coalition against Aethelstan was shattered. Although it

A Viking longship, from the Anglo-Saxon codex Cotton MS Tiberius, around 1050.

was nearly 20 years before the Viking kingdom of York was definitively conquered, the chances of a new Viking conquest of Wessex were much diminished by Brunanburh.

9

The 'Great Army' (or *micel here*). Although the Vikings had first overwintered in England in 850 on the Isle of Thanet, making their raiding the next spring much easier (as they did not have to cross the North Sea), the threat of the invaders only became critical in 865 when a new large force arrived in England. Probably numbering at least several thousand, the 'Great Army' (or *micel here* in Old Norse), progressively conquered the main Anglo-Saxon kingdoms, beginning with York in 866 (which they assaulted on 1 November, the Feast of All Saint's Day, when they knew the defences would be laxer) and then East Anglia in 869 and Mercia in 874. Garrisons were left to defend these new conquests and so when the Great Army, by then led by Guthrum, invaded Wessex in the early 870s, its numbers were diminished, contributing to its defeat by Alfred in 878. By then the raiders, with parts of the army having been on campaign for more than a decade, had begun to settle down and divide the land between them. While other large Viking hosts invaded in the 870s and 890s, none had as large an impact as the Great Army before the invasion led by Sweyn and Cnut in 1013.

10

Kent. As the closest point in England to continental Europe, Kent was a natural conduit for influences, including trade and invaders, to enter Britain. Kent was where Pope Gregory I sent the first Christian mission to the Anglo-Saxons; he is said to have seen fair-haired slaves being sold in the market at Rome and upon being told they were Anglo-Saxons quipped they were *Non Angeli, sed Angli* ('Not Angels, but Angles'). The pope then despatched a group of monks led by Augustine, prior of St Andrew's Abbey in Rome, to bring Christianity back to England (where it seems largely to have disappeared after the collapse of the Roman province the previous

century). Augustine arrived at Canterbury, the capital of the kingdom of Kent in 597, where their reception was greatly assisted by the king's wife Bertha, who was Frankish, already being a Christian. Soon after, King Aethelberht himself was baptised by Augustine, who the pope had appointed England's first archbishop, with his see at Canterbury, and from there the progressive conversion of all the main Anglo-Saxon kingdoms over the next century proceeded.

11

Eirik Bloodaxe. The Vikings first captured York in 867, but initially they ruled it through English puppet kings. By the mid-870s, however, a line of Viking monarchs had imposed itself, beginning with Halfdan Ragnarsson. These monarchs established a thriving community of Scandinavians and held off attempts by the rulers of Wessex to push north until Aethelstan's defeat of a Viking-Scottish coalition at Brunanburh in 937 allowed him to chase out King Guthfrith and take York. Aethelstan's death in 939 enabled a Viking comeback under Guthfrith's son Olaf, and control then swung several times between Wessex and the Norsemen until in 952 Eirik, who rejoiced in the nickname 'Bloodaxe', took it for the Vikings once more. His reign proved ephemeral because the people of York expelled him just two years later and as he retreated north he was killed, at a place called Stainmore, by a certain Earl Maccus.

Genius Question

Emma of Normandy. Cnut (or Canute) initially invaded England in summer 1013 in the army of his father, the king of Denmark, Sweyn Forkbeard – and, having driven King Aethelred from Wessex, assumed the crown of England in 1014 following Sweyn's death. After a complex struggle involving the returned Aethelred and his son Edmund Ironside, Cnut definitively secured the English kingship in 1016. To reinforce his rule, he married Aethelred's widow, Emma, the daughter of Duke Richard the Fearless of Normandy, who became a key figure in securing the loyalty of the Anglo-Saxon nobility to the new regime. After Cnut's death in 1035, when Harald Harefoot, his son by another wife, became king, Emma tried to promote the cause of Alfred and Edward, her sons by Aethelred, but their attempted seizure of the throne ended in Alfred's murder and Edward's flight back to Normandy. In 1040 she managed to get Harthacnut, her son by Cnut, recognised as king, and when he died in 1042 she promoted the cause of Edward (later known as Edward the Confessor), making her the wife and the mother of two English kings.

Emma, from the Encomium Emmae Reginae ('In Praise of Emma'), eleventh century.

1

Their names in English – 'black pool'. Dublin was founded in 841 by Viking raiders from Scandinavia who needed a fortified harbour (or *longphort*) to beach their ships. The original Gaelic name *dubh linn* (or 'black pool') is derived from the deep pool formed by where the city's Poddle stream met the River Liffey. The Irish capital's modern name in Gaelic is Baile Áth Cliath, which means 'town at the ford of the hurdles' and refers to its location on an important medieval trade route. Dublin's English 'namesake' Blackpool, known for its Pleasure Beach and

iconic tower, which opened in 1894, gets its name from a drainage ditch which once flowed through the area and over a peat bog, lending the water a rather muddy hue.

2

Máel Morda, king of Leinster. Fought on Good Friday 1014, the Battle of Clontarf was the culmination of a long period of expansion of the Dal Cais kingdom of Brian Boruma (or Boru), which saw him become High King of Ireland by 1002. Fearful of Brian's ambitions, a coalition emerged against him, led by Sihtric Silkenbeard,

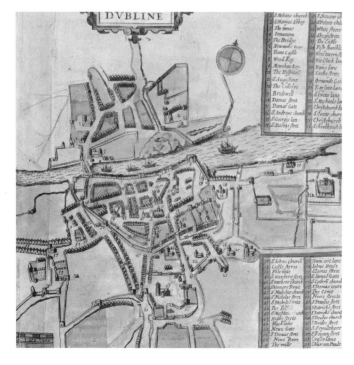

A map of Dublin, from *Civitates orbis terrarum*, by Braun and Hogenberg, 1600-23.

the Norse king of Dublin, and King Máel Morda of Leinster. Both sides gathered allies, with the force arrayed against Brian including the Viking rulers of Orkney and the Isle of Man. Among the dead in the clash that followed was Brian – slain, it was said, while praying in his tent – and his eldest son and heir Murchad, while on the other side Sigurd the Stout, Earl of Orkney, and Brodir of Man both fell. The Leinstermen and Dublin Norse eventually fled and were slaughtered in great numbers, leaving the political power of Viking Dublin neutered, but creating a succession crisis in Dal Cais that shattered the legacy of Brian.

3

Strongbow. The English invasion of Ireland began in 1169, when a group of Anglo-Norman mercenaries was called over by Diarmait mac Murchada, the deposed king of Leinster, to help restore him to his throne. Successful in their mission, the group was joined by a further wave of Anglo-Normans in 1170 led by Richard de Clare, the Earl of Pembroke. He managed to insinuate himself into Diarmait's favour, marrying his daughter Aoife and being declared the heir to the Leinster kingdom. Unfortunately, de Clare's growing pretensions aroused the ire of Henry II and led to the king intervening with an official English force in October 1171, beginning 750 years of British involvement in Ireland. De Clare's nickname only appears a century after his death and has nothing to do with his prowess at archery, but seems to be a corruption either of Striguil (the early medieval name for Chepstow), which lay within his lands, or of a Norman-French word meaning 'fancy trousers'.

4

Boycott. Formed in 1879, the Irish Land League campaigned against excessive rent rises and the ensuing evictions imposed on tenants by largely English landowners. Its first president, Charles Stewart Parnell, inveighed against the injustices and sought to raise funds to help beleaguered tenant farmers buy out their landlords. An ineffective Land Act of 1881 did little to resolve the situation, and Parnell turned his fire on

the worst cases, such as Charles Cunningham Boycott, agent of the 3rd Earl of Erne in Count Mayo. Parnell instructed him to reduce his rents by a quarter and when Boycott refused, Parnell and the Land League encouraged his tenants to withhold their rent and refuse to carry out labour for Boycott. This strike gave rise to the term 'boycott', although the man himself remained in place as agent until 1886, and it was not until the 1903 Land Purchase Act began to break up huge estates owned by absentee landlords that the iniquities symbolised by Boycott began to subside.

5

Stormont. Originally built in the 1830s for the Cleland family – and remodelled in 1858 in a baronial style that gave it its appellation of 'Castle' – Stormont. When Ireland was partitioned in 1921, the British government, needing a home for the Northern Ireland parliament to represent the six counties that had remained in the United Kingdom, purchased Stormont for £21,000. From then until direct rule from Westminster was imposed during the Troubles, it was the official residence of the Prime Minister of Northern Ireland, and then the headquarters of two short-lived Northern Ireland Assemblies in 1973-74 and 1982-86, and then from 1998 – with several periods of suspension – of the current iteration.

6

Belfast. Long one of Ireland's most notable products, linen has been woven there from the late Bronze Age. Industrialisation led to an upsurge in production and a rise in exports, and by the 1870s Ulster linen had become dominant, with over 14,000 looms in use in the province, boosted when the American Civil War cut off supplies of raw cotton and led some textile manufacturers to turn to the flax used to make linen. At the centre of this manufacturing and trade was Belfast, the largest linen centre in the world. Mounting costs, the effect of World War Two, which cut off flax supplies from Russia, and the appearance of lower-cost competitors decimated the Northern Irish linen industry – one of whose Belfast mills, York Street, had employed over 5,000 people – and by the 1960s 'Linenopolis' was no more.

7

Oscar Wilde. Dublin-born Wilde, one of the most famous of Irish writers, and the author of dramatic masterpieces such as *The Importance of Being Earnest* (1895) and the novel *The Picture of Dorian Grey* (1891), came from a literary family. His mother Jane was a well-known nationalist poet, who wrote for *The Nation* newspaper under the nom-de-plume Speranza (the Italian for 'hope'). She also turned to retelling Irish folktales after the death of her husband in near bankruptcy led the family to move to London in 1879, where her legendary literary soirées and wit did much to form the character of her son.

Oscar Wilde.

8

The island of Iona. The Book of Kells is an illuminated gospel book, dating from around AD 800, which has resided in the library of Trinity College Dublin since the 1660s; its lavish depictions of the evangelists and 'carpet page' of intertwining knots and roundels are among the glories of medieval manuscript art. Produced in the Insular style prevalent in Scotland, northern England and Ireland in the centuries around this date, candidates for its place of origin include the Abbey of Kells in County Meath and Lindisfarne Abbey off the northeast coast of England. It was, however, most likely produced in the mother abbey on the island of Iona, off the coast of Argyll in Scotland, whence the monks fled around 825 in the face of persistent Viking raids, carrying the monastery's treasures with them to the daughter house at Kells.

9

White Star Line. Famously sinking on the night of 14-15 April 1912 after hitting an iceberg, with the loss of over 1,500 passengers and crew, the *Titanic* was laid down in March 1909 at Harland & Wolff's shipyard in Belfast. It was part of White Star Line chairman J. Bruce Ismay's response to his great rival Cunard's new ships, the *Mauretania* and *Lusitania*. With its 16 watertight bulkhead compartments said to render it 'unsinkable', *Titanic* was the second of White Star's *Olympic*-class liners and Ismay accompanied the ship on her maiden voyage. There were not enough lifeboats on *Titanic* for all those aboard (as maritime regulations at the time did not insist on it) and women and children were given priority. Nonetheless, Ismay managed to get aboard one just before the ship finally went down, a fact for which he was much vilified in the press in the aftermath of the disaster.

10

'Silken' Thomas. Appointed his father's deputy in February 1534 when Gerald, the 9th Earl of Kildare, was summoned by Henry VIII to London (to die there in the Tower of London on 2 September), Thomas renounced his allegiance to the English Crown and declared a crusade to restore Catholic supremacy in Ireland. His rebellion faltered when a siege of Dublin failed, and his stronghold Maynooth Castle surrendered in March 1535, effectively ending the Kildare rebellion. He surrendered five months later and was taken to London, where he was executed on 3 February 1537. The nickname 'Silken' was bestowed on Thomas for the richness of the clothing in which he and his retinue dressed themselves.

11

Maria Edgworth. After moving to Ireland as a teenager, Maria Edgworth observed the interactions between her estate-owning father and the Irish peasantry, which informed the early children's tales she wrote for her 21 brothers and sisters. Later, she turned to more political themes, focusing on abuses of absentee English landowners, which she chronicled in *The Absentee* (1812), *Patronage* (1814) and *Ormond* (1817). In her *Practical Education* (1798) she championed a more scientific approach to education focused on age-appropriate material built gradually on a firm foundation of knowledge. Poor reviews for her edition of her father's *Memoirs* in 1820 dissuaded her from any further literary ventures until *Helen* in 1834. One of the most famous English-language novelists in the early nineteenth century, her star soon waned until her rediscovery in the twenty-first.

Genius Question

Boxing. Ireland has competed in the Summer Olympics since 1924 in Paris, and won its first medal, a gold in the men's hammer-throw, at the 1928 Amsterdam games. However, Ireland's most successful Olympic sport has been boxing, at which the country has won 16 medals (up to 2016), including Michael Carruth's gold at the 1992 Barcelona men's welterweight, and Katie Taylor's first place in the women's lightweight competition at the 2012 London Olympics. Although Ireland has sent athletes to seven winter games (up to 2018), it has yet to win a medal.

Prime Ministers

1

Sir Robert Walpole. Walpole, who served as prime minister for 20 years and 315 days (from April 1721 until February 1742), was also the first person to hold the role. His official title was First Lord of the Treasury and his political skill in navigating the turbulent waters of British politics in the early Hanoverian era (when George I lacked both English and long-standing aristocratic supporters) enabled political parties to gain ground and helped him to recover from a spell in the Tower of London, for corruption in 1712, to become chief minister under both George I and George II. Walpole survived early crises such as the South Sea Bubble, a financial investment scandal, in 1720 and maintained his position through assiduous management of the House of Commons until entanglement in a needless war against Spain in 1739 (dubbed the War of Jenkins' Ear, because the casus belli was the mutilation of a Welsh sea captain's ear by the Spanish) combined to force his resignation.

2

'Hubble-bubble'. Thomas Pelham-Holles, the 1st Duke of Newcastle, acquired his distinctive nickname on account of his reputation for hurrying everywhere (the word describes a commotion or flurry of activity). One of Britain's richest landowners, with an income estimated at over £40,000 a year, he was a 30-year veteran of political intrigue when he finally became prime minister in 1754. Early defeats in the Seven Years' War with France, which broke out in 1756, led to his resignation, although he returned the following year. George III, who became king in 1760, disliked the duke, and he was finally forced out of office two years later.

3

Archibald Philip Primrose, the Earl of Rosebery, Liberal prime minister from 1894 to 1895. A staunch defender of the British Empire, Rosebery cut his political teeth as William Gladstone's manager in the Midlothian Campaign of political speeches in 1879–80. His divided Cabinet and a Tory-dominated House of Commons meant his tenure in office was brief. He drifted further from the Liberal mainstream in later life, supporting British involvement in the Boer War and becoming the leader of the 'Liberal Imperialists' who bitterly opposed Irish Home Rule. As a result, he did not hold high political office again.

4

Theresa May. James Chuter Ede, the Labour MP for South Shields, was Home Secretary for all of Clement Attlee's term as prime minister in 1945–51, but he never rose higher. Theresa May served on London's Merton Council before being elected as MP for Maidenhead in 1997. After several Shadow Cabinet positions and a stint as Conservative Party chairman, she was appointed Home Secretary in May 2010, a position she held until June 2016, gaining a reputation as a hardliner on public order and immigration issues. In the aftermath of Britain's referendum vote to leave the European Union (EU) and David Cameron's resignation as prime minister, she was elected Conservative Party leader and appointed prime minister. Her premiership was dominated by attempts to secure an exit agreement with the EU acceptable to her own party and the EU's negotiators, a task made more difficult when she called a general election in 2017 in a bid to gain a bigger majority, but ended up with in a minority government forced into an informal coalition with Northern Ireland's Democratic Unionist Party. After two more years of gruelling negotiations and parliamentary defeats, she resigned in June 2019.

5

Henry Addington, 1st Viscount Sidmouth. Tory prime minister from 1801 to 1804, Addington was MP for Devizes in Devon, but made little impact until his election as Speaker in 1789, an office he held for 12 years. He succeeded William Pitt 'the Younger' as prime minister, negotiating the Peace of Amiens in 1802 that promised an end to the war. When that collapsed in 1803, so did Addington's administration and he resigned in May 1804. He returned to high office as Home Secretary in 1812, earning a reputation as a harsh reactionary, who championed measures intended to prevent any revolutionary infection in Britain, including the Six Acts, which gagged newspapers and banned protest meetings. His ten-year tenure also saw the Peterloo Massacre, when 11 people (perhaps even as many as 20) were killed because cavalry charged a mass meeting in Manchester called to demand parliamentary reform.

'The Plumb-pudding in danger;- or - State Epicures taking un Petit Souper', by Gillray, 1805.

6

The Earl of Rosebery. Rosebery (prime minister from 1894 to 1895) was something of an anomaly even in aristocrat-dominated nineteenth-century British politics. While many other prime ministers, including Disraeli and Earl Grey served in the Commons before their elevation to the peerage, or received titles later in their career, the only other nineteenth-century prime minister who sat exclusively in the House of Lords was Lord Aberdeen, prime minister from 1852 to 1855.

7

Oldham. Churchill, who served two terms as prime minister, from 1940 to 1945 and 1951 to 1955 (his tenure as wartime leader securing his reputation as one of Britain's greatest prime ministers), began his Commons career as MP for the northwest constituency of Oldham in 1900. He was deselected by the local Conservative Party after his defection to the Liberals, and then rapidly won the seat at Manchester North West, which he served for two years. In 1908 he transferred to Dundee, a seat he held for 14 years. Relationships with his Scottish constituents became strained by his neglect of the seat and Churchill, hampered by appendicitis, lost in the 1922 election, but he bounced back as MP for Epping in 1924, and then

from 1945 to 1964 for its subdivision of Woodford. At his resignation, he was the longest-serving MP in the modern political era, having been an MP for nearly 64 years.

8

George Canning. Prime minister from April to August 1827, Canning had served as Foreign Secretary from 1807 to 1809, before his star temporarily fell after a feud with Lord Castlereagh. Foreign Secretary again from 1822 to 1827, Canning ably guided British foreign policy, but when he finally reached the highest office – after his predecessor as prime minister, Lord Liverpool, had a stroke – his own health collapsed and he died after just 119 days in office. Although several other prime ministers have had shorter terms (including Lord Rockingham for 96 days in 1782), they had second or subsequent terms in office and so their total time in office exceeded that of Canning.

9

Spencer Perceval. Appointed prime minister in 1809, Perceval had a turbulent time in office; weak support in the House of Commons meant his administration was constantly unstable, while opposition from the Prince Regent further undermined his authority. On 11 May 1812, the Commons was considering measures to alleviate the economic depression blighting the North of England. Perceval was running late and as he entered the Commons lobby, a bystander pulled a pistol from his pocket and shot the prime minister at point-blank range in the chest. The assassin was John Bellingham, who blamed Perceval for failing to secure him compensation for his five-year incarceration in a Russian debtors' prison. Perceval was survived by 12 children, only one of whom, a son also called Spencer, followed him into politics, serving as an MP in three parliaments.

10

Boris Johnson. Prime minister from July 2019, Johnson was born in 1964 on the Upper East Side of Manhattan, New York City, where his father was studying Economics at Columbia University. Although Andrew Bonar Law (prime minister from 1922 to 1923) was born in New Brunswick, Canada, in 1858, it was at the time a British possession. Lord Shelburne and the Duke of Wellington were both born in Dublin, but it was during the period of British rule in Ireland. As a result, Johnson is the only prime minister to have been born in non-British territory, in his case entitling him to United States citizenship, which he only renounced in 2016.

11

Arthur Balfour. Prime Minister in succession to his uncle Lord Salisbury, Balfour served in the role from 1902 to 1905. Initially better known as a philosopher, even he did not at first take his political career seriously, remarking: 'I am more or less happy when being praised, not very comfortable when being abused, but I have moments of uneasiness when being explained.' By 1891 he was First Lord of the Treasury and seen as Salisbury's natural heir. His premiership included measures on Irish land reform and an Education Act, the negotiation of the Entente Cordiale with France in 1904, and the Licensing Act of the same year, which paid pub landlords to close down (so reducing the oversupply of licensed premises). He resigned in 1905, but returned to the Cabinet during World War One as Lloyd George's Foreign Secretary, a tenure in office for which he is most famous, because in November 1917 he wrote the letter later known as the Balfour Declaration, which pledged British support for Zionist efforts to establish a Jewish homeland in Palestine.

Genius Question

Stanley Baldwin. Conservative prime minister from 1923 to May 1924, from November 1924 (after the collapse of Ramsay Macdonald's short-lived first-ever Labour government) to 1929, and again from 1935 to 1937, Baldwin served under George V, Edward VIII and George VI. The latter part of his premiership was blighted by the growing spectre of German power and debates over how far and fast Britain should rearm, and in May 1937 his replacement was Neville Chamberlain.

Britain in Pictures (part two)

1

'White' (Whitehaven, Whitehall and Gilbert White). Whitehaven, on the Cumbrian coast, was the site of a Benedictine monastery from 1120, but owed its real development to the establishment of a quay for a small fishing village in 1633. It grew rich on the coal trade (the chimneys of collieries can be seen in the distance in this mid-nineteenth century view of the port), with sugar, rum and the slave trade adding to the mass of shipping jostling in its harbours. The West Pier Lighthouse shown on the engraving was built in 1832.

Originally the street leading to the royal palace built by Henry VIII in the 1530s, Whitehall was widened by Oliver Cromwell, but was bordered at the time by private residences until their leases reverted to the Crown and the thoroughfare became associated with the government departments which now line it. Horse Guards, shown here in an 1826 engraving, replaced an earlier barracks for the Household Cavalry that had become dilapidated. It was rebuilt between 1750 and 1760 by William Kent in the Palladian style that he became the principal promoter of in Britain (his other buildings include Holkham Hall in Norfolk) and appears in numberless tourist photographs as one of the spots where bearskin helmeted sentries of the Queen's Guard may be snapped.

Gilbert White was an early British naturalist and parson of Selborne in Hampshire, whose love of nature – which led him to remark 'Earthworms, though in appearance a small and despicable link in the chain of nature, yet, if lost, would make a lamentable chasm' – has caused him to be labelled the first British ecologist. His *The Natural History and Antiquities of Selborne*, published in 1789, is a lovingly crafted account

of the animals and plants he observed over his decades at Selborne, presented in the form of over 100 letters.

2

Crystal Palace. The Great Exhibition, which took place between May and October 1851, was held in a building that was soon dubbed the 'Crystal Palace' for its astonishing architecture inspired by the greenhouses which its architect Joseph Paxton had designed for the 6th Duke of Devonshire at Chatsworth House. Exactly 1,851 feet (564m) long, in a nod towards the date, its cavernous interior enclosed three large elm trees already on the site, as well as a 27-foot-high (8-m) coloured glass fountain and

Crystal Palace opens in Hyde Park, 1 May 1851.

14,000 exhibits from around the globe. It took 28 miles (45km) of guttering and 9,000 square feet (836sqm) of glass to build and it was opened to great fanfare (including a massed rendering of the 'Halleluiah' chorus from Handel's *Messiah*) on 1 May. Once the exhibition closed, the Crystal Palace was dismantled and then transported and re-erected on a site at Sydenham Hill in South London, where it stood until it was almost totally destroyed in a catastrophic fire on the night of 30 November 1936. Its former grounds now house a dinosaur park.

3

They were all imprisoned at one time or another. There was a darker side to Sir Thomas Malory, whose *Le Morte d'Arthur*, the first English prose version of the chivalric legend of King Arthur and his knights, was published by William Caxton in 1485, some 15 years after the author's death. Although elected as an MP in 1443, he was accused in 1451 of an attack on the Duke of Buckingham and then of extortion and burglary in his local area of Warwickshire. After escaping custody by swimming a moat, he was finally tried in 1451 and incarcerated in Marshalsea Prison in London for a year. His crimes may have had a political nature, as they were aimed at prominent Lancastrians and in 1461 he was pardoned by the new Yorkist king, Edward IV.

Christopher Marlowe, a literary prodigy, whose short life yielded several masterpieces, including *Dido, Queen of Carthage, The Jew of Malta* and *Doctor Faustus*, before his murder aged 29 in 1593, had several brushes with the law. In 1589 he was briefly imprisoned after a brawl in which a neighbour died, and in 1592 he was detained in the Netherlands on charges of counterfeiting. In May the following year he was arrested during an investigation of a libellous tract attacking French Huguenot refugees. Although he was released, ten days later he was killed during another drunken brawl. Daniel Defoe, who is most famous today for his novel *Robinson Crusoe*, published in 1719, was better known to his contemporaries as a political pamphleteer. His venomous wit proved his undoing in 1703 when

his satirical pamphlet 'The Shortest way with Dissenters', heaping ridicule on the persecution of Nonconformist Protestants (of whom Defoe was one), led to his arrest, conviction and sentence to indefinite detention until he had paid a large fine, as well as three stints in the pillory (although his popularity was such that instead of pelting him with rotten fruit, the mob threw flowers and began a riotous party drinking to his health.) His *A Journal of the Plague Year* was published in 1722 as part of the bitter debate about what measures should be taken to prevent the pestilence then raging in Marseilles from reaching Britain. Although purporting to be a journal, Defoe was only five years old at the time of the 1665 outbreak in London it described and so could hardly have recalled much about it.

4

All appear in the titles of a Shakespeare play (*Julius Caesar, The Merchant of Venice* and *The Taming of the Shrew*). The fertile pen of Britain's greatest playwright produced at least 39 plays (and possibly, if collaborations with others are included, a few more than that). *Julius Caesar* was first performed in 1599, at a time when the succession to the unmarried Elizabeth I was unclear, and its account of the assassination of the great Roman general by Brutus and the turmoil that follows is a warning against political instability. *The Merchant of Venice*, written around 1598, tells of the consequences of a debt owed by Antonio to a Jewish moneylender named Shylock and is set against an Italian backdrop of the type Shakespeare quarried for several of his other plays. *The Taming of the Shrew*, written around 1590, is one of Shakespeare's finest comedies, turning on themes of love, marriage, deception and disguise and centring on the attempt by Petruchio to win the hand of, and tame, the gloriously independently minded Katherina (the 'shrew' of the title).

1

Ely. Ely, in a low-lying district of the fens, was long accessible only by boat, hence its designation as an 'island'. It derives its name from the Old English *eilge*, or 'eel district', and was the site of an early Anglo-Saxon abbey founded by St Etheldreda in 673. It formed a centre of resistance to William I after the Norman Conquest, but then received a magnificent Romanesque cathedral begun in 1083. Oliver Cromwell lived in Ely for ten years from 1636, but by then it had entered an economic decline.

2

Cardigan. An open-fronted knitted top, traditionally fastened with buttons, the cardigan was name for Lord Cardigan, the British commander at the Charge of the Light Brigade in 1854 (a disastrous charge against a battery of Russian guns caused by military incompetence but much romanticised after the event as an act of heroic bravery). It was said he devised it as a convenient way of keeping warm in the cold Crimean winter, which would not, like longer coats, risk getting caught in campfires. The Welsh town of which he was the 7th Earl grew up around the castle built by the Normans in 1093 as they encroached on the Welsh Marches, dismantling Welsh independence piecemeal before its wholesale demolition by Edward III in the 1280s. Deriving later prosperity from the herring trade, Cardigan was for a brief time in the nineteenth century the leading port of Wales, eclipsing even Swansea and Cardiff.

3

St David's ('St David' on the map). The life of the sixth-century Welsh holy man Saint David (or Dewi Sant) is shrouded in uncertainty, much of

it set down in a late-eleventh century life by a monk named Rhygyfarch. His father was said to be a prince of the kingdom of Ceredigion. In around 550 he established his monastery, dying some 40 or 50 years later and becoming the subject of a cult venerating his memory. He was canonised by Pope Callixtus II in 1120 and became regarded as the patron saint of Wales. The settlement that grew up around his monastic foundation took on his name, although it subsequently dwindled to become Britain's smallest city.

4

Dunwich ('Dunwiche'). Now a small Suffolk village, for a time Dunwich was the capital of the Anglo-Saxon kingdom of East Anglia and one of England's ten largest towns. The coastal position that had gifted it prosperity as a port proved Dunwich's undoing, as a series of storms in 1286–87 and 1328 swept much of the town into the sea, with a further great tempest in 1347 delivering the coup de grâce. Neglect of its sea defences had probably left it vulnerable and further coastal erosion, which continues into the present (the church of All Saints finally toppled into the sea in 1919), prevented any chance of a return to its former glory. It is said that when conditions are right, it is possible to hear the ghostly sound of church bells chiming in the submerged part of the town.

5

Flint ('Fflynt'). Flint in North Wales, just 13 miles (21km) from Chester, is said to owe its name either to *fluentum*, the Latin for 'tide' or 'flood', or the bed of gravelly flint on which, around 1277, the Normans built a castle, around which the present town grew up. As a bridgehead of

English influence, it was the target several times of Welsh attacks – Dafydd ap Grufudd's forces besieged it in 1282, shortly before his final defeat by the English, while the garrison was forced to burn it in 1295 to prevent it falling into the hands of Madog ap Llywelyn's rebels (although their successors a century later resisted a siege by Owain Glyndŵr in 1400). In 1969 the town hosted Wales's first National Eisteddfod.

6

Sandwich. The sandwich is said to have been invented for John Montagu, the eighteenth-century 4th Earl of Sandwich who needed a snack that he could consume without leaving the gaming tables. Sandwich, which was originally called Lundenwich, was established around 664 to replace the old Roman port (and fort) at Rutupiae (Richborough), which had decayed and silted up, as a principal port in Kent. Its easy access to France proved a double-edged sword and in 1217 Prince Louis of France landed there as part of his failed bid to unseat King John and the French returned in 1457 and burned it to the ground, murdering the mayor. Later in the mid-sixteenth century Elizabeth I granted Flemish refugees the right to settle there, so that by 1565, of 420 households in the town, 129 were Walloons. Among the valuable skills they brought was market gardening, and they cultivated celery in England for the first time. The town's most famous resident was Thomas Paine, the author of the revolutionary tract *Common Sense*, who lived in Sandwich for a short time in 1759.

7

Glastonbury. Glastonbury and its abbey became steeped in Arthurian legend during the Middle Ages, particularly after the late twelfth-century French poet Robert de Boron alleged in his *Estoire du Graal* ('History of the Grail') that Joseph of Arimathea came to Britain bearing the Holy Grail, the cup from which Jesus drank at the Last Supper. He was said to have reached Glastonbury, where he decided to rest, striking his staff into the ground, from which a miraculous thorn tree immediately appeared. The legend

tells that Joseph then founded a church, Britain's very first, just a few years after the Crucifixion. Glastonbury Abbey, in whose grounds a winter-flowering thorn tree grew until it was cut down by parliamentary soldiers in 1647, is in truth not quite so venerable, having been founded by King Ine of Wessex in 712.

8

Rochester, Chester and Winchester ('Rouchestre', 'Chestre' and 'Winchestre') – all include 'chest'. Rochester, Chester and Winchester all derive the last part of their name from *castrum*, the Latin for a fort, which, during Anglo-Saxon times was corrupted to '-caester' and came to mean any fortified point. Rochester was in Roman times called Durobrivis, and was a way station on the road to London, its name later being abbreviated to Robrivis or Roibis and then Roibis-caester. Chester had been a Roman legionary fort, founded around AD 70 as Deva. A legion remained stationed there until at least the end of the third century. Winchester began life as the tribal capital of the Celtic Belgae, and became known as Venta Belgarum during the Roman occupation. Abandoned after the Romans left in the early fifth century, it was refounded in the seventh century, becoming the capital of the kingdom of Wessex, known as Ventacaester or Wintancaester.

1

Colours associated with medieval dyeing. As England became the centre of a thriving textiles industry from the Middle Ages (helped by climatic conditions which made the raising of sheep highly profitable), so individual towns became known for the colours traditionally used to dye cloth. In Coventry this was blue, and in Lincoln the dyers used green. The Lincoln colour, whose exact shade cannot be reconstructed, was made by mixing woad (which lends a blue colour to the fabric) with the plant known as dyer's weed, which is yellow. The first reference to it comes in 1182, when the Sheriff of Lincoln is recorded as having bought a length of green cloth. It may thus have been the Sheriff, rather than his arch-enemy Robin Hood, who was clad in 'Lincoln green'.

2

Five, but also two 'ancient towns' and seven 'limbs'. The Cinque Ports is a confederation of south coast ports, which acquired trading privileges and exemption from taxes as a result of their maritime service to the Crown. The confederation's origins probably lie in the reign of Edward the Confessor (r. 1042–66), and it initially comprised the towns of Sandwich, Dover, Hythe, New Romney and Hastings, their number (five) giving rise to the name (from the Norman French for five). To these were later added the two 'ancient towns' of Rye and Winchelsea and seven major limbs (Tenterden, Lydd, Folkestone, Faversham, Margate, Deal and Ramsgate), together with a number of associated towns such as Pevensey and Seaford. The original five ports first received a charter in 1155 granting them privileges in return for providing ships to the royal fleet, but their importance gradually

declined after the fourteenth century as other ports rose to prominence and because silting and storms, which changed the coastline, damaged some of their harbours, and in the case of New Romney literally left it high and dry after a storm in 1287. The Cinque Ports lingers on as a ceremonial grouping, the position of its highest official, the Warden, being occupied by Queen Elizabeth, the Queen Mother from 1978 to 2002.

3

St Albans. Verulamium was already a tribal centre of the Catuvellauni at the time of the Roman invasion of Britain in AD 43, and it grew to be one of the largest towns of the Roman province, complete with a Roman theatre and walls built between AD 250 and 300 as the security of the empire's outermost regions grew less certain. It gained its modern name from Alban, a resident of the town, who was executed in the third or fourth century when he offered his life to the magistrate in place of a Christian priest who was due to be put to death for his faith. As Alban was led to his execution, a spring is said to have miraculously appeared to quench his thirst. St Albans Cathedral was built to his martyrdom, the first Christian martyr in Britain.

4

Manchester. Granted to the city in 1842, Manchester's coat of arms includes a globe peppered with seven bees as a symbol of the industriousness of the city, which had become a main hub of the Industrial Revolution, its prosperity founded on the burgeoning cotton mills (of which it boasted 99 by 1830). The theme is enlarged upon in the city's Latin motto on the coat of arms, *Concilio et Labore*, which means 'by Wisdom and by Work'.

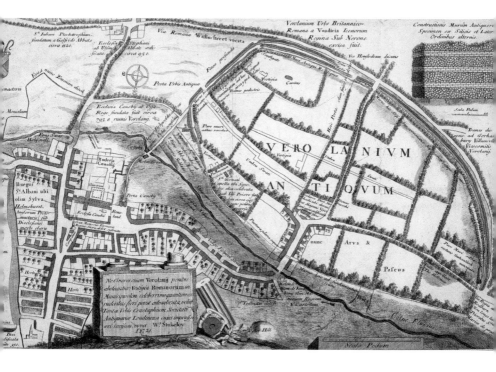

Verulamium Antiquum, by William Stukeley, 1721.

5

Fort by the River Taff. Cardiff owes its distant origins to a fort established by the Romans in the mid- AD 50s to keep down the restive Silures, who were vigorously resisting the conquest of Wales. It was long a ruin when the Norman aristocrat Robert FitzHamon built a new castle in its shattered shell around 1081. Around this a small market town grew, which became known as Caerdyf ('the fort by the River Taf', which flows by the castle), and eventually Cardiff (or Caerdydd in Welsh). A relative backwater after Tudor times, the development of the South Wales coal industry brought it renewed prosperity (by 1913 it was the largest coal-exporting port in the world) and its choice as the site of the Welsh National Assembly (or Senedd) from 1999 gave it a new role as a political capital.

6

1482, when it was captured by Richard Duke of Gloucester. The most northerly town in England,

Berwick-upon-Tweed was bitterly contested with Scotland for centuries. The first recorded transfer of the town took place in 1176 when William the Lion of Scotland ceded it to Henry II of England, but Richard I gave it back to the Scots to raise funds for his crusade in 1190. Edward I retook it in 1296, nearly destroying the town, and Berwick went back and forth between the two countries for the next two centuries, always suffering in the periodic border wars between them. Finally, in 1482, Richard of Gloucester (who was to become King Richard III the following year) captured Berwick, and the union of England and Scotland in 1603 put paid to any thoughts of Scottish reconquest. A story that Berwick was notionally at war with Russia from the end of the Crimean War until 1966 rests on memories of its uncertain legal status and an erroneous belief that it was specifically mentioned in the declaration of war against the Russians in 1854, but accidentally left out in the Treaty of Paris which ended it in 1856. In reality, Berwick was mentioned in neither document.

7

Trowbridge. Wiltshire is named for Wilton, an ancient town that was a principal seat of the kings of Wessex from the ninth century, but its county town has since 1889 been Trowbridge. A tiny settlement of 24 households at the time of Domesday Book, it grew as a centre for the textile trade from the fourteenth century and by the 1800s overshadowed its more venerable neighbour. When Wiltshire county council was formed after the Local Government Act of 1888, Trowbridge was chosen as its seat. Perhaps the town's most famous son or daughter is Isaac Pitman, born there in 1813, whose inspirational motto 'time saved is life gained' led him to devise the form of shorthand that bears his name.

8

Norwich. After the postal reforms of 1840, which introduced a uniform penny post and led to an increase in the volume of mail, the problem of delivering letters to the correct address – especially in London, where many streets bore the same name – became pressing. In 1857 a scheme divided the capital into ten postal districts (EC, WC, NW, N, NE, E, SE, S, SW and W). The NE and S districts were abolished after a report drafted by the novelist Anthony Trollope in 1866, but the system was broadly successful and was gradually extended to other towns, with the sub-district (such as W1) appearing during World War One. Finally, it was realised a more finely gradated system was needed and in 1959 postcodes with a full set of letters and numbers, indicating individual streets, was introduced, with the first trial taking place in Norwich. The modern version of postcodes appeared in 1966, sometimes indicating individual houses, beginning in Croydon. Ironically, the last town to receive these codes, a century after its pioneering role, was Norwich.

9

York. Long considered the capital of the North of England and the site of the country's second archbishopric, York was founded by the Romans in AD 71 as a legionary fortress, which they knew as Eboracum (probably from a Celtic root meaning 'Place of the Yew tree'). Although abandoned after the Roman withdrawal from Britain in 410, by the seventh century it had become an important centre of the Anglo-Saxon kingdom of Northumbria (whose king, Edwin, was baptised in 627 by St Paulinus, after which the first version of York Minster was established). It was at this time that the original Latin name was corrupted to become Eoforwic, a form that did not last long, since in 866 the city was conquered by the Vikings, who further mangled its name to become Jorvik, the form from which the modern York descends.

10

Belfast. Cavehill, the 1,207-foot (368-m) basalt hill that overlooks Belfast, derives its official name from the many caves dotted about its cliffs, but its nickname 'Napoleon's Nose' comes from its profile, which is said to resemble the face of the French emperor. The hill houses a Mesolithic stone cairn, an early medieval defensive promontory fort known as McArt's fort, and it is said that on a clear day it is possible to see the Isle of Man from its summit.

11

Glasgow, Newcastle, Manchester. The first image shows Glasgow in 1810, as elegant families walk along the banks of the Clyde, one carriage escorted by British redcoat troops. In the foreground is the Victoria Bridge, Glasgow's oldest, originally a wooden structure built in the fourteenth century and for over 300 years the only Clyde crossing, and in the background is the Glasgow Bridge, originally built by William Mylne in 1772 and in a later incarnation the first bridge in the city to be lit by electricity. The second view shows Newcastle upon Tyne in 1819, as seen from Rope Walk in Gateshead, its busy port bustling with sailing ships shown at a period when the city was just beginning to escape the economic stagnation caused by its overdependence on the coal-carrying trade. The third image is of Manchester and the new Exchange building constructed in 1809.

Illustration of Belfast and surrounding countryside.

Designed as a centre for the burgeoning cotton trade, its cost was underwritten by 400 members who each contributed £50 for the elegant Grecian-style building. It became a victim of its own success and was replaced by a larger Royal Exchange in 1867.

Genius Question

St Davids. Although the City of London (at a traditional one square mile, though in reality around 10 per cent larger) is Britain's smallest city by area, its population (8,760 in 2015) is nearly five times that of the Welsh city of St Davids (at 1,840 people). St Davids was long regarded as a city under the historical yardstick that any settlement with a cathedral merited the title. Technically it lost its status in 1886, when its borough corporation was abolished, and without its own government it could not be a city. The historical status quo was restored in 1994 when the Queen granted St Davids a new city charter.

ROUND

17

Land of Dreaming Spires

1

William of Ockham (anagram of 'mow mafia hillock'). The fourteenth-century English Franciscan friar William of Ockham lectured on logic before he was summoned to Avignon in 1324 to answer charges of heresy. A proponent of nominalism (that general designations such as 'city' or 'father' have no reality beyond the individual objects), he also taught that the papacy's power was limited by natural law, which got him into trouble with Pope John XXII, who excommunicated him. Ockham is best known for the principal of 'Ockham's razor', which teaches that 'entities are not to be multiplied beyond necessity' (that is, that the simplest solutions should be considered first), although this is a general principle of much medieval philosophy and is not unique to Ockham's works.

2

The British Library's Reading Room. The communist ideologue Karl Marx came to London in August 1849 after his incendiary journalism in the wake of the 1848 revolutions in Europe had led to his expulsion from Prussia and France. Perennially short of funds, he was supported in England by his friend Friedrich Engels (who had to bail him out when Marx and his family were evicted for failing to pay the rent). So poor he could scarcely afford the coffin for one child who died and ridiculed by the London communist group for being a 'paper revolutionary', Marx did the only thing he could: he wrote drafts of what would become *Das Kapital* in the splendid round Reading Room of the British Museum (which then housed the British Library). The work was laborious, and it took until 1867 for volume 1 to be published. The other two volumes were only published a decade after his death.

3

Thomas Hobbes. One of the founders of English political philosophy, Thomas Hobbes lived at a time when questions of the roots of sovereignty and the rights by which a monarch ruled were much debated. Just two years after the execution of King Charles I, an unprecedented act of regicide, Hobbes published his best-known work *Leviathan*. In it he develops an early form of social contract theory, in which he posits that people originally lived in a state of nature, in which there were no laws or obligations beyond the bonds of family, and that the state (and the sovereignty of a ruler) came about by a voluntary (but permanent) act of the giving up of the liberty they then enjoyed in exchange for the security that a ruler, and a government, could provide. It is as part of his description of that state of nature that he describes mankind's unhappy lot as 'solitary, poor, nasty, brutish and short'.

4

Pneumonia caught while stuffing a chicken with snow. Parliamentarian and statesman – he was attorney general and lord chancellor under James I – Francis Bacon was also an influential scientist: his *Novum Organum*, published in 1620, sets out the basis of the scientific method, by which facts are established through experimentation and conclusions drawn from these (rather than, as previously, derived from pure reason). After his disgrace in 1621, when he was convicted for corrupt acceptance of gifts from litigants, he continued to devote himself to experimentation and one day in 1626, while travelling in his carriage through a snowy Highgate, he took it into his head to see if snow could be used to preserve

Title page to *Leviathan* by Thomas Hobbes, 1651.

Non est potestas Super Terram quæ Comparetur ei Job 41. 24.

LEVIATHAN
or the
MATTER, FORM,
and POWER of
A COMMON WEALTH
ECCLESIASTICAL
and
CIVIL.

Written by
Thoˢ. Hobbs
1651.

meat. He obtained a chicken locally and duly stuffed it, but in the process caught a chill, which developed into pneumonia and after two or three days it proved fatal.

5

St Andrews. Founded in 1410, its establishment of resolved a tricky situation for Scottish students who had previously had to go south of the border to Oxford or Cambridge, or even further afield to Paris in search of an advanced education. The wars with England from the late thirteenth century had cut off the first avenue and then a schism in the Catholic Church in which Scotland supported the anti-Pope Clement VII, while France adhered to the Roman candidate Urban VI, made Paris suddenly an unfriendly environment for Scots. The new university obtained a papal bull (and so full recognition as a degree-granting body) from Clement's successor, Benedict XIII, in 1413. St Andrews remained Scotland's only university until 1451 when it acquired a rival in Glasgow. With the foundation of Aberdeen in 1495 and Edinburgh in 1583, Scotland had four such bodies, a number which England exceeded only in 1900.

6

A riot. The centuries-long rivalry between Oxford and Cambridge, therefore, began in a violent disturbance. Cambridge University has a variety of spurious foundation legends, from the Spanish prince Cantaber, said to have established it in AD 317 accompanied by a coterie of Greek philosophers, to King Arthur and Edward the

Elder. On more secure historical ground is the account of the Oxford scholars who in 1209 fled after one of their number had killed a townswoman, provoking a violent reaction in which three of the students were hanged. Most of the student body then fled, travelling eastwards until they reached Cambridge. There they and their academic masters established a new university, which is first mentioned in documents in 1226 and had by the 1230s received royal and papal recognition.

7

Edinburgh. While there are dozens of universities where a student can take a degree in psychology, there is only one university-level course in parapsychology. Established in 1985 through a bequest from the author Arthur Koestler, who was fascinated by the paranormal, the university's Koestler Parapsychology Unit describes the discipline as 'the scientific study of the capacity attributed to some individuals to interact with their environment by means other than the recognised sensorimotor channels', including extra-sensory perception and telekinesis, and offers courses at undergraduate, postgraduate and doctoral levels.

8

Roger Bacon. The thirteenth-century English Franciscan Roger Bacon was a polymath with an extraordinary range of interests. Escaping from the stifling intellectual bounds of the

Roger Bacon's writing on optics, late 1200s.

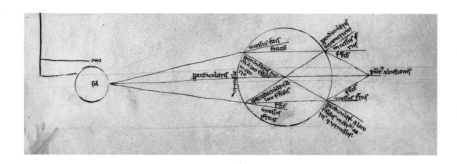

trivium, the medieval scholastic curriculum focused on grammar, logic and rhetoric, Bacon became a firm believer in experimentation and did work on astronomy, alchemy, astronomy and mathematics; he was the first European to describe gunpowder, and even put forward the idea of a mechanical flying machine. Although his experimentation earned him clerical disapproval, he was forced into becoming a Franciscan friar in 1257, which largely ended his scientific career. Bacon's reputation was such that he earned the posthumous accolade *Doctor Mirabilis* ('the marvellous doctor').

9

Jeremy Bentham. Bentham went to Oxford aged 12 to study law, but instead devoted himself to a life of philosophy, developing the doctrine of utilitarianism, which began from the principle that 'Nature has placed mankind under the governance of two sovereign masters, pain and pleasure' and that actions should be judged not by conventional moral principles, but on whether they produced the largest amount of pleasure for the largest number of people. Bentham left instructions that after his death (in 1832) his body should be preserved as an 'Auto-Icon' and displayed dressed in his own clothes. Unfortunately, the mummification process for the head went awry and it was replaced with a wax effigy. However, most of Britain's greatest utilitarian is still on view in the atrium of University College London.

10

Philippa Foot. The 'trolley problem' is an ethical and philosophical dilemma concerning whether it is morally acceptable to sacrifice the life of one person to save a large number of people. The scenario concerns a runaway trolley speeding down a railway track. A bystander sees that there are five people trapped on the track in its path and that pulling a lever will divert the trolley onto another track and save them. But then he notices that there is one person on the new track who will certainly die if the trolley is diverted. What is the ethical thing to do: to act and kill one and save five, or do nothing and let the five die and

the one live? Foot, born in Lincolnshire, studied Politics, Philosophy and Economics at Somerville College, Oxford, becoming a Fellow of the college and remaining attached to it for the rest of her academic career, although from the late 1960s she divided her time between there and the United States. Her work focused on moral judgements and whether morality can be rationally based, articulated in works such as *Natural Goodness*, a preoccupation that gave rise to the formulation of the 'trolley problem'.

11

John Stuart Mill. A child prodigy, who by the age of eight could read Herodotus's *History* in the original Greek, and two years later had devoured the dialogues of Plato, John Stuart Mill moved remorselessly on through Aristotle and the whole canon of classical philosophy and then onto modern political economists such as David Ricardo and Adam Smith. Heavily influenced by Jeremy Bentham, the English utilitarian philosopher, Mill went beyond these many sources of inspiration to produce a theory of liberty of the individual in opposition to the demands of the state. His works on logic and philosophy, including *A System of Logic* (1843), *On Liberty* (1859) and *Utilitarianism* (1861), made him perhaps the most influential English philosopher of the nineteenth century.

Genius Question

Bertrand Russell. Mathematician, philosopher and humanitarian, Russell was one of the founders of analytical philosophy and his great *Principia Mathematica*, the first part of which was published in 1910, sought to create a consistent logical basis for mathematics. An ardent pacifist, he was jailed during World War One for his anti-war activism, and later campaigned for nuclear disarmament as well as vigorously against authoritarian regimes and their suppression of freedom of opinion. His citation for the 1950 Nobel Prize for Literature noted that the award was 'in recognition of his varied and significant writings in which he champions humanitarian ideals and freedom of thought'.

A British Miscellany *(part two)*

1

He had been dead for three months. Edward Legge was elected MP for Portsmouth unopposed on 15 December 1747 in a by-election brought about by the fact that his predecessor, Thomas Gore, had also been elected MP for Bedford in the general election that summer and had chosen to take his seat there. Legge was a Royal Navy officer – the Portsmouth seat was effectively in the Admiralty's gift – and as far as anyone knew was serving in the West Indies, to where he had been sent as commodore of the Leeward Islands (to replace Fitzroy Henry Lee about whose drunken behaviour the council of Antigua had

complained). Because of the delays inherent in communication across the Atlantic, when all messages had to be carried by ship, word only reached England a few days after Legge's election that he had died in the West Indies on 15 September.

2

Field Marshal, by the Duke of Wellington. Field Marshal has been the most senior rank in the British Army since George Hamilton, the 1st Earl of Orkney, was promoted to it in 1735 (although by then, at 68, his active military career was long over). Arthur Wellesley made his reputation in

Duke of Wellington, illustration from *History of the French Revolution, and of the Wars Produced by that Terrible Event,* by Christopher Kelly, 1817.

the Peninsular War in Spain against Napoleon's armies, winning a string of victories, and in June 1813 inflicting a devastating defeat on a French force at Vitoria, for which he was awarded his promotion to Field Marshal (after he had recovered from a fit of temper when his troops looted the French baggage train instead of pursuing their fleeing enemy, earning them the insult 'the scum of the earth' from their commander). Already a marquess, he was elevated to duke in 1814 after winning another signal victory at Toulouse. After he finally bested Napoleon at Waterloo in 1815, his reputation was meteoric, and a grateful nation awarded him with political office, culminating in his appointment in 1828 as the Prime Minister (a role he previously said he would be 'worse than mad' to accept). The struggle to push through Catholic Emancipation in the teeth of opposition from his own Tory party undermined his administration and he lost office in the election of 1830.

An omnibus, by John Thomson, c.1870s.

3

The 1820s. Before George Shillibeer began his horse-drawn omnibus service in 1829, urban transport in Britain – and especially in London – had been a chaos of hackney cabs and sedan chairs for hire and private carriages. Shillibeer, a coachbuilder who had seen large passenger carriages operating in Paris, where he had been commissioned to build one, saw an opportunity back home in London. On 4 July 1829 he began a horse-drawn service from the Yorkshire Stingo Tavern near Paddington to the Bank of England, carrying up to 20 passengers each paying a shilling a trip. Originally, he intended to call his vehicles 'economists', but in the end opted for the more euphonious 'omnibuses'. The fare was expensive and the route was forced to skirt then north of the City of London to Islington before heading south to avoid infringing the monopoly that hackney carriages had on transporting passengers. Although the monopoly was abandoned in 1832, rival services and high taxes forced Shillibeer into bankruptcy twice, and he was given a prison sentence when over 100 gallons of smuggled brandy were found secreted

at his home. Unable to make money out of buses, Shillibeer became an undertaker, but still could not resist designing a novel funeral carriage.

4

Wandsworth Prison. The last judicial executions in Britain were carried out on 13 August 1964 at Strangeways Prison in Manchester and Walton Prison in Liverpool of two men convicted of murder during a bungled robbery. The death penalty for murder was abolished in Great Britain on 9 November 1965 by the Murder (Abolition of the Death Penalty) Act, although the sentence remained on the statute book for Northern Ireland until 1973. Even so, the death penalty remained technically an option for several offences, but gradually these anomalies were removed: it was abolished as a sentence for arson in a naval dockyard in 1971, and for piracy with violence and high treason in 1998 (with the highly archaic practice of beheading for the latter offence being outlawed in 1973). Because of these vestiges and the possibility the death sentence might be restored, the gallows at Wandsworth Prison in London were retained, and tested every six months in case they might be needed once more. Only in 1993 was it finally dismantled, and sent to the National Justice Museum in Nottingham.

5

They all begin with 'Her' – Hereford Cathedral, Hereward the Wake and Herbert Asquith. Traditionally founded in 696, Hereford Cathedral's current building retains vestiges of a Norman structure built from 1107 and is notable for the Hereford Mappa Mundi, the finest surviving medieval world map, and the largest extant chained library in the world. It also has a very early copy of Magna Carta made in 1217. Hereward the Wake was an Anglo-Saxon rebel against the Norman occupation of England after 1066. Although many colourful legends have accreted to his story, the historical core suggests that he rebelled in expectation of support from King Sweyn Estrithson of Denmark, who planned to invade England in 1070. The invasion proved abortive and Hereward and his ally Morcar, the former Anglo-Saxon earl of Northumbria, retired to the fenland fastnesses around Ely, where they carried out a desperate but futile guerrilla resistance for some months. Herbert Asquith was prime minister from 1908 to 1916, but his government was undermined by a scandal involving the undersupply of munitions to the army in World War One and the failures of the Gallipoli campaign and he resigned in December 1916. Although Asquith was replaced by David Lloyd George, another Liberal, he depended on Conservative support and Britain has never had another majority Liberal government.

6

Den Watts. The first episode of *EastEnders* was broadcast on 19 February 1985, watched by an audience of 13 million people. In the opening scene Den Watts (who later attracted the nickname 'Dirty' Den), Arthur Fowler and Ali Osman kick down the door of a flat belonging to Reg Cox, a local man who has gone missing, only to find him unconscious and dying. Watts then utters the show's first lines, 'Cor, it stinks

in 'ere, don't it?' Watts, the original landlord of the Queen Victoria public house, was a regular fixture on *EastEnders* for the next 13 years, then returned in 2003, before his on-screen character was murdered in 2005.

7

The Pilgrimage of Grace. Henry VIII's Reformation legislation – and in particular the Dissolution of the Monasteries, which began in 1536 – caused especial resentment in the religiously conservative North of England, where it was seen in part as an attempt by the government to exert greater control from London. Riots broke out in Lincolnshire in early October, but then a larger rebellion erupted in Yorkshire, led By Robert Aske, a local lawyer. The rebel host, by then 30,000-strong, took York on 16 October and looked set to march south, but delaying tactics by Thomas Howard, Duke of Norfolk, who commanded the king's forces, and the promise of a pardon and other concessions to the rebel leaders, which caused Aske to instruct his followers to disperse, led the revolt to fizzle out. Aske and around 250 other leading rebels were then arrested and executed, with Aske's hanging on 12 July 1537 at Clifford's Tower in York marking an end to the most serious uprising of Henry VIII's reign.

8

Kirkwall on Orkney. Founded in 1137 by Rognvald, the Viking earl of Orkney to honour his pious (and martyred) uncle St Magnus, Kirkwall Cathedral came under the jurisdiction of the Norwegian archbishop of Nidaros until 1472, thereafter the Catholic archbishop of St Andrews, and then after the Reformation it became a see of the Presbyterian Church of Scotland. The contrasting locally quarried red and yellow sandstones of its Romanesque architecture create a striking effect in a building known as the 'Light of the North'.

9

As the centre of the Somerset Case, which restricted slavery in Britain in 1772. James

Somerset was an enslaved African who had been bought by Charles Stewart, a British customs officer in Boston, who then brought him to London in 1769. Two years later Somerset escaped, but was recaptured and taken to a Jamaica-bound ship to be transported to a plantation there. Somerset's English godparents – he had in the meantime converted to Christianity – took a case on his behalf to the court of the King's Bench, arguing that he was being unlawfully imprisoned. After repeated adjournments, the abolitionist lawyer Granville Sharp powerfully argue that the law of England determined that Somerset could not be transported against his will, and Lord Mansfield, the Chief Justice, agreed. Somerset was set free, and although the case did not actually abolish slavery in Britain, it made it illegal for slaves held there to be transported overseas and gave a powerful boost to the cause of abolitionists. .

10

Mary Wollstonecraft. Philosopher and early feminist, Wollstonecraft led a wildly unconventional life, escaping from the early confines of being a ladies' companion and governess, which was the normal fate of respectable young women of modest means in the late eighteenth century. She earned money by writing novels, children's tales and reviews, and she spent three years from 1792 in France during the full fury of the Revolutionary Terror that claimed the lives of many of her acquaintances there. Her *A Vindication of the Rights of Woman*, published in 1792, argues that women have the same fundamental rights as men and should be educated to the same level as men to allow them to take a fuller role in society. She died in 1797 of puerperal fever shortly after giving birth to her daughter Mary, who would go on to become the author of *Frankenstein* and wife of the poet Percy Bysshe Shelley.

11

Mary Wollstonecraft (1759), Jane Austen (1775), Charlotte Brontë (1816). A leading proponent of social equality and equal education for women,

Wollstonecraft became part of a radical group of reformers that included Thomas Paine and William Blake. Jane Austen's six published novels – notably *Pride and Prejudice* – contain delicate and vivid depictions of middle-class life, its constraints and conceits, during the Regency Period. Charlotte Brontë was the eldest of three talented literary sisters who lived with their parson father at Haworth on the Yorkshire Moors. Charlotte's masterwork *Jane Eyre* (1847) was followed by *Shirley* (1849) and *Villette* (1853), before her early death aged 38 in 1855.

Genius Question

They were all briefly part of the British Empire. The eighteenth century saw Britain gain a number of territories in Europe, whose status as British possessions proved ephemeral. Minorca was awarded to Britain in 1713 under the terms of the Treaty of Utrecht (by which Spain also ceded Gibraltar to the British), but was then occupied by the French from 1756 to 1763, when British rule was restored. Spain retook the island in 1782, and has held it ever since apart from a brief British reoccupation from 1798 to 1802. Among the more surprising legacies of the British period in Minorca are the sash windows which grace many of its Georgian era buildings. Corfu (or Kerkyra in Greek) became British in 1815 after the defeat of Napoleon (whose forces had taken it from the Venetians in 1797), but it was ceded to Greece in 1864 on the occasion of the coronation of the new Greek king, George I. The period of British rule bequeathed Corfu, almost uniquely in Greece, a cricketing heritage, and it is home to the Hellenic Cricket Federation. Heligoland, an archipelago in the North Sea off the coast of Denmark and Germany, became British when a naval task force captured it in 1807, and remained so until 1890 when it was ceded to Germany in exchange for recognition of a British protectorate over Zanzibar in East Africa.

ROUND
19 On the Move

1

Ermine Street. Linking the cities of Londinium (London) and Eboracum (York), Ermine Street was one of the main spines of the Roman province of Britannia, going by way of Lindum (Lincoln). Its name has nothing to do with the rodent whose fur was much prized by the later British aristocracy, but is derived from the Earningas, an Anglo-Saxon people who lived in the vicinity of Royston in Hertfordshire.

2

Ten miles per hour (mph). Set by the Locomotives on Highways Act of 1861, the measure was more to do with locomotives and steam-powered traction engines damaging roads than with speeding automobiles (which had yet to be invented). The rate was further reduced in 1865 to 4mph, with the further hindrance of requiring a man with a red flag to walk 60 yards (55m) ahead to warn less nimble riders and pedestrians of the engine's snail-like approach. The Locomotives on Highways Act of 1896 increased the legal speed limit, in mid-November, to 14mph and removed the need for the flag-wielding escort, an occasion celebrated by the enthusiasts of the Motor Car Club by a drive from London to Britain, a rally which became an annual event from 1927.

3

Dagenham (anagram of 'ma hanged'). From the breaking of ground by Henry Ford's son, Edsel, in 1929, the car plant at Essex in Dagenham was one of the jewels of the British car-making industry. Its 70-year career of manufacturing motor vehicles, which came to an end in 2002, saw over ten million vehicles leave the assembly line, the first being an AA truck in 1931 and the

last a Ford Fiesta on the factory's final day of car manufacturing. Built after 22,000 concrete piles had been driven into marshland to stabilise it, the site boasted its own hospital, foundry, power station and railway in its heyday. It sat alongside the Becontree Estate, the largest council estate in Britain, which housed many of the Ford workers, including 2,000 the company transported on special trains down from Manchester in 1931 to staff the new production lines.

4

1935. The bane of learner drivers through the decades, the driving test was first introduced in March 1935 and became compulsory three months later. It was not before time; politicians had become increasingly concerned about the carnage on Britain's roads, with 7,343 people killed in car accidents the year before (a notable toll considering the era's lower-power vehicles and the fact there being only 2.4 million of them on the road). Around 246,000 people applied for the first round of tests, with a pass rate of 63 per cent, and the honour of being the very first to pass went to a certain Mr Beere, who paid 37.5p for the privilege of taking a test that included knowledge of hand signals (a skill only dispensed with in testing in 1975).

5

The sixteenth century. Although the eighteenth century was the golden age of British canal-building, beginning with the Duke of Manchester's Bridgewater Canal between Runcorn and Leigh in the 1760s, improving Britain's waterways for navigation was already a process several centuries old. The first pound locks with vertical gates and rising water levels were installed on the Exeter Canal, a stretch constructed to bypass a difficult

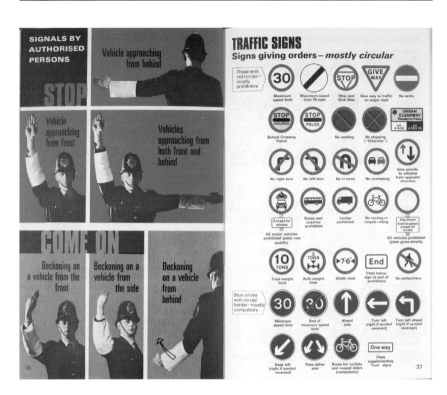

Signals and signs from *The Highway Code*, 1968.

section of the River Exe, in 1566. At their height in the mid-nineteenth century there were over 3,700 miles (6,000km) of navigable canals in Britain, linking hubs of the Industrial Revolution to sources of raw material and ports nationwide, after which canals were steadily overtaken by the more flexible railway and then the motor car, leading to their gradual neglect and the diminution of the network, until they were finally nationalised in 1947.

6

The trial opening of the Metropolitan Line, London's first underground line on 9 January 1863. The stretch of line between Baker Street and Paddington formed part of the very first section of the London Underground. Built to solve the increasing problem of congestion on Victorian London's roads, the two-year construction project involved 'cut and cover' (in essence, digging an enormous hole, crafting the tunnel and then covering it over), which itself caused massive disruption. On the day before the Metropolitan Line's public opening, 600 grandees enjoyed a subterranean gala, a special inaugural trip on the train and a feast at Farringdon Station, although the prime minister, Lord Palmerston, declined his invitation on the grounds that at 78 he would soon be spending the rest of eternity below ground. On the first public day, 30,000 passengers travelled, despite fears that they would be asphyxiated by noxious fumes, or, according to one evangelical minister, transported to Hell (a feeling with which many modern commuters may sympathise), and during its first year in operation the Underground proved itself a resounding success by carrying over nine million people.

7

He was the first Black person to hold a British pilot's licence. William Robinson Clarke (known as 'Robbie') was born in Kingston, Jamaica, and after World War One broke out, he paid his own passage to Britain to contribute to the war effort, joining the Royal Flying Corps in July 1915. Although he was employed as an air mechanic, he was keen to fly and in December 1916 secured a place on a pilot training course. In April 1917, he won his 'wings', becoming Britain's first qualified Black pilot and the following month was posted to 4 Squadron operating out of Abeele in Belgium, flying R.E.8 biplanes. Despite a near escape when he was shot in the spine and barely managed to nurse his aircraft home, Clarke survived the war.

He returned to Jamaica, but there were no further opportunities to fly and he finished his career in the building trade.

8

A stagecoach service from Manchester to London. Although stagecoaches (so-called because they covered a number of intermediate stops or 'stages' along their route) had been introduced in Scotland in the early seventeenth century, they were still a rather haphazard form of transport, plagued by delays, appalling roads and the danger of highwaymen, who took full advantage of the published schedules posted by the stagecoach proprietors. In 1754 a Manchester company introduced the 'Flying Coach' with a superior

An advertisement by the Austin Motor Co Ltd for the Austin 'Twenty' car, 1919.

carriage that was advertised as covering the distance to London in a mere four-and-a-half days. Even into the 1760s it took three days for travellers to travel to Birmingham and six for the bone-shaken passengers to reach Edinburgh, perhaps explaining the huge enthusiasm in later decades for improved turnpike roads and passenger railways.

9

Hendon in northwest London. Built on a plot of land purchased by aviation pioneer Claude Grahame-White in 1911, the initially very promising development of Hendon aerodrome, dubbed by its founder as 'the Charing Cross of aviation', was stifled by World War One, during which it was requisitioned by the Royal Naval Air Service (and then taken over by the fledgling Royal Air Force in 1922). It was never returned to civilian aviation. Instead an airport was established at Croydon and then, in 1930, the land that was to become Heathrow Airport was purchased from the vicar of Harmondsworth for the princely sum of £15,000.

10

The 1890s. On 17 August 1896, while taking a stroll in Crystal Palace Park, Mrs Bridget Driscoll was struck by a vehicle while crossing Dolphin Terrace inside the park. In theory it should not have been going at great speed, because the then speed limit was 4mph, although Mrs Driscoll's daughter May claimed the driver had been weaving around erratically and ignored the umbrella that her mother put up as a warning sign. Testimony from one of the passengers in the vehicle indicated the driver had frantically rung his bell, but that Mrs Driscoll remained rooted to the spot and was knocked over. The verdict of the subsequent inquest was one of accidental death.

11

1976 and 2003. The first passenger-carrying supersonic commercial aircraft, Concorde was the fruit of co-operation between Britain and France, which shared the development and production costs. Capable of cruising at around 1,350mph (almost 2,180kmph), it cut the flight time between London and New York to three hours, promising a new era of rapid transatlantic travel. The first scheduled services were between London and Bahrain and Paris and Rio from January 1976 (with routes to Washington, DC, following soon after and New York City late in 1977). Restrictions on its speed in inhabited areas (because of the supersonic boom it created) and high operating costs meant Concorde was a loss-maker for airlines (while return tickets cost to New York cost around $8,000), and after an accident in 2000 when an Air France Concorde crashed during take-off, killing 113 people, the aircraft was retired and made its final passenger flight from New York to London on 24 October 2003.

Genius Question

Between 1924 and 1970. On 25 September 1924, Malcolm Campbell set the British land-speed record over a mile distance when recording 146mph (235kmph) in his Sunbeam *Blue Bird* car at Pendine Sands in Wales. He bettered that the next year, reaching 150.7mph (242.6kmph), but lost the record to Henry Segrave, only to regain it in 1927, when he also broke the world land-speed record in reaching 174.8mph (281.3kmph) over a mile, again at Pendine Sands. The British record stood until 1970 when Tony Densham hit 207.6mph (334kmph) at a circuit at Elvington in Yorkshire in his *Commuter* dragster.

Making Money

1

The sixpence. First minted in 1551, during the reign of Edward VI, the sixpence was worth half a shilling (the equivalent now of 2.5p) and continued in circulation until the British coinage was decimalised in 1971. It contained actual silver (over 90 per cent until 1920, and then 50 per cent until 1946 when it was replaced by cupro-nickel), and came to be regarded as a symbol of good fortune – a coin was traditionally slipped into a bride's shoe before the wedding ceremony. The nickname 'the tanner', which arose in the early 1800s, is believed to come from the Romani word *tawno*, meaning something small.

2

The English East India Company. Spices such as cloves and nutmeg, which could only be grown on the tiny Banda Islands in the East Indies, were in great demand in Europe in the fifteenth and sixteenth century and small quantities fetched a fortune. Because the trading routes to the East were controlled by the Ottoman and Mughal empires, Europeans pushed into the Indian Ocean by force, establishing a string of trading posts there. The English were late into the game, but in 1600 the East India Company (EIC) gained a charter from Elizabeth I giving it a monopoly on the spice trade. Although the initial results were good, the EIC's Dutch rival, the VOC, defended its interests in the East Indies aggressively and after a massacre of EIC officials on Amboyna in 1623, the English withdrew. Instead, they concentrated on India, where in Surat the company had gained a foothold that would eventually grow to encompass most of the subcontinent. As a result, the directors of what came to be informally known as 'John Company' grew rich on the trade in cotton, silk, pepper, indigo, tea and (latterly) opium, with their headquarters on Leadenhall Street the centre of an empire that rivalled that of the British Crown.

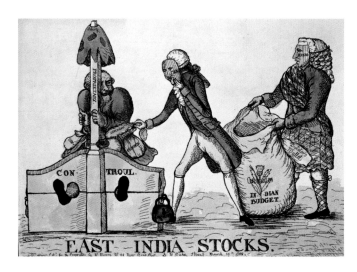

'East-India Stocks', an anonymous caricature about the East India Company, London, 1788.

3

25 per cent. In June 1975 the United Kingdom's rate of inflation, as recorded by the Retail Price Index, soared to 25 per cent. It was fuelled by a credit boom, caused by a relaxation on personal borrowing in the early 1970s, and the effects of the oil crisis, which followed the Yom Kippur War of 1973 between Israel and its Arab neighbours when an OPEC oil embargo caused the oil price to quadruple with a knock-on effect on the inflation rate in industrialised countries. As workers demanded higher wages to compensate – average earnings in the UK rose by 28 per cent in 1974 – Britain found itself gripped by stagflation (low growth and high inflation). It took eight years of attempts to negotiate wage restraints, the labour reforms of the Thatcher government from 1979 onwards and a serious recession in 1981 to squeeze inflation out of the economy, before it dropped to an average of 4.5 per cent in 1983.

4

Eight. The Bank of England is the only body authorised to issue banknotes in England and Wales. In Scotland, there are three banknote-issuing banks: Bank of Scotland, Clydesdale and RBS; while for Northern Ireland there are four: Bank of Ireland, Ulster Bank, Danske Bank and First Trust Bank. The notes issued in each of these three territories are not legal tender in the others (that is, English banknotes are not legal tender in Scotland), but because – strictly speaking – legal tender only applies to the payment of debts, in practice it's up to shopkeepers which notes they choose to accept.

5

A speculative mania that ruined thousands of investors. The South Sea Company was set up in 1711 to trade with Spanish possessions in South America, and as a means to fund Britain's national debt by forcing the government's creditors to take the company's stock in exchange for their loans. It ran into trouble two years later when the Treaty of Utrecht between Britain and Spain restricted the company to sending one vessel a year, but the issue of more stock in 1720

led to a frenzy that pushed its price from £128 a share in January to £1,000 in early August. Those who realised the surge was not backed by any commercial reality sold out at the top, while many less well-connected individuals were ruined. One investor was Sir Isaac Newton, who supposedly said: 'I can calculate the movement of the stars, but not the madness of men.'

6

Henry III. Gold coins were of limited practical value in the Middle Ages because they could not be used in everyday transactions and silver pennies were the most common form of coinage. The appearance of the Florentine florin in 1252, Europe's first properly circulating gold coin for centuries, set off a flurry of competition among European monarchs keen not to be outshone by the Italian mercantile republic. Henry III of England ordered his agents to buy up large quantities of gold and in 1257 a number of gold pennies, equivalent in value to 20 silver pennies, were struck. Unfortunately, the quantity of gold in the coin was worth more than its face value and gold pennies soon disappeared from circulation or were melted down. A successful gold coinage in England had to wait until Edward III issued the gold noble in 1344.

7

Silver platters. The *birrus Britannicus* was a type of hooded woollen cloak that was very popular in Britain (unsurprising given the rainy climate) and was noted by several ancient authors. Britain was also renowned for the quality of its hunting dogs (in aristocratic Celtic folklore the dog plays an important role, and the hero Cúchulainn was known as the 'Hound of Ulster'). High-quality luxury ware such as silver plates tended to be imported into Roman Britain from workshops in Gaul and elsewhere and they appear in many buried hoards, such as the Mildenhall Treasure dating from the fourth century that was found in Suffolk in 1942, which includes 30 silver bowls and platters, notably the 'Great Bowl', which weighs almost 18 pounds (8kg) and is about 24 inches (60cm) in diameter.

8

Domesday Book. Although William of Normandy had conquered England in 1066, it was difficult to understand the country's true worth and, more importantly, how much revenue he could extract from it. At Christmas 1085 the king commissioned a survey of his realm, in which inspectors took sworn evidence from local juries about the ownership of each piece of land, both at the time of the survey and at the time of Edward the Confessor, the livestock on it and the rent it yielded. Within a year the returns were collated, transcribed and bound into two volumes (Little Domesday and Great Domesday). Although parts of the north of England (and London, because of its tax exemptions) were missing, Domesday was the most comprehensive land survey of the Middle Ages.

9

1799. First introduced to raise funds for the war against Revolutionary France, Prime Minister William Pitt the Younger expected that income tax, levied on incomes over £60 at 1 per cent and then on a sliding scale up to 10 per cent for those earning more than £200 annually, would be a temporary measure. It was indeed abolished in 1816, but then reintroduced in 1842 by Robert Peel, and has been a feature, if not a much-loved one, of Britain's financial system ever since.

10

Jonathan's Coffee House, Change Alley. Although the Elizabethan merchant Thomas Gresham established the Royal Exchange in London in 1570, as a centre for financial and mercantile exchange on the model of the Amsterdam Bourse he had seen in the Netherlands, stockbrokers who dealt in the buying and shelling of share in companies were excluded. Instead, they traded informally in the streets around, most notably one that became known as Change Alley. In 1698, trader Jonathan Castaing published a list of stock and commodity prices at his coffee house, which then became a centre for stock trading. Finally, in 1773 a new building at nearby Sweeting's Alley, with a dedicated dealing room, became the

ancestor of the modern London Stock Exchange whose flagship FTSE 100 share index contains companies valued at approximately £2.2 trillion.

11

They have all appeared on the £10 banknote. Nursing pioneer Florence Nightingale was the face of the £10 note from 1975 to 1991, when she was supplanted by the novelist Charles Dickens who appeared on notes issued between 1991 and 2000, before in turn being replaced by the pioneer of evolutionary theory Charles Darwin, who featured on them between 2000 and 2017. The new plastic polymer notes first issued in 2017 bear the portrait of the novelist Jane Austen. Traditionally, Bank of England banknotes did not bear any portraits at all, not even the monarch's and the first portrait of Queen Elizabeth II did not appear until 1960. The first banknote to carry the face of a historical character was the £20 note issued in 1970 with that of William Shakespeare. The selection of the figures to appear is now made by an advisory committee, which picks a field of endeavour, invites nominations from the public and creates a shortlist, from which the Governor of the Bank of England makes a final selection.

Genius Question

They are all companies founded by Quakers. Such non-conformist groups were persecuted after the Restoration of Charles II, with the Corporation Act of 1661 laying down that all officials had to take Anglican Communion. Although the authorities ceased active persecution after 1689, the Act remained in force until 1826; denied careers in public life, Quakers turned to business, in which they prospered thanks to their close-knit community and a reputation for integrity. What became Barclays Bank was founded by John Freame and Thomas Gould, two Quaker goldsmiths, in 1690; Cadbury's by John Cadbury in 1824, when he set up a grocery shop in Birmingham that sold cocoa and drinking chocolate; Cyrus Clark initially made rugs in Street in Somerset in 1825, before branching out into slippers (from carpet offcuts) in 1828, and then on to the shoes for which it is best known.

Medieval, Tudors & Stuarts

1

Henry IV (13 years), Henry II (34 years), Henry III (56 years). Henry IV, otherwise known as Henry Bolingbroke or Henry of Lancaster, reigned from 1399 to 1413. The first king of the House of Lancaster, he derived his claim to the throne as the son of Edward III's third son John of Gaunt. He fell out of favour with Richard II after forming a cabal of Lords Appellant in 1387 that ousted the king's previous favourites and was forced into exile in 1398. He returned in 1399 and, with his former noble allies, usurped the king. This left him vulnerable and his reign was blighted by rebellions by Owain Glyndŵr in Wales, the Percy Earls of Northumberland in northern England and by Thomas Mowbray, heir to the duchy of Norfolk.

Henry II, who reigned from 1154 to 1189, was the son of Matilda, Henry I's daughter, and Geoffrey of Anjou, and he added to the already substantial domains of his father, the lands of Eleanor, heiress to Aquitaine, when he married her in 1152. The Angevin Empire thus created occupied the king for much of his reign, and he spent only 14 years in England. His rule there, in which he engaged in a comprehensive legal reform by the Assize of Clarendon (1166), which established formal juries and regular circuit courts, contrasted with that in France, where constant trouble with his sons, notably the future Henry III, and noble revolts left his domains in turmoil. Above all, he is remembered for his quarrel with Thomas Becket, whom he appointed

Thomas Becket before Henry II, a fifteenth-century miniature from *Annales monasterii sancti Albani*.

Archbishop of Canterbury, and in whose martyrdom in 1170 he was implicated.

The longest-reigning monarch until George III, Henry's 53-year reign began when he was just nine years old. The early years were dominated by regents, and it was only in 1234 that he began to rule personally, a period that saw increasingly fractious relations with his barons. Eventually, when he demanded money for a papal war in Sicily in return for his son, Edmund, being granted the throne of the island, the barons forced him into signing the Provisions of Oxford (1258), ceding part of his power to a 15-man privy council. It all ended in a virtual mirror image of the baronial revolt in his father John's reign, this time led by Simon de Montfort. Although de Montfort was ultimately defeated and killed at Evesham in 1265, the concessions the Crown had been forced to make helped ultimately establish the beginnings of a real parliament in England.

2

Chancellor to Henry II. Thomas Becket already had a track record in the Church when Henry II noticed the efficiency of the young archdeacon and trusted aide to Theobald of Bec, the Archbishop of Canterbury. Appointed royal Chancellor in 1155, he proved an able administrator and when Theobald died six years later, Henry thought Becket the ideal replacement to help him stamp his authority on the English Church. It was a terrible mistake because Becket proved more loyal to Pope Alexander III than to his royal patron. In particular, he angered Henry by refusing to allow clerics accused of crimes to be tried in royal courts. Forced into a six-year exile in 1164, Becket infuriated Henry further by excommunicating the Archbishop of York just as he returned to England in December 1170. In a fit of rage, the king reputedly said: 'Will nobody rid me of this turbulent priest.' Four of his knights took this seriously, travelled to Canterbury and murdered Becket in the cathedral, an act of impiety that caused outrage and led to pilgrims flocking to a shrine to him that sprang up. Although Henry was absolved in 1174, Becket's murder has forever been a stain on his reputation.

3

The Peasants' Revolt. Richard II's wars with France in the 1370s left him chronically short of money and led him to impose a poll tax (per head of population) in 1377 and 1379. Resentment at legal controls on wages introduced by the Statute of Labourers in 1351, following the Black Death, also festered and when a new poll tax, at a shilling a head, was levied in 1381 tax collectors were at first turned away. When they returned, rebellions erupted in Kent and East Anglia. A host of peasants and artisans gathered, led by Wat Tyler, a cleric named Jon Ball and Jack Straw (or Rackstraw). They entered London on 13 June, ransacked the palace of John of Gaunt and murdered the unpopular Chancellor, Archbishop Simon of Sudbury. An alarmed Richard II agreed to meet the rebels at Smithfield, but during a fracas Wat Tyler was cut down. Deprived of their leader, the disoriented rebels agreed to the king's order to disperse on the promise of concessions, which never manifested. Instead, the remaining rebels were rounded up and the attempt to impose the poll tax abandoned.

4

Milford Haven. Henry VII, who was the great-great-grandson of John of Gaunt, became the leading Lancastrian pretender to the throne of England only because most of the other claimants had perished during the Wars of the Roses. As the popularity of Richard III, the Yorkist king, was waning, Henry gathered a small force and made contact with allies in England. He landed, though, in Wales, the homeland of his father Owain's family, the Tudors, after a six-day voyage from France. On arriving in Pembrokeshire, on 7 August 1485, he is said to have kissed the ground and recited a psalm. Perhaps it gained him divine favour, for just 15 days later he defeated and killed Richard III at Bosworth Field in Leicestershire, so winning the throne of England and beginning the Tudor dynasty.

5

Lambert Simnel. Although Henry Tudor's route to the throne had seemed providential, with his victory over Richard III giving him an easier-than-expected route to the throne, he was dogged for several years by Yorkist pretenders. The most prominent real Yorkist claimant, Richard III's nephew, the ten-year-old Edward, Earl of Warwick, had been incarcerated in the Tower of London, which meant Henry's steps were dogged instead by fake pretenders conjured up by Yorkist sympathisers. Lambert Simnel, who may have been a baker's son, was put forward as the Earl of Warwick, claimed to have escaped the Tower and was crowned 'King Edward VI' in Dublin. John de la Pole, Earl of Lincoln, assembled a force of mercenaries, but the project collapsed when it was defeated at Stoke Field on 16 June 1487 and Simnel captured. He was treated with surprising leniency and put to work turning a spit-roast in the royal kitchen. The next false pretender, Perkin Warbeck, who had masqueraded as Richard Duke of York (murdered in the Tower in 1483), was not treated so kindly and was executed in 1499 after involving the Earl of Warwick, who was still imprisoned, in a plot to escape.

6

Lord Howard of Effingham. The 130-ship fleet that Philip II of Spain despatched in May 1588 to exact vengeance on Elizabeth I for years of raiding Spanish possessions in the New World (and a provocative raid by Francis Drake on Cadiz in 1587) was supposed to link up with an invasion force stationed in Flanders under the Duke of Parma. The Spanish Admiral, the Duke of Medina Sidonia, was not an experienced sea commander, and allowed himself to be caught in a game of cat-and-mouse with the smaller English fleet along the Channel. That fleet was actually led by Lord Howard of Effingham, a far less effective propagandist and self-publicist than Drake, who was his second-in-command. It was Howard's idea to send in fireships to scatter the Spanish fleet harboured in Calais Roads, after which they were more easily picked off and defeated at the Battle of Gravelines on 8 August. Drake spent more time trying to secure better prizes of captured Spanish vessels than in co-ordinating strategy, but his force of personality meant he got more

credit afterwards from the queen (and from public opinion down the ages).

7

The proposed marriage of Prince Charles (the future Charles I) to the Spanish Infanta Maria Anna. In 1618, James I feared diplomatic isolation after the outbreak of the Thirty Years' War, whose early stages embroiled his own daughter, Elizabeth (who was married to Frederick V, the Protestant Elector of the Palatinate, who found himself in conflict with the Austrian Habsburgs). In search of allies, James turned to the other branch of the Habsburg family, in Spain, and began secret negotiations for the marriage of his son Prince Charles to Maria Anna, daughter of Philip III. The talks were protracted but, finally, in 1623 Charles travelled in disguise, accompanied by the Duke of Buckingham, to push matters to a conclusion in person in Madrid. The enterprise went badly wrong: Maria Anna disliked Charles, the Spanish expected the price of the alliance would be the restoration of Catholicism in England and the match was, politically, enormously unpopular in the English Parliament. In October, Buckingham and Charles slunk back to England and the furious prince called on his father to declare war on Spain. Rather than open up James's options, the 'Spanish match' had closed them down and he was forced to turn to France and a marriage alliance between Charles and Henrietta Maria, daughter of Henri IV, which was concluded the following year.

8

Pride's Purge (anagram of 'pureed sprig'). By 1648, King Charles I had in effect lost the Civil War with Parliament after the defeat of his Scottish Presbyterian allies at Preston in August had closed off his last hope of a military victory. Even so, the members of the Long Parliament (which had been sitting since 1640) continued to negotiate with the king (who had been in captivity in 1647) hoping to preserve some element of monarchical rule. Finally, the patience of the army, and in particular its commander Oliver Cromwell, snapped, and on the morning of 6 December

Colonel Thomas Pride was despatched with a contingent of troops to bar from entering the Commons Chambers those MPs who favoured persisting with the talks with the king. Pride's Purge excluded 140 MPs, of whom around one-third were actually arrested, leaving around 200 more compliant members to continue sitting and do Parliament's bidding in breaking off negotiations. The Rump Parliament, as it was disparagingly known, continued to sit until 1653, when Cromwell did away with it altogether.

9

Killiecrankie. The deposition in 1688 of the Stuart James II in favour of the Dutch Protestant William III had not gone down well with Stuart loyalists, especially in Scotland, the cradle of the dynasty. When the Scottish parliament recognised William as king on 11 April 1689, the Jacobites (taking their name from Jacobus, the Latin for James) raised the standard of revolt. Led by John Grahame, Viscount Dundee, they enjoyed initial success, and won a resounding victory at Killiecrankie on 27 July. However, Dundee's death in the battle, supply problems which meant the

Highlanders in the Jacobite forces dispersed, an unfocused strategy and English concessions to moderates (including hefty bribes to Highland chiefs) meant the uprising fizzled out.

10

The Medway Raid in 1667. By 1667, England was embroiled in a second war with the Dutch, its long-time allies, whose growing maritime power had begun to threaten England's own pretension to dominate the seas of northwest Europe. Although the English won an initial victory at Lowestoft in 1665, they failed to trap the remnants of the Dutch fleet, which escaped. A Dutch victory at the Four Days' Battle the following year was balanced by an English one in the St James's Day Battle. But the losses suffered by the English fleet and Charles II's growing inability to finance the prolonged war provided an opening for the Dutch. On 9 June 1667 a Dutch fleet led by Michiel de Ruyter appeared off Sheerness, captured the fort and then broke through a chain blocking

The Spanish Armada, from the Sheares Bible, 1701-31.

the Medway and fell on the unsuspecting and unprepared English fleet. Fifteen English vessels were destroyed in the carnage, including three of the navy's largest warships, the *Royal Oak, Loyal London* and *Royal James*. Most insulting of all, the English flagship, the *Royal Charles,* named for the king himself was captured and towed back to Holland. It was England's worst-ever naval disaster, of which the diarist Samuel Pepys wrote: 'And, the truth is, I do fear so much that the whole kingdom is undone.'

11

As part of the Gunpowder plot in 1605. Guy (or Guido) Fawkes's attempt to assassinate James I in order to replace him by his young daughter Elizabeth (who it was believed would be more sympathetic to English Catholics) has made him one of the more controversial figures in British history. Fawkes became involved with Robert Catesby a young Catholic nobleman in 1603 and gradually the pair hatched a plot to smuggle barrels of gunpowder into a basement in the Houses of Parliament and detonate them as the king was opening Parliament. However, they and their co-conspirators were betrayed, and in the early hours of 5 November Fawkes was arrested. Although he refused to give up the names of his confederates, even under severe torture, they were tracked down to Holbeche House in Staffordshire where Catesby and several of the other were killed in a skirmish. Seven of the survivors were hauled back to London and sentenced to death by hanging, drawing and quartering and they were executed on a scaffold in Old Palace Yard, Whitehall, on 30-31 January 1606. In the image, Fawkes is third from the right and Catesby second from the right.

Genius Question

The Prayer Book Rebellion. Also known as the Western Rebellion, the uprising erupted in Devon and Cornwall in response to the quickening pace of the English Reformation. The dissolution of the monasteries between 1536 and 1541 had already angered traditionalist sentiment. Under Edward VI, the religious atmosphere became even harsher, with the banning of processions and the closing down of shrines to saints. In 1549 a new prayer book was imposed by the Act of Uniformity, in effect making many of the traditional forms of church service illegal. Trouble erupted in Sampford Courtenay in Devon, where an angry mob of parishioners began to march on Exeter, gathering more to their ranks as they went. It turned into an open rebellion with attacks on local gentry and a demand for a restoration of the old Catholic rites. After a skirmish at Crediton, and a failed siege of Arundel, the rebels, by then led by the landowner Humphrey Arundell, began to retreat and were defeated in August at Clyst St Mary and Clyst Heath, with thousands killed and hundreds more massacred after the battles. The rebellion collapsed, Arundell was captured, and hung, drawn and quartered the following January, while the vengeance exacted on Cornwall left it even more politically marginalised than before.

The *Book of Common Prayer,* 1559.

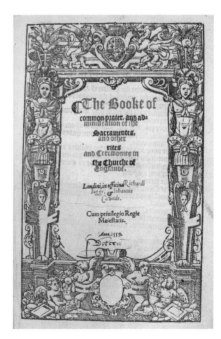

Kings & Queens *(part two)*

1

The Tudor. Of the five Tudor monarchs, three (Henry VII, Henry VIII and Edward VI) were male and two female (Mary I and Elizabeth), giving a proportion of 40 per cent. In second place comes the Stuart dynasty (as rulers of England), with five men (Charles I, James I, Charles II, James II and William III) and two women (Mary II and Anne).

2

'The Maypole', and 'the Elephant and Castle'. When George I arrived from Hanover in 1714 to take up the English throne after the death of his heirless cousin Anne, he brought not a wife – he had incarcerated his own, Sophia Dorothea, in Ahlden Castle on account of her affair with a Swedish cavalry colonel – but two mistresses. The difference in physique led wags to dub the slim Ehengard Melusine 'the Maypole' and the more portly Sophia Charlotte 'the Elephant and Castle'. George, not generally a demonstrative man, showered them with honours, with Sophia becoming Countess of Darlington and Countess of Leinster, and Melusine – who had three illegitimate daughters with George – becoming Duchess of Munster, Countess of Dungannon and Duchess of Kendal, as well as Princess of Eberstein. Sophia died two years before George, in 1725, but Melusine survived him, living the last 15 years of her life at Kendal House in Isleworth by the River Thames.

3

Mary Queen of Scots, aged six days. Mary was only a week old when her father James V died, in November 1542. Being female and too young to rule in her own right, Mary became the object of a series of proposed marriage alliances throughout her childhood, as successive regents wavered

between pro-English and pro-French factions at court. Finally, Mary was smuggled to France where she married the Dauphin, François, in April 1558. When his father Henri II died in a tournament the following year, Mary found herself queen of both Scotland and France, but the premature death of her young husband in December 1560 led her to return to her Scottish kingdom. Arriving in August 1561, she made a series of unsuitable marriages with Scottish nobles, and when forced to abdicate in favour of her young son James, Mary escaped to England in May 1568. There she was incarcerated by her cousin Elizabeth I and executed in 1587 for conspiring with the English queen's enemies. Despite succeeding to the Scottish throne seven days after birth, she had spent only 12 of her 45 years in Scotland.

4

James I. Already king of Scotland, James succeeded his childless cousin Elizabeth on the English throne upon her death in March 1603. He had high hopes that he could make the personal union that now united the two kingdoms into a reality and from 1604 he styled himself 'King of Great Britain'. James even designed the first version of the Union Jack, but resentment at the Scottish favourites he brought to court with him, and his tendency to ignore Parliament, made him unpopular. As a result, England and Scotland remained resolutely legally separate kingdoms for the next 100 years, only finally becoming formally Great Britain by the Act of Union in 1707 during the reign of James's great-granddaughter Anne.

5

A title according to eight Anglo-Saxon kings with the status of overlord. Literally meaning 'Wielder of Britain', the title was given by the *Anglo-Saxon Chronicle*, one of our leading contemporary sources for English history before the Norman Conquest, to a ruler who exercised dominion over other kings. The *Anglo-Saxon Chronicle* lists eight Bretwaldas: Aelle of Sussex (488–514), Ceawlin of Wessex (560–592), Aethelberht of Kent (590–616), Raedwald of East Anglia (600–624), Edwin of Deira (616–633), Oswald of Northumbria (633–642), Oswy of Northumbria (642–670) and Egbert of Wessex (820–839).

The title was never a formal one (and most of its holders would have been unaware, despite their ambitions to regional hegemony, that they held it at all). The list also has glaring omissions: because the *Anglo-Saxon Chronicle* was compiled in Wessex it studiously ignores the claims to recognition of the rulers of Wessex's arch-rival Mercia, most notably Penda, who dominated the north and the Midlands in the seventh century, and Offa, one of the very greatest of Anglo-Saxon rulers who even fancied himself the equal of Charlemagne, and built Offa's Dyke to delineate the border with the Welsh in the late eighth century.

6

Edward I. The black granite block in Westminster Abbey that marks the tomb of Edward I is inscribed with two Latin phrases. 'Pactum Serva', or 'Keep the Promise', an injunction to fidelity; and 'Scottorum Malleus' ('Hammer of the Scots'), a reference to Edward's Scottish campaigns, which began in 1296 and led to the temporary subjugation of Scotland to English rule after his defeat of William Wallace. Edward was still on campaign and on the point of launching yet another attack on Scotland, when he died, aged 68, at Burgh-by-Sands near Carlisle in 1307. His body lay in the local St Michael's Church – in part built from Roman stone reclaimed from the nearby Hadrian's Wall – before being taken back south to its final resting place.

7

James II. Although James I was crowned king of Scotland (as James VI) in 1567 at the tender age of 13 months (when a special infant-sized sceptre and crown had to be used), and then again as king of England in 1603, and his son Charles had an English coronation at Westminster Abbey in 1626 and a Scottish one at Holyrood in 1633, James II was the only king to have two coronations in England. His wife, Mary of Modena, was a Catholic and James had himself converted to Catholicism in 1669 – and so on 22 April 1685 a coronation was held at Whitehall Palace according to Catholic rites, and another the following day at Westminster Abbey, conducted with an Anglican ceremony. There were a series of evil omens: the crown almost went missing during the coronation procession to Whitehall and the royal champion fell off his horse in full armour. It was perhaps a sign of James's ultimate fate. Tired of his promotion of Catholicism and fearful of his growing closeness to France, in 1688 Parliament invited the impeccably Protestant William of Orange to intervene. The Dutch Stadtholder invaded with a fleet that, blown by a 'Protestant Wind' to Torbay, struck such panic into James that he fled without making serious efforts to counter the invasion, allowing William, and his wife Mary (James II's daughter by a previous marriage), to take up the vacant throne.

8

Henry I. Although the exact count varies, Henry had at least 26 children, and possibly as many as 29. Twenty-five of these were illegitimate by various mistresses. His legitimate son William Adelin died when the *White Ship* in which he was travelling sank off Barfleur in 1120, together with a clutch of nobles and several of his illegitimate half-siblings. As a result, the heir apparent became Henry's daughter Matilda. When Henry's nephew disputed the succession in 1135, the resulting civil war lasted for 18 years. Henry's wife Matilda of Scotland was the great-granddaughter of the Anglo-Saxon king Edmund Ironside, as a result of which Queen Elizabeth II is the lineal descendent both of the Norman conquerors of England and the Anglo-Saxon royal house which they displaced.

9

Queen Bertha of Kent. The daughter of the Merovingian Frankish king Charibert I, Bertha was sent to England in the 580s as the bride of King Aethelberht of Kent, part of a diplomatic initiative to bind the two kingdoms more closely together. Bertha was a Christian, as the Franks had converted almost a century earlier under Clovis, but her new husband was a pagan, and so part of the agreement on their marriage stipulated that she be free to practise her religion. Encouraged by her personal chaplain Liuthard, who she brought with her, Bertha converted a derelict building that dated from Roman times into a chapel dedicated to St Martin. When Augustine arrived in Kent in 597 on a mission to convert the English, sent by Pope Gregory I, Britain's first Christian queen was in a powerful position to assist him.

10

Edward VIII. Edward VIII, or Prince Albert as he had been called up to then, succeeded his father George V on 20 January 1936. After his abdication that December, when he refused to give up his relationship with the American divorcée Mrs Wallis Simpson, he was succeeded by his brother George VI. His successor was his daughter Elizabeth II (and therefore not a king).

11

It is the longest run of succession from father to son in British history. Although it might seem that a king succeeding his father on the throne is the normal course of events, in fact it is far from common in British history. The throne has passed directly through three male generations on only three occasions (Henry IV, Henry V and Henry VI; Henry VII, Henry VIII and Edward VI and Edward VII, George V and Edward VIII) or four if the succession from James I to Charles I and Charles II is counted (ignoring the interregnum of 11 years after Charles I's execution in 1649). The longest sequence began with King John, who succeeded his brother Richard in 1199 and was followed by Henry III (r. 1216-72), Edward I (r. 1272-1307), Edward II (r. 1307-27) and Edward III (r. 1327-77). The 178-year run was broken when Edward III was succeeded by his grandson Richard II (his son, Edward the Black Prince having died the year before of dysentery).

Genius Question

William III. The 'gentleman in velvet' in question being a mole. William of Orange, the hereditary Stadtholder of Holland in the Netherlands, had become king of England in 1688. In February 1702 William went riding in the grounds of Kensington Palace, where his horse stumbled on a molehill. The king was thrown and broke his collarbone. An infection set in, followed by a fever, and a few days later he died. William's inveterate foes, the Jacobites, who supported the continued rule of the deposed James II and his son James Francis Stuart, were delighted, hoping the Stuarts would now be restored and took to toasting 'the little gentleman in the black velvet waistcoat'. The event is commemorated in William III's equestrian statue in St James's Square in London, where the molehill can be clearly made out beneath the horse's left hind hoof.

Buildings & Architecture

1

Sir Giles Gilbert Scott. Long a landmark on the south bank of the Thames, Battersea Power Station was originally due to be built by the Manchester architects Halliday and Agate, but furious opposition by local residents to a coal-burning power station on their doorsteps led to the bringing in of the reassuringly knighted Sir Gilbert Scott (already the architect of Liverpool Cathedral, and later to go on to design the New Bodleian in Oxford, Cambridge University Library and Bankside Power Station). Begun in 1929, the power station was decommissioned in 1983 to become the subject of successive failed redevelopment schemes, until a plan for its regeneration as a retail, residential and cultural space was finally agreed in 2012. In May 2021 the first residents moved in to the regenerated site.

Battersea
Power Station,
photographed
from the River
Thames.

2

Edinburgh Waverley. Waverley Station has its origins as North Bridge Station, the terminus of the North British Railway, which arrived in Edinburgh in 1846 as it pushed its route from Carlisle northwards. For a while it had two competitors, in the General Station (for the Edinburgh and Glasgow Railway) and Canal Street Station (for the Edinburgh, Leith and Granton Railway), and from 1854 the three collectively became known as 'Waverley'. Ironically, although named for Sir Walter Scott's great cycle of Scottish novels, the character of Edward Waverley in the novels is in fact an English soldier. Three became one in 1868 when the North British bought out the other two, demolished their stations and built a new one on the present site, which retained the 'Waverley' appellation. The clock of the Balmoral Hotel, which has overlooked the station since 1902, is permanently set three minutes fast – so tardy travellers won't miss their train.

3

The first residential 'tower block' in Britain. Britain faced a housing crisis by the early 1950s, as many houses had been damaged or destroyed during World War Two, and the state of much of the rest in urban areas left much to be desired. The solution was to build upwards and the Lawn building, the first of a new generation of tower blocks, was completed in 1951 in Harlow, Essex. Designed by Frederick Gibberd, it had ten floors, with four flats on each and was designed so each of them had a south-facing balcony. Tower blocks mushroomed in the 1960s, some reaching over 30 storeys, but fell out of favour after the catastrophic partial collapse of the Ronan Point block in Newham, East London, in 1968. Even so, the Lawn has been a Grade II listed building since 1998.

4

Brixworth. Early Saxon stone churches are comparatively rare – many were built in timber and rotted away, others were destroyed during the Viking invasions, or fell into disuse as population patterns changed. All Saint's Brixworth is the largest we have left, with a nave over 60 feet (18m) in length. Built in part from Roman tiles and masonry from Lactodurum (Towcester) and other nearby settlements, it probably dates to around 700; it was, oddly, not mentioned by name in any of the Anglo-Saxon chronicles or charters from the period (although there are references to unspecified dependent houses of the abbey at Medeshamstede, or Peterborough). The first secure mention of the church only comes in the early twelfth century when the chronicle of Hugh Candidus, a monk at Peterborough, refers to it as a daughter house of Medeshamstede.

5

Zaha Hadid. Iraq-born Hadid studied at the Architecture Association in London and established an architectural practice in the city in 1979. Her bold plan for the Peak Leisure Club, with its striking hillside diagonal structure, won her attention. This and other fragmented designs led to her being labelled a 'deconstructivist', although at first she struggled to get her blueprints actually built. Greater success came in the late 1980s and 1990s with a series or projects in Germany and the Mind Zone for the Millennium Dome in Greenwich. In 2000 she built the Lois & Richard Rosenthal Center for Contemporary Art in Cincinnati, Ohio, its appealing curved structure creating what Hadid said she hoped was a welcoming 'urban carpet'. Her design for the Heydar Aliyev cultural centre in Baku (2012) won her the 2014 London Museum Design of the Year award, while at her death in 2016 she had 36 projects in progress, including Qatar's 2022 World Cup stadium.

6

Winchester. The historic royal centre of the kings of Wessex, Winchester received its first church, the Old Minster, shortly after King Cynegils was baptised in 635. Despite several enlargements, by the time of the Norman Conquest the church was clearly inadequate. Walkelin, the bishop appointed by King William

I in 1070 to replace the previous Anglo-Saxon incumbent Stigand, resolved to build a grand new church in the Norman Romanesque style popular in his homeland. Work began in 1079, using masonry from the demolished minster and limestone from local quarries, and was complete by 1093. Although subsequently expanded and embellished, notably by William of Wykeham (the founder of Winchester School) in the fifteenth century, it forever remains associated with Walkelin, whose career thereafter prospered to such an extent that in 1097 he served as joint regent for William II for three months before his death.

7

John Nash. As eighteenth-century British towns were adorned with elegant housing in squares laid out on their urban estates by aristocratic families with an eye to the profit to be made by leasing them out, John Nash became one of the most sought-after architects to implement the fashionable Neoclassical style. As well as swathes of Regency London, including notable terraces around Regents Park and Regent Street, he also redesigned the Royal Pavilion at Brighton between 1815 and 1822, and remodelled the state rooms at Buckingham Palace between 1825 and 1830 (although Nash's extravagant spending led William IV to fire him). Earlier in his careeer, he practised in a rather different area of architecture, when he built the new Hereford County Gaol between 1792 and 1796.

8

Sir Christopher Wren. Wren is better known for his design for the new St Paul's Cathedral and 51 other churches to replace those destroyed in the 1666 Great Fire of London, but his first major commission was the Sheldonian Theatre at Oxford. The university acquired the patch of land just after the Restoration and entrusted the task of building a venue for its public ceremonies to Wren, who, only in his late 20s, had just been appointed Professor of Astronomy. Turning his agile mind to architecture – he had already undertaken the more

The Royal Pavilion, Brighton, by John Nash, 1827.

minor task of designing Pembroke College Chapel in Cambridge in 1663, a job given to him by his uncle, the Bishop of Ely – he based the buildings on Roman models, but had to design a 75-foot (23-m) roof truss in the Sheldonian to avoid the load-bearing columns that would have ruined the drama of the central space.

9

The Great East Window of York Minster. Depicting the start and end of time, with its illustration of the Creation story from the Book of Genesis and the Apocalypse and Second Coming of Christ, the Great East Window of York Minster is both among the more ambitious medieval stained-glass windows and the largest, with over 311 glazed panels. It was constructed in 1405-08 by the master glazer John Thornton on the instructions of Walter Skirlaw, the bishop of Durham, who had hoped to become (but never did) Archbishop of York. The window has survived the ages, and has been restored a number of times, most recently between 2008 and 2012 as part of an £11 million project that installed ultra-violet-filtering secondary glazing to protect the original stained glass.

10

The Festival of Britain. Intended as a 'tonic for the nation' after the trials of World War Two and to act as a showcase for British enterprise, industry and culture on the centenary of the Great Exhibition of 1851, the Festival of Britain opened in the summer of 1951. Among the structures built to cater for, and awe, the 8.5 million people who flocked to it were the Dome of Discovery (featuring improving exhibits on the 'Land' and the 'Sea'); the Skylon, a cigar-shaped steel tower suspended in an aluminium frame; and the Royal Festival Hall, a squat concrete building with a 2,900-seat auditorium, whose

opening concert in May was attended by King George VI and which has since established itself as one of London's principal cultural venues.

11

Durham (1093), Ripon (1154), York Minster (1220). Although the first church on the York site was built in 627 by St Paulinus after he baptised King Edwin of Northumbria, the current Minster structure was begun in 1220 under Archbishop Walter de Grey (who obtained the canonisation of one of his predecessors, William FitzHerbert, in 1226 in order to provide a resident saint for his foundation). Durham, too, had an Anglo-Saxon church – this one built to house the relics of St Cuthbert after the monks of Lindisfarne fled the island in 875 to avoid Viking raiders – but a new stone church, the basis of the present cathedral, was begun in 1093 by Bishop William de St Carileph. Ripon Cathedral was founded by St Wilfred in 672, and the saint was buried there. His crypt still survives under the edifice of the current church, whose construction was started by Archbishop Roger de Pont l'Eveque in 1154.

Genius Question

The Royal Victoria Hospital, Belfast. Belfast's Royal Victoria Hospital (or RVH) and its successor institutions have served the city since 1799. In 1903 it became the first public building in the world to have a mechanical air-conditioning system, providing much needed relief to patients and staff alike, when it was installed by local firm Sirocco Works. It used a design invented by the company's founder Sir Samuel Cleland Davidson, but wasn't quite the world's first air-conditioning unit (which was installed a year earlier in Brooklyn, New York, by Willis Carrier to solve the problem of humidity causing the ink to bleed in a printworks used to produce *Judge*, a illustrated humour magazine).

1

Britannia. The personification of Britannia first appeared on Roman coins during the reign of Hadrian (r. 117–138) as a symbol of the new province, often in a rather submissive mode. After disappearing (together with a monetary economy) when the Romans left the island in 411, Britannia did not feature again on British coins until 1672, when Charles II reintroduced the figure, which was by now regarded as a symbol of Britain's martial excellence and dominance of the seas, a place she has occupied in national sentiment ever since. (The coin shown is a 1730 penny of George II.)

The cartoon shows Britannia racing up the River Thames past Parliament in a British warship drawn by dolphins. The year of its publication, 1909, was one of increasing tension with Germany, which the previous year has passed a fourth Naval Bill to increase production of warships to a level that dangerously threatened Britain's previously unchallenged naval supremacy.

Thomas Arne, was one of mid-eighteenth century England's most prolific composers, his musical inclinations already having become clear at school, where he spent most of his time studying the violin, much to his father's horror. As a Roman Catholic, he was barred from many musical posts, and did not compose liturgical music. Instead, he turned to the stage, with compositions created for David Garrick's Shakespearian performances at Covent Garden. 'Rule Britannia!', with the words of James Thomson and David Mallet set to music by Arne, was first performed in 1740 as an air for *Alfred: A Masque*, a celebration of another iconic figure from British history, as well as the reputed founder of the English navy.

2

All were the mothers of two English kings. One of the most powerful women of the Middle Ages, Eleanor of Aquitaine had already been queen of France, as the wife of Louis VII, for 15 years before their increasingly fractious marriage ended in an annulment in 1152. The same year, Eleanor married Henry, Duke of Normandy, who in 1154 succeeded his grandfather Henry I as king of England. Bringing with her the lands of Aquitaine and Anjou, Eleanor provided a massive boost to England's prestige. She bore Henry five sons: Henry 'the Young King' died of dysentry in 1183 during a rebellion against his own father in France; Richard (later nicknamed 'the Lionheart') succeeded Henry II in 1189, although he spent little time in England; the youngest son John became king in 1199, although his loss of virtually all England's French possessions and his forced concession of Magna Carta to an alliance of rebellious barons permanently tarnished his memory.

Henrietta Maria was the daughter of Henri IV of France and Marie de Medici. She became the wife of Charles I in 1625 after his attempts to arrange a more politically convenient marriage alliance with Spain foundered. Headstrong, lively and insistent on openly practising her Catholicism at a time of rising anti-Catholic feeling in Britain, she alienated many at court and in the country. She fled to France in 1644 as the civil war, which had erupted, turned against her husband and did not return until 1660 when the first of her sons came to the throne as Charles II. She found she did not much care for her adopted country and returned to Paris, making only a few brief visits thereafter, and she had been dead for 16 years by the time her second son to become king, James II, ascended to the throne in 1685.

Princess Mary of Teck was the daughter of the Prince of Teck, a member of the German ruling house of Württemberg. First engaged to the Duke of Clarence (the elder son of the future Edward VII), tragedy struck Mary when he died a few weeks later, but ultimately in 1893 she married his younger brother George, Duke of York, who in 1910 became King George VI. A steadfast partner, she supported the king through the horrors of World War One and the social changes which followed it. She helped the monarchy weather the storm that threatened to engulf it when her eldest son, Edward VIII, abdicated, after just a few months reign, in December 1936 to marry the American divorcée Wallis Simpson. She then supported her second son, George VI, in his unexpected role as king and through World War Two. She died in March 1953, just over a year after the accession of her granddaughter, Elizabeth II, to the throne.

3

The Cabinet. Although the first MP of Black heritage was arguably John Stewart, the Conservative MP for Lymington between 1832 and 1847, it took until May 2002 for there to be a Black member of the Cabinet, when Paul Boateng was appointed Chief Secretary of the Treasury. Of mixed Scottish and Ghanaian heritage, he had politics in his blood, as his father had been a Cabinet Minister in the post-independence government of Kwame Nkrumah in the early 1960s. A solicitor and barrister by profession, Boateng served on Walthamstow Council and as chair of the Greater London Council's Police Committee, before being elected MP for Brent in 1987. He stood down from Parliament at the 2005 general election and served as High Commissioner to South Africa, before being elevated to the House of Lords in 2010.

Born in Chard, Somerset, Margaret Bondfield became active in politics after becoming friendly with a woman's rights activist who came into the shop where she worked as a draper's assistant. By 1899, aged just 26, she had become the first female delegate to the Trades Union Congress, and was appointed its first female chairman in 1923. She worked tirelessly to promote child welfare and women's rights and was Chair of the Adult Suffrage Society before World War One. In December 1923 she was elected MP for Northampton and was appointed parliamentary secretary in the Ministry of Labour (making her the first female junior minister). She lost her seat in the 1924 election, but was returned for Wallsend in the 1926 by-election there. After Labour became the largest party following the 1929 election, Bondfield was appointed to the Cabinet as Minister of Labour at a time when rising unemployment was straining government budgets. She lost at the 1931 election, but continued her fight for women's rights, even after her formal retirement from her trade union positions in 1938.

Princess Mary of Teck, from *The Sketch*, 19 July 1893.

1

Winchcombe. In the late evening of 28 February 2021, a meteorite came to land with a thump in a driveway in Gloucestershire. By then it was 10.6 ounces (300g) in weight, the rest having burned up as it descended. The Winchcombe meteorite was a rare specimen, the first to be found in Britain since 1991, and one of only 51 (out of 65,000 known meteorites) to be a carbonaceous chondrite, a type particularly rich in complex organic compounds. It fell on an ancient community, well known for the nearby Belas Knapp Neolithic barrow, which dates to around 3000 BC and which was the site of an Anglo-Saxon abbey founded in 798. In the seventeenth century it was the centre of an unlikely tobacco-growing industry, which Samuel Pepys records the Life Guard was sent to suppress in 1667.

2

Tewkesbury ('Tewkesburye' on the map). The fields outside here saw one of the climatic battles of the Wars of the Roses, in which the Lancastrians' made a last roll of the dice, their cause already harmed by the death of the Earl of Warwick (a defector from the Yorkists) at the Battle of Barnet in April 1471. At about the same time, another large Lancastrian force led by Queen Margaret and Prince Edward had landed in Dorset and marched north to link up with Jasper Tudor in Wales. When Gloucester barred its gates to them, they were forced towards Tewkesbury in search of a crossing of the Severn. There, on 4 May, the Lancastrian army wilted under a rain of Yorkist arrows and a charge led by the Duke of Somerset was smashed. In the rout that followed, Prince Edward was killed, leaving the 'white rose' of the Yorkists in firm control of England for the next 12 years.

3

Over Slaughter and Nether Slaughter. The names of these rather murderous sounding, but picturesque, Cotswold villages is actually derived from the Old English *slothre*, meaning a muddy place. Modern-day Upper Slaughter is best known for its Old Mill museum, while Lower Slaughter's Copse Hill Road was named in a 2011 poll as being the most romantic street in Britain.

4

Cheltenham. This spa and market town has been the host of the UK government's top-secret Government Communications Headquarters (GCHQ), responsible for intercepting telecoms and Internet communications, since 1951. The town dates to the ninth century, but its period of prosperity began in unlikely fashion in 1716 when Gabriel Davis Mason noticed a flock of pigeons pecking at salt near a spring on a meadow he owned. Suspecting they were attracted by mineral salts, he built a shed and pump, and within 30 years it was an established spa. George III's visit in 1788 set the seal of elite approval on the town and left it with a rich legacy of Regency buildings. Horseracing added to the town's attractions from 1815, and it is now the scene for the Cheltenham Festival, a mainstay of the equestrian calendar. Among its famous residents were Arthur Harris, the World War Two commander of Bomber Command, and Gustav Holst, composer of *The Planets* suite, who were both born in the town.

5

Gloucester ('Glocester'). Thomas of Woodstock was the fifth son of Edward III and was awarded the title Duke of Gloucester in 1385. He became the leader of the 'Lords Appellant', during the Merciless Parliament of 1388, which sentenced many of Richard II's leading supporters to death, but in 1397 when the king regained power he was arrested in Calais, and murdered while in detention, most likely on the king's orders. Humphrey of Lancaster, the 2nd Duke of Gloucester, was the fourth son of Henry IV and the uncle of Henry VI, during whose minority he acted as Lord Protector. Although generally popular, and an effective commander during the Hundred Years' War, his wife Eleanor of Cobham was accused of witchcraft in 1441 and convicted and sentenced to exile. Six years later Humphrey himself was arrested on charges of treason and died while in captivity, some claimed by poisoning. Perhaps the most unfortunate of all the dukes of Gloucester was Richard, who took advantage of the disappearance and likely murder of the young King Edward V in the Tower of London (quite probably at his command) to seize the throne himself as Richard III. His reign was short lived and came to an end two years later at Bosworth Field with his defeat and death in battle against the forces of Henry Tudor.

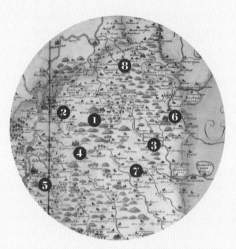

6

Stow-on-the-Wold ('Stow on the Wowld', an anagram of 'old west town who'). Although an ancient market town, it has a more contemporary connection because John Entwistle, bass guitarist of The Who, owned a house there from 1978 for the last 26 years of his life. The town, which lies on the ancient Fosse Way, was originally called St Edwardstow, possibly after the Anglo-Saxon royal martyr Edward, murdered in 978 while visiting his half-brother Ethelred at Corfe Castle. It saw the last skirmish in the first phase of the English Civil War, when 3,000 royalists under Sir Jacob Astley were defeated a mile north of the town on 21 March 1646, and has been the site of a renowned twice-yearly horse fair held on the feasts of St Edward the Confessor (24 October) and St Philip and James (12 May) since they were granted a charter by Edward IV in 1477.

7

Comptonabdale Hampnet. The small village of Compton Abdale, known for its church dedicated to St Oswald, with its wolf-like gargoyles and painted table of St George slaying the dragon, was occasionally known as Compton-in-the-Hole in the eighteenth century. It stood on an important Roman junction on the 'White Way' from Cirencester and the remains of a Roman villa were found south of the village in 1931.

8

Buckland ('land', as opposed to 'sea'). The village derives its name from 'book-land', or an area whose tenure depended on a charter (or 'book'); 'folc-land' was held according to customary right. The charter in question was that granted by Coenred of Mercia in 709 to Edburga, the abbess of St Peter's Abbey in Gloucester. It later became a Benedictine abbey and remained active until it was suppressed by Henry VIII's commissioners in 1546 during the general Dissolution of the Monasteries. It was then given to Sir Richard Gresham, a former Lord Mayor of London, who also acquired the lands of Fountains Abbey in York, and whose son Thomas Gresham established the Royal Exchange in 1571. A resolutely independent place, Buckland was recorded in a survey in 1266 as having 29 villeins and 14 bordars (both categories of free peasant) but, unusually, no unfree serfs at all.

1

For Valour. Before the 1850s, there was no medal to recognise heroic actions by ordinary servicemen (although officers could receive preferment, patronage and even ennoblement). Queen Victoria ordered this rectified during the Crimean War, and in 1857, just after it ended, the first 62 awards were made for exceptional bravery in the face of the enemy. The medals inscribed 'For Valour' were made of bronze, but probably not, as was once thought, from cannon captured from the Russians during the Siege of Sebastopol. Later medals, after World War One, may well have been struck from metal recovered from Chinese cannon captured during the Second Opium War in 1856–60. The medal, Britain's most prestigious, has been awarded 1,358 times (including three second awards), the very first to Mate Charles Lucas for picking up a live shell that had landed on the deck of his ship, HMS *Hecla*, on 21 June 1854, and throwing it overboard, and the most recent to Lance Corporal Joshua Leakey of the Parachute Regiment for bravery in an action in Afghanistan in August 2013.

2

The South Pole, 17 January 1912. Robert Falcon Scott was an obvious choice for a British push to reach the South Pole that set out in 1910 – he was already a veteran of the Antarctic, having commanded the *Discovery* expedition in 1901–04. But poor planning, the breakdown of the motorised sleds Scott hoped to rely on, and loss of their ponies in the bitter cold, which led to having to man-haul their supplies, all slowed the British down. When Edgar Evans, Lawrence Oates, Edward Wilson, Henry Bowers and Scott himself arrived at the Pole on 17 January they found a flag already there, planted a month earlier by the rival Norwegian expedition of Roald Amundsen. On the five-man party's gruelling trip back Evans died first, then Oates, crippled with frostbite, left his tent in a driving blizzard believing his death would help the others get to safety more quickly. Scott and the other two struggled on for five more days before setting up a final camp. Their supplies exhausted and trapped by appalling weather, they perished less than 11 miles (18km) away from a food depot that might have saved them.

3

1940. Inscribed 'For Gallantry', Britain's highest medal that can be awarded to civilians (and for military bravery not in the presence of the enemy) was instituted by King George VI in September 1940, when it was clear there was a need for an award to recognise the courage shown by many civilians during the Blitz. The George Cross has been awarded 408 times (although 245 of those were in exchange for gallantry medals which pre-dated its institution), including to the island of Malta in 1942. The most recent recipients were Major Dominic Troulan for gallantry shown during a terrorist attack on the Westfield Shopping Mall in Nairobi, Kenya, in 2013, and to the National Health Service in 2021 for its actions during the COVID-19 pandemic.

4

Grace Darling. The daughter of William Darling, a lighthouse keeper on the Farne Islands off the coast of Northumberland, Grace was keeping a lookout from the Longstone Rock lighthouse on the night of 7 September 1838 when she caught sight of the SS *Forfarshire* which, with its boilers leaking, had tried to come in close to land and had become wrecked on the rocks. Grace raised the alert and she and her father rowed through treacherous seas and a driving gale to rescue nine passengers and crew. When her actions became known, Grace was acclaimed as a heroine and awarded a Silver Medal by the Royal National Lifeboat Institute (Queen Victoria even sent her £50). Tragically, she died of tuberculosis four years later, aged just 27.

5

Ernest Shackleton. An experienced Polar explorer, Shackleton had breached the record for the most southerly point reached, when he came within 112 miles (180km) of the South Pole in January 1909 during his *Nimrod* expedition. In August 1914 he returned to have another try, but his vessel, the *Endurance*, became trapped in pack ice. After drifting for ten months, the vessel was crushed by the force of the ice, and the expedition survivors, after some weeks on an ice floe, rowed to Elephant Island in the South Shetlands. Shackleton took five men and sailed in the *Endurance*'s lifeboat the 800-plus miles (1,300km) to South Georgia. They then had to cross a mountain range in South Georgia's interior

Shackleton, from *The Antarctic Book*, 1909.

E·H· SHACKLETON·

to reach a whaling station, where they raised the alarm. It took four attempts to reach Elephant Island, but finally, on 30 August 1916, four-and-a-half months after he had left them, Shackleton returned to rescue his crew. During all of it, he lost not a single man.

6

Jack Phillips, chief radio operator of the *Titanic*. Accompanying the White Star Line's SS *Titanic* on its fateful first (and final) voyage were two radio operators, 25-year-old Jack Phillips and his assistant 22-year-old Harold Bride. Together they manned the 'Marconi Room' (named for the company that made the transmitter used by the pair to relay messages). Much of the traffic was initially routine communications with other ships, or messages from passengers to their loved ones or business partners back home, until at around 12.15am the wireless operators tapped out the message: 'We struck an iceberg, sinking.' Jack Phillips, who had graduated from the Marconi Telegraphy School in 1906 and who had turned 25 just two days before the *Titanic* sank, carried on signalling to the end, together with Harold Bride, who made it onto a lifeboat at the very last minute. Phillips's last signal – 'Engine room full up to boilers' – was sent at 1.45am, just minutes before the boat went under the icy North Atlantic waters. With it went Phillips and just over 1,500 other crew and passengers.

7

Geoff Hurst. On their way to the 1966 World Cup Final, England had enjoyed home advantage to top their group in the first stage and then beat Argentina in the quarter-finals and Portugal in the semis to advance to an eagerly anticipated final with West Germany. The West Germans opened the score in the 12th minute when Helmut Heller shot past England goalkeeper Gordon Banks. West Ham forward Geoff Hurst evened the score in the 18th minute after an England free-kick, but the scores ended level 2–2 after 90 minutes. Hurst scored twice more in extra time, the first a controversial shot that the Germans claimed (and continue to maintain) never actually crossed the line after it bounced off the crossbar. The 4–2 final score made England World Champions for the first and (so far) only time.

8

The Samaritans. Appointed Rector of St Stephen's Walbrook in London in 1953, Chad Varah used the position to launch a service to help those contemplating suicide, an issue that had concerned him since the funeral he had conducted in 1935 of a 14-year-old girl who had taken her life. Acquiring the number MAN 9000 to make it memorable for callers in distress, he took the first call on 2 November 1953. The service struck a chord and was soon expanding, until today the Samaritans have over 20,000 volunteers, who between them spend over a million hours each year answering calls from those in distress.

9

The slave trade. Born in West Africa, probably in what is now Nigeria, around 1745, Equiano – who was known for much of his life as Gustavus

Frontispiece to *The Interesting Narrative of the Life of Olaudah Equiano, or Gustavus Vassa, the African,* c.1789.

Vassa – was kidnapped aged 11 by slave-traders and enslaved. Taken to Virginia, Equiano was bought by a Royal Navy captain Michael Pascal, and then in 1765 sold on to an American merchant, who allowed him to trade on his own account and earn the £40 to buy his freedom the next year. Equiano made his way to England, where he worked as a deckhand on various voyages, until he finally settled in London in the 1780s and became active in the abolitionist movement. Popular for his first-hand account of the impact of slavery, in 1789 he published his memoir to great acclaim. Equiano died in 1797, ten years before the slave trade in Britain and its empire was abolished, and it was 1833 before slavery was entirely ended there.

10

Sir Douglas Bader. Douglas Bader joined the RAF as a cadet in 1928, but his career almost ended in 1931 when his plane crashed while performing a low-level acrobatic manoeuvre and his injuries were so severe he had to have both legs amputated. Although he tried to remain in the RAF he was invalided out in 1933, only to rejoin in October 1939 just after the outbreak of World War Two. Posted to a Spitfire squadron, he fought in the Battle of France and the Battle of Britain, scoring 23 confirmed kills before his plane went down on 9 August 1941 while in combat with a German Messerschmitt Bf 109 over northern France. Bader was captured by the Germans and, despite his disability, initially managed to escape through a window from the hospital where he was being treated. He was held in several POW camps before being sent to the notorious Colditz Castle for high-risk prisoners in August 1942. Liberated from there in April 1945, he remained in the RAF until the following year when he joined Shell, ultimately becoming Managing Director of Shell Aircraft. *Reach for the Sky,* a biography of Bader written by Paul Brickhill, was published in 1954 and made into a feature film released in 1956 with Kenneth More playing Bader. It won a BAFTA award for the best British Film and secured Bader's fame as one of Britain's best-known Battle of Britain fighter pilots.

11

Edith Cavell. The daughter of a Norfolk clergyman, Cavell had several jobs as a governess in the area before accompanying the Francois family to Brussels, where she stayed five years. She then returned to England, where she trained as a nurse at the London Hospital, and, following posts at a number of hospitals, went back to Brussels in 1907, where she became matron in charge of a nursing training school. When World War One broke out and the German Army occupied Brussels, most British nurses returned home but Cavell remained. Stray British soldiers who had been cut off in the Allied retreat began to make their way to her training school where, together with a network of assistants, she helped them make their way to neutral Holland. In early August 1915 she was betrayed and arrested. In October she was sentenced to death by a military court, and despite appeals from the United States embassy she was executed by firing squad a week later.

Lord Horatio Nelson (1758-1805).

Genius Question

The Battle of Calvi, 1794. Horatio Nelson, who rose to become Britain's most enduring naval hero, went to sea in 1770 aged 12 - a not uncommon age to begin a naval career in the era - and at first served principally in the Americas, as part of the British fleets during the American Revolutionary War and in the Caribbean. He received his first command, of HMS *Badger*, in 1778, but saw more frequent action after the outbreak of war with Revolutionary France in 1793. Sent to the Mediterranean in October that year with orders to blockade the French garrison on Corsica, he masterminded the capture of Bastia in May 1794, and then in July took command of the land assault on Calvi in the northwest of the island. During an inspection of the forward British batteries on 12 July, Nelson was struck in the right eye by flying debris, blinding him. The town surrendered a month later, and Nelson lived to fight another 11 years, losing his right arm in an attack on Spanish positions on Tenerife in 1797, famously assaulting Copenhagen in 1801 after raising a telescope to his blind eye to avoid obeying the signal hoisted by his commanding officer Sir Hyde Parker to withdraw, and then dying in 1805 at Trafalgar, the victory that sealed his reputation.

1

The Jaffa Cake. Beloved of generations of sweet-toothed Britons, the Jaffa Cake, with a sponge base covered in tangerine-flavoured jam and coated with chocolate, was first manufactured by Edinburgh-based McVitie's in 1927. It takes its name from the Jaffa oranges grown from the mid- nineteenth century in Palestine, from where 500,000 crates of the fruit were being exported by 1905. In 1991 the UK government took McVitie's to court, claiming that the Jaffa was a chocolate-covered biscuit, on which VAT was payable, and not a chocolate-covered cake (on which it was not). McVitie's won and so the Jaffa Cake remains a cake.

2

Kedgeree (anagram of 'greed eek!'). A distinctly acquired taste, kedgeree is a traditional British breakfast dish composed of flaked smoked fish (generally haddock), rice, hard-boiled eggs, parsley, curry powder and butter. It is said to have been based on *khichari*, an Indian dish of spiced lentils and rice brought back by returnees from the British Raj in India in the nineteenth century. First mentioned in a Scottish cookbook in the 1790s, it is said to have been a favourite dish of Queen Victoria (although that didn't stop her having the last Mughal emperor Bahadur Shah – who was partial to *khichdi*, another Indian version of the dish – from being deposed in 1857 following the Indian Mutiny).

3

1908, on Glasshouse Street, near London's Piccadilly Circus. The growth of Chinese cuisine in Britain, by now almost ubiquitous, was at first slow. First showcased at the 1884 International Health Exhibition in South Kensington, early restaurants were informal affairs aimed at the tiny Chinese community, mainly composed of dock-workers. As immigration from Hong Kong took off in the 1950s, the numbers grew and the more entrepreneurial set up new takeaway restaurants aimed at the native British market. The first was John Koon's Lotus House in Bayswater, which opened in 1958, and by 2015 there were over 2,700 Chinese restaurants in the United Kingdom.

4

Battenberg Cake. The Hesse town of Battenberg was the seat of Counts of the Wittgenstein family in the thirteenth and fourteenth century. Although their line died out, the title was revived in 1851 for Julia, the wife of Prince Alexander von Hessen-Darmstadt, whose non-noble birth had caused a scandal. In 1884 their son Louis married Princess Victoria of Hesse, the granddaughter of Queen Victoria, and in their honour a new cake, with four sponge panels alternately coloured pink and yellow, held together with jam and covered in marzipan, was baked. The Battenberg cake was born.

5

1671, at a feast given by Charles II. British monarchs have always had a taste for the exotic. Henry VIII had a penchant for seagulls and Queen Victoria is said to have offered a prize to anyone who could bring back a pomelo from Malaysia fresh enough for her to eat. But Charles II topped it all at a St George's Day Feast in Windsor when he served ice cream for the first time (but only to guests on his personal table!). It was a real novelty – iced sorbets had appeared in Europe only in the 1660s, and the addition of sweetened milk in Naples in 1664 created the first modern ice cream. The dessert was an instant hit with Britain's aristocracy and once Domenico Negri opened the first real ice cream parlour, The Pineapple, on London's Berkeley Square in 1757, a wider public could enjoy the delights of a range of ice cream flavours, including ginger brandy and lemon.

6

The Roman period (from AD 43 to 411). The Romans had a very eclectic palette, including sea urchins, ostrich and a pungent sauce of rotting fish called garum. Oddest of all was the edible dormouse, which they fattened in special terracotta jars, called *gliraria*, in which the hapless rodents had nothing to do but eat and try to run up the inside of their prison. Once fat enough they were killed and served in dormouse pies, stuffed with pork and garnished with fennel. The edible dormouse has had its revenge in Britain: in 1902 some escaped from a collection on Lord Rothschild's estate at Tring in Hertfordshire and have since become an established pest, munching their way through anything they can find, including electric cables.

7

Spotted dick. A sponge pudding laced with sultanas (hence the 'spotted'), the name of Spotted Dick has been the subject of endless jokes. First appearing in 1849 in *The Modern Housewife*, a cookery book by Alexis Soyer, the 'dick' part of the name seems to derive either from a dialect word for dough, or from a corruption of 'puddick', a regional word for pudding.

8

Rabbit. When the Romans came to Britain, they brought with them as many of the components of the Mediterranean diet as they could manage to grow in their new province's comparatively chilly climate. This included cherries, cucumber, almonds and lentils, as well as a whole range of other foods, including plums, mulberries, celery and coriander. Rabbits were introduced by the Normans for their meat and fur after their conquest of England in 1066. However, analysis

in 2017 of a tiny bone found at Fishbourne Roman Palace in West Sussex indicated that it was from a rabbit. There was no sign of the rabbit having been butchered for meat, so it may have been a pet. So the Romans could have kept rabbits in Britain, but there is no evidence they ate them.

9

Cawl (Wales), Haggis (Scotland) and none (England) – Cawl, a stew of leeks, beef or lamb, potatoes, carrots and other vegetables, was first recorded as long ago as the eleventh century. Haggis, traditionally made from a sheep's stomach stuffed with offal, oatmeal, suet and onions is first mentioned around 1500 in a poem by William Dunbar as part of a flyting, a kind of poetic insult competition in which he included the charming barb: 'The gallows gape for your disfigured dimples, As you gape for haggis, like a ravenous mew.' Its origins, though probably

Frontispiece to *Modern Domestic Cookery*, 1851.

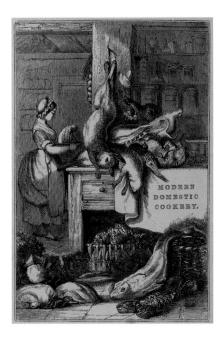

lie centuries earlier. England has no universally recognised national dish, although claims have been made for roast beef and Yorkshire pudding, fish and chips, and even chicken tikka masala.

10

They are both reputed to have killed a king (lampreys for Henry I, and peaches for John). The Middle Ages was not exactly a safe period for monarchs, with the hazards of assassins, royal rivals, invaders and disease ever present. Even the dining table presented another, albeit less expected, mortal threat. In 1135 Henry I was tucking in at a feast. Age – he was in his 60s – had not diminished his appetite and he indulged in a heroically large portion of lampreys, an eel-like fish. It was all too much for him and he fell sick and died several days later, it was said of 'a surfeit of lampreys'. His great-grandson John had had a turbulent reign, having fallen out with his barons and being forced into agreeing Magna Carta in 1215. In September 1216, as he campaigned to mop up the rebel barons (in alliance with Prince Louis of France), he enjoyed a meal of peaches near Lynn (now King's Lynn) in East Anglia. They seem to have been contaminated and the king contracted dysentery. He ended his life in sorry fashion, losing his baggage train as he crossed The Wash on his way back westwards and dying in agony at Newark Castle in Nottinghamshire on 19 October.

11

1170. A hard white or off-white cheese, which is Britain's most popular (accounting for around half the total market), Cheddar was traditionally produced in the caves around Cheddar Gorge where the humidity helped maturation and to earn its name the cheese had to be made within 30 miles of Wells Cathedral. Cheddar was first mentioned in 1170, when Henry II is recorded as purchasing 10,240 pounds (he clearly had a taste for it!). It remained popular among British monarchs: during the reign of Charles I the cheese was monopolised by the court and not available outside the royal table, while Queen Victoria was given a giant wheel of cheddar, weighing over 1,200 pounds (nearly 550kg) and nine feet four inches (285cm) in diameter, as a wedding gift.

Genius Question

Coffee. Allegedly discovered in the ninth century by an Ethiopian goatherd whose flock became rather excitable after chewing on the berries from a bush, coffee reached England via the Ottoman Empire in the mid-seventeenth century. The first coffee house opened in Oxford in 1650, followed two years later by one on London's Cornhill. Before long they were the go-to places for gossip, intrigue and business (the Lloyd's of London insurance market opened up in one in 1668). The 3,000 coffee houses that the capital boasted by the 1670s were not so popular with the wives of the men who spent almost every waking hour there and in 1674 *The Women's Petition Against Coffee* was published, a vicious diatribe against the baleful influence of the 'nauseous puddle'.

A pamphlet *The Women's Petition Against Coffee*, objecting to the new 'liquor', 1674.

THE
WOMEN'S
PETITION
AGAINST
COFFEE.

REPRESENTING
TO
PUBLICK CONSIDERATION
THE
Grand INCONVENIENCIES accruing
to their SEX from the Excessive
Use of that Drying, Enfeebling
LIQUOR.

Presented to the Right Honorable the
Keepers of the Liberty of *VENUS*.

By a Well-willer ———

London, Printed 1674.

1

Lord North. A member of the landowning aristocracy, North entered Parliament aged just 22 in 1754. He enjoyed rapid promotion, helped by his speech calling for the expulsion of the radical MP John Wilkes, and earned appointments as the Chancellor of the Exchequer in 1767 and the prime minister in 1770. He mishandled the government's response to the growing demands of the American colonists for greater liberties: the Coercive Acts he championed in the wake of the Boston Tea Party in 1773 simply pushed them into open revolt. Early British successes were not followed up, and the entry of the French into the war in 1778 left Britain on the defensive. By 1781, with the surrender of General Cornwallis and the main British land force at Yorktown, it was clear the war was lost. North resigned in March 1782 after a very rare vote of no confidence in Parliament.

2

Poaching. An economic downturn in the early 1720s led to an upsurge in poaching in the royal forests by men desperate to eke out a livelihood. The English upper classes were sensitive about poaching and an Act went through Parliament aimed at poachers who went about their business in disguise (one group was know as the 'blacks' because of blackened faces, and so lent their name to the measure). The penalties imposed by the Waltham Black Act were draconian: more than 50 offences became punishable by death, including not just poaching, but damaging orchards, burning haystacks and harbouring poachers. Over the next 80 or 90 years a huge range of further capital crimes were added, until around 350 carried the death penalty. So many people were convicted and hanged that calls for the reform of what was referred to as 'the Bloody Code' mounted, and from 1832 the capital offences were gradually removed from the statute book, beginning with forgery and cattle rustling.

3

An early steam locomotive. Richard Trevithick's experiment with high-pressure steam in the late 1790s enabled him to produce an engine that could power a piston, which he used to develop a working steam locomotive, the *Puffing Devil*, in 1801. Although it carried passengers, Trevithick could not drum up enough interest in its larger potential, his engines being mainly confined to use in mines. In 1808 he built a new locomotive, the *Catch Me Who Can*, which he ran for the paying public on a circular track in Bloomsbury. Unfortunately, the weight of the locomotive caused the rails on which it ran to subside, and the train derailed several times. As a result, the public's interest dwindled and a despondent Trevithick abandoned the development of locomotives altogether.

4

John Edmonstone. Charles Darwin's five-year scientific odyssey aboard the *Beagle* might not have had quite the same impact if he did not have the ability to preserve the specimens he encountered (notably the Galapagos finches, which prompted him to formulate his ideas concerning evolution and the natural selection of species). The man from whom he acquired this delicate skill was John Edmonstone, a former slave on a timber plantation in Demerara, Guyana, who accompanied his master Charles Edmonstone to Scotland in 1817, where, once free, he earned his living as a taxidermist preparing specimens for the zoological department of Edinburgh

University. In 1825 Darwin went to Edinburgh to study Anatomy and Zoology, but found the lectures dull. He left after two years, but had spent his spare time to better effect, having taken lessons in taxidermy from John Edmonstone, who charged him a guinea a day for a two-month course. Darwin professed him 'a very pleasant and intelligent man' and used what he had learned well: he brought back over 500 preserved bird skins from South America, of which London's Natural History Museum still holds nearly 200.

5

Josiah Wedgwood. Wedgwood came from a long line of Staffordshire potters, but it was only when he went into business on his own account in the 1750s that he rose to fame. His technical innovations, in particular basalt, a black background which lent itself to imitations of Greek vase painting, led to huge demand for his work at a time Neoclassicism was much in vogue. As well as British aristocratic patrons, Wedgwood came to the attention of foreign nobility and among the more prestigious commissions was the 'Green Frog Service' ordered by the Russian empress Catherine in 1773. Each of its 952 pieces was adorned with a green frog, as a reference to their Kekerekeksiny Palace destination (its name means 'frog swamp' in Finnish).

6

Limehouse, East London. London's Chinese community dates to the 1780s, when crew members aboard clippers carrying tea from China began to visit the port of London and sometimes to settle. The most convenient locations were by the docks in Shadwell and Deptford, but by the 1880s the tiny community had coalesced in Limehouse, which by 1914 supported 30 Chinese-owned businesses, mainly in the catering and laundry trade. As other avenues for employment were closed off to them, the Chinese began to move into the restaurant business. With the decline of the docks and the wartime devastation

wrought on the area, many Chinese people moved the focus of their activities to Soho, where London's current Chinatown is situated.

7

Warren Hastings. The son of a clergyman, Warren Hastings arrived in India in 1750 to seek his fortune in the service of the East India Company. The expansion of the company's territories after the victory against the nawab of Bengal at Plassey in 1757 provided new opportunities and ultimately Hastings rose to be Governor of Bengal in 1771, and then two years later the first British Governor-General of India. His clashes with members of his council sent from London to help supervise him and the exigencies of wars against the Marathas in the 1770s and Mysore in 1780 led him to resort to some dubious practices to raise funds, and when he returned to London in 1785 a clamour arose in which he was accused of embezzling a fortune. Most notable among those calling for his impeachment was Edmund Burke, whose tirades against the former governor during the trial, which dragged on for seven years between 1788 and 1795, became notorious. In the end, Hastings was acquitted, but he never shook off the taint of the accusations against him.

'Impeachment Ticket. For the Trial of W-rr-n H-st-ngs Esqr', by Gillray, February 1788.

8

New Lanark. Welsh textile manufacture and social reformer Robert Owen had strong views on the moral imperative to improve the lot of workers in the cotton industry in which he made his fortune. Having managed mills near Manchester, in 1799 he married the daughter of the proprietor of the New Lanark Mill, southeast of Glasgow. He moved to Scotland and reformed the working practices in the mill, reducing the length of the working day, abolishing the practice of using orphans as labourers, establishing sick pay and setting up a model village for his workers, with medical care and a school for their children. He later became committed to a broader social reform, setting up several model communes in the United States, notably New Harmony in Indiana, and in 1834 helping to establish the Grand National Consolidated Trades Union.

9

Martello Towers. Fearing invasion from France, in 1803 the British government decided to build a line of forts along the south coast to stem the advance of any invading army. Named after Fort Mortella in northern Corsica (where the British had won a victory against France in 1794), work on the first towers began in 1805. Each was to be garrisoned by an officer and 24 men, hardly enough to dent a determined attacker's progress, but the bureaucracy needed to sanction their construction meant that by the time the line of 75 forts was largely complete in 1812, the real threat of invasion was over. As a result, the Martellos never fired a shot in anger.

10

Riots by agricultural workers against the introduction of mechanical threshing machines. Enclosure of much Common Land in the half-century before 1820 and then a series of poor harvests aggravated poverty among agricultural labourers, many of whom struggled to feed their families. The introduction of mechanical threshing machines, which threatened to put many of them out of work, incensed rural sentiment even further. Protests started in Kent in the summer of 1830, where threatening letters signed 'Captain Swing' were sent to farmers and magistrates calling for a rise in wages, reduction in tithes and the removal of the machines; if not, the farmers would 'swing' on gallows set up to punish them. As the movement spread into East Anglia, hundreds of machines were destroyed. Although the authorities promised concessions, these were never enacted, and around 500 'Captain Swing' rioters were deported to Australia.

11

The Peterloo Massacre. By the summer of 1819, the movement for social, and in particular parliamentary, reform was gathering momentum. On 16 August there was a mass assembly organised by the Patriotic Union Society at St Peter's Field in Manchester. Rattled by the 60,000-strong crowd and fearful of a French-style revolution, the local authorities sent in a unit of local militia to disperse the assembly. Against the sabre-wielding yeomanry, many of the unarmed demonstrators panicked, causing a crush, and as chaos escalated the magistrates sent in a regular British Army unit, the 15th Hussars. In the carnage that ensued, 11 people were killed and hundreds injured. The incident was followed by a series of acts clamping down on the rights to assembly. In the end, though, the reform movement raised sympathy for the cause of widening the suffrage, contributing to the rise of Chartism.

Genius Question

The Times newspaper. Founded as the *Universal Daily Register* by John Walter, the newspaper changed its name to *The Times* exactly three years later, on 1 January 1788 (reputedly because Walter was annoyed that people kept missing the 'Universal' out of the name). Since then it has been published continuously, save for a break in 1987–88 during an industrial dispute. It earned its nickname 'the Thunderer' in Victorian times, for its outspoken challenges to authority, and has employed an array of notable correspondents, including the historian E.H. Carr and the Soviet spy Kim Philby.

1

Richmond Park. At around 2,500 acres, Richmond Park is by far London's largest park, dwarfing Hampstead Heath's 790 acres and Hyde Park's comparatively puny 350 acres. The park has long been a royal hunting preserve (it is to this day home to herds of red and fallow deer), dating back to the time of Edward I (r. 1272-1307), and was enclosed within a wall (that still exists) by Charles I in 1637. Its existence as a public park dates back to a court case in 1758 when John Lewis, a Richmond brewer, who objected to paying for a ticket to enter the park, took his case to the Surrey Assizes and won, after which gates and stiles were installed to allow the public free pedestrian access. The park had its own entirely independent police force until this was amalgamated with the Metropolitan Police in 2005.

2

The Russian ambassador. The first St James's Park pelicans were a gift from the Russian ambassador to Charles II in 1664, intended to curry favour with a king known to be interested in exotic wildlife. The pelicans have lived there continuously ever since, their numbers boosted by periodic imports (because they tend not to breed in small communities). In the 1960s the birds almost sparked a Cold War incident, when the US ambassador decided to donate a number of American pelicans and the new arrivals started to behave aggressively towards their 'Russian' peers. It turned out, on closer inspection, that the American pelicans were the wrong sort, a different species entirely, so explaining their violent rivalry with 'the Russians'. The most recent pelican influx was a gift from the city of Prague in 2013, and there are currently six resident pelicans in St James's Park.

3

Yugoslavia. In July 1941, as Axis forces mopped up the last remaining independent military forces in the Balkans, they invaded Yugoslavia, causing the 17-year-old King Peter II to flee to London (via Athens and Cairo) to set up a government-in-exile there. The king took up residence with Queen Alexandra in a suite in Claridge's Hotel. When his wife was about to give birth four years later, Prime Minister Winston Churchill apparently offered to temporarily assign Yugoslav sovereignty to their suite so that the baby could claim to have been born on Yugoslav soil. So it was that Crown Prince Alexander initially held Yugoslav, but not British, nationality until stripped of it by the new communist government of Josip Tito in 1947. Alexander returned to Yugoslavia in 1991, and now lives in the Royal Palace in Belgrade.

4

The eleventh century. After William the Conqueror's defeat of Harold II Godwinson at Hastings in 1066, he and his Norman followers began to build castles to dominate their new realm. At first made of wood, one of the first stone strongholds was in London, where the White Tower, the nucleus of the Tower of London, was begun around 1078. Complete by about 1100, it became a jail for high-status prisoners, both foreign – such as Charles Duke of Orléans held there for 25 years after the Battle of Agincourt in 1415 – and native, such as Guy Fawkes who was tortured there before his execution in January 1606.

5

Charles Dickens. One of Britain's best-known writers and the author of 15 novels, Dickens moved into the Georgian terraced house on

Doughty Street with his family in March 1837. The Holborn property was a step up for the Dickens family – only 13 years before his father had been slung into Marshalsea Debtor's Prison – and cost the princely annual rent of £80, paid for by his earnings from the publication of the first part of *The Pickwick Papers*. During his time there he wrote *Oliver Twist*, *Nicholas Nickleby* and part of *Barnaby Rudge*. As his fortunes rose even higher, Dickens moved out in 1839 to a larger flat on Devonshire Terrace, and then in 1851 to an 18-room residence on Tavistock Square, before his final move – out of London to Gad's Hill near Rochester in 1860.

6

Pall Mall. Of French origin, the ball and mallet game pall mall takes its name from the Italian *palla* ('ball') and *maglio* ('mallet') and crossed over into Britain from France in the early seventeenth century. The game came to be played on a court in an alley just inside the walls of St James's Park and became popular with the aristocracy. Samuel Pepys, in his diary, records that in April 1661 he saw the Duke of York (later King James II) playing 'Pelemele' there. The game gradually fell out of favour and aficionados of mallet and hoop eventually created croquet,

which reached the zenith of its popularity in the 1860s. Although pall mall the game and the court on which it was played have long ago disappeared, both are still remembered by the name of the modern street lined with private members' clubs.

7

Thirty-two. The current number dates back to 1965, when the London Government Act 1963 came into effect, abolishing the mess of county, municipal and metropolitan boroughs that had hitherto governed the capital's districts. Some of their names are ancient indeed, dating to Anglo-Saxon times, such as Southwark (listed in the Domesday Book as *Sudweca, or* 'south work', the southern defences of London) and Lambeth, whose name comes from *hithe*, a landing place for lambs. The London Eye also has 32 compartments, a number chosen by its designers so that there would be one to represent each of the London boroughs.

8

The Vintners' and Dyers' Livery Companies. Ever since the twelfth century the British monarch has had the right to claim ownership of all swans on the River Thames. In the

View near Richmond, London, 1811.

fifteenth and sixteenth century two of the livery companies, the medieval guilds which came to dominate commerce in the capital, acquired the right to a share of the birds. The Vintners' Company (whose members ran the wine trade) and the Dyers' Company (whose members, as its name suggests, specialised in dying cloth) still retain that right and in the third week of July the ceremony of Swan Upping takes place in which representatives of the companies and the queen (the sovereign's Swan Uppers clad in scarlet) sail down the river in skiffs and take a swan census, inspecting the birds for disease, counting the cygnets and marking those which are the property of the Vintners and Dyers.

9

Richmond-upon-Thames. Carved out of parts of Surrey and Middlesex by the local government reorganisation of 1965, Richmond is the perfect riposte to those ambivalent about whether North or South London is superior. Richmond also has a river frontage of over 21 miles (34km), and more than half its area is parkland, lending it a far more rural feel than many of the other London boroughs.

10

The café. Coffee had long been a popular drink in Arabia and the Ottoman Empire and gradually percolated its way westward into the Habsburg lands of Austria and beyond. In 1652 Pasqua Rosée, the Greek manservant of an English merchant named Daniel Edwards, came with his master back to Britain. He established a coffee ship in St Michael's Alley, Cornhill, the first in London (although not quite the first in Britain, which opened two years before in Oxford). Before long, imitators proliferated and by 1674 there were more than 3,000 coffee shops in England, the distant ancestors of today's chains such as Starbucks, Costa Coffee and Café Nero.

11

John Gower. Although William Shakespeare, who lived in the local parish, has a monument in Southwark Cathedral, he was actually buried in Stratford-upon-Avon (although the grave of his brother Edmund is in the cathedral). John Gower, who died in 1408, and was a contemporary of Geoffrey Chaucer, lived the last part of his life in the priory at the cathedral and is best known for his *Confession Amantis* ('Confession of the Lover'), in which the despairing lover of the title invokes Venus and Cupid to help him and is regaled with scores of tales of lovers from classical and biblical history in a poem that extends to over 33,000 lines.

Genius Question

George IV. The district, originally called Battlebridge, took its modern name from a monument to George IV erected at the crossroads of Euston Road, Grey's Inn Road and Pentonville Road. The structure, standing 60 feet (18m) high and with an 11-foot (3.3-m) statue of the monarch topping it off, was generally unpopular, derided by Walter Thornbury (the biographer of JMW Turner) as a 'ridiculous octagonal structure' and a 'hideous monstrosity'. Complaints that its vast bulk obscured the view of carriage drivers did not help and in 1845 it was removed, but the area, and the railway station that was built in 1851, kept the name of the unlamented 'King's Cross'.

Demolition of the King's Cross monument in 1845.

1

Skara Brae, Orkney. Five thousand years ago, Orkney hosted one of the most thriving Neolithic communities in Britain, living at Skara Brae on the Bay of Skaill, a small village of round houses that was home to around 50 people. Each dwelling, sunk into the ground for better insulation, had a suite of furniture, such as dressers, beds and storage chests, all made out of stone. The pastoralists who lived in Skara Brae herded sheep and cattle and also feasted on seafood. The village was eventually abandoned around 2500 BC after the climate grew too cold to eke out even a basic existence and it was covered over by a mound of drifting sand and soil until exposed in a great storm in 1850, although it was not until the late 1920s that the site was finally scientifically excavated.

2

Mary Somerville. Born in Jedburgh in the Borders in 1780, her family did not encourage her education, but the determined autodidact lapped up every book she could find, and even had her younger brother's tutor teach her Latin, Greek and geometry. She became fascinated with mathematics and its application to astronomy. After her first husband died in 1807, she married William Somerville, who did approve of her academic achievements, and once they moved to London she mixed in circles which included the mathematician Charles Babbage and the astronomers William and Caroline Herschel, and begin to publish on scientific subjects. In 1836 she included calculations in one of her books showing that irregularities in the recorded orbit of Uranus might indicate there was another planet, which ultimately led to the discovery of Neptune. Somerville College, Oxford, was named for her in 1879 and includes among its alumnae Margaret Thatcher, Indira Gandhi and Dorothy Hodgkin.

3

Selkie. Creatures whose origins probably lie in myths of Viking Norse settlers of Scotland's islands, the selkies were seal-folk who had the ability to transform themselves into human form by shedding their seal-skins, by tradition on Midsummer's Eve. Anyone who found a skin and took it had the selkie in their power because it could not then turn back into a seal. There are tales of young women who drowned who were said to have been taken to sea by selkie-lovers and of fishermen who found the skins of female selkies and then took the selkie as a wife. Almost invariably the selkie later found the skin and departed back to her former life as a seal.

Mary Somerville (1780-1872).

4

Lorne sausage. Also known as the square sausage or sausage slice, the Lorne sausage was traditionally said to have been named after the comedian Tommy Lorne who was active around the time of World War One. Adverts for the slab-like beef sausage appeared, though, as early as 1896, so its appearance as a Scottish breakfast staple and its name probably owes more to the former district of Lorne, an area now within Argyll and Bute.

5

The Darien Scheme. As other nations established colonies in the New World, and the Navigation Acts, which outlawed non-English ships from trading with English colonies, prevented Scottish vessels from doing business in India (or in English North America), Scottish merchants were keen not to be left behind. In 1695 a proposal was drawn up to settle a Scottish colony at Darien

A plan of the harbour at Darien, by J. Watson, 1743.

on the Isthmus of Panama, thus giving Scotland a toehold in the lucrative transatlantic trade. Unfortunately, lukewarm support in England and the opposition of William III meant that few funds were raised there, and the new Company of Scotland for Trading in Africa was forced to rely almost entirely on Scottish subscribers. It did all too well, supping up over £400,000 in funds, a huge proportion of the available capital in Scotland. The expedition to Darien, in 1698, was a disaster because the site of 'New Edinburgh' proved to be a malarial swamp and had to be rapidly evacuated; three-quarters of the 1,200 colonists died and none returned home in time to stop a second expedition setting out in 1699 with another 1,000 settlers. Fractionally more successful than the first venture, the refounded colony attracted the attention of the Spanish authorities who forced its evacuation the following year. The huge expense crippled the Scottish economy and saddled Scotland with a massive debt, which made many Scots more favourably disposed to the eventual union with England in 1707.

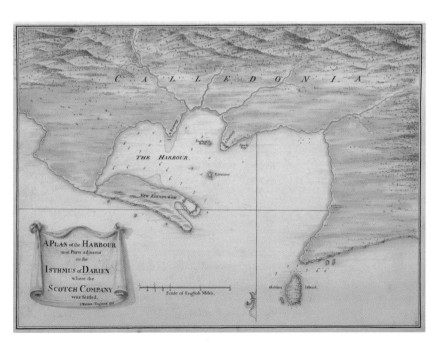

6

Nine. The first Stewart king was Robert II, who was the son of Robert the Bruce's daughter Marjorie, but whose father Walter was the hereditary High Steward of Scotland, from whence the dynasty he founded in 1371 derives his name. Robert II died in 1390 and the subsequent Stewart monarchs were Robert III (r.1390-1406), James I (r.1406-37), James II (r.1437-60), James III (r.1460-88), James IV (r.1488-1513), James V (r.1513-42), Mary (r.1542-67) and James VI (r.1567-1625, from 1603 also as king of England). Blighted by a large number of minorities – Mary was only a week old when she became queen – it was also said of the Stewarts that they were good rulers in youth but turned bad in old age.

7

'The Skye Boat Song'. In the aftermath of the Jacobite defeat at Culloden on 16 April 1746, Charles Edward Stuart ('Bonnie Prince Charlie') fled westwards, always in hiding to evade government troops until he reached the Hebrides in mid-May. Then, on 28 June, he took a boat arranged by Flora Macdonald over to Skye, disguised as 'Betty Burke', an Irish maid. Finally, on 19 September, he and his close companions boarded a French vessel sent to rescue him, which conveyed the prince to exile in France (and then Italy). He would never return to Scotland. The song that commemorates the event appeared long after; the words, by Sir Harold Boulton, were set to a traditional air and were first published only in 1884. Robert Louis Stevenson so much disliked them that he penned his own version in 1892, which appears as part of the theme tune to the television series *Outlander.*

8

Aminatta Forna. Established in 1987 by the Commonwealth Foundation to recognise the work of poets and novelists resident in the Commonwealth, by 2011 the prize had been won by Australian writers eight times, but that year the first Scottish recipient was Aminatta Forna, born in Bellshill to Sierra Leonean and Scottish parents. The events surrounding the imprisonment and death of her father, who had become involved in politics after the family moved to Sierra Leone, formed the backdrop to her first book *The Devil that Danced on Water* (2002). Her third novel *The Memory of Love* (2010) deals with the experiences of three Sierra Leonean men living in London and secured her the Commonwealth Writer's Prize. Aminatta

Seal of Robert II
of Scotland, 1386.

Forna has also been shortlisted for the Samuel Johnson Prize, the Women's Prize for Fiction and in 2017 was awarded the OBE for services to literature.

9

Inchtuthil. The Roman conquest of Britain, which began in AD 43, reached its culmination exactly 40 years later at Mons Graupius, somewhere in the Highlands, where the legions defeated a confederation of Caledonian tribes led by Calgacus, whom Tacitus tells us declared in a speech before the battle that the Romans made 'a desert and declared it peace'. Afterwards the Roman set to pacifying their northernmost province, establishing a legionary fortress at Inchtuthil on a plateau overlooking Strathmore that would dominate the entrances to the Highlands. Then in 86 a crisis erupted on the Danube, where the Dacians had attacked across the river into the province of Moesia, causing Emperor Domitian to pull back the II Adiutrix Legion from Britain to face the emergency. There were no longer sufficient troops in Britain to garrison Inchtuthil and there began a gradual retraction from the advanced Roman positions in Scotland. The fortress was dismantled and the soldiers abandoned the area, leaving only a million iron nails buried in a pit, to avoid their falling into the Caledonians' hands and be forged into weapons, as a testimony of the legionary headquarters that never was.

10

The Watt (James Watt). One of the pioneers of the Industrial Revolution, James Watt, from Greenock in Renfrewshire, patented his improved steam engine in 1769. A separate condenser made the engine vastly more efficient and soon it spread from its original use, for pumping water out of mines, to service in the cotton mills that were beginning to proliferate in Britain. The watt, a unit of power equal to an energy transfer of one joule per second, was named after the inventor in 1882, and is now the official unit under the International System of Units (SI).

11

First Secretary of State for Scotland. Born into a venerable Scottish noble family, John Erskine, 6th Earl of Mar, supported English interests in the Scottish parliaments of the early eighteenth century. In the memorable words of the biographer John Gibson Lockhart he 'returned like the dog to his vomit, and promoted all the court of England's measures with the greatest zeal imaginable' in 1704, after his patron the Marquis of Queensberry's return to influence following a brief fall from royal grace. He was appointed a commissioner for the negotiation of the Union and as a reward for his labours in 1713 became the first Secretary of State for Scotland, an office established to represent the country's interests at Westminster. When George I became king in 1714, Erskine defected to the Jacobite cause and became the principal leader of the 1715 uprising. Forced into exile, he nonetheless in 1719 accepted a pension from George I, his frequent changes of allegiance earning him the nickname 'Bobbing John'.

Genius Question

Macbeth. The real Macbeth, a rather different character from the one depicted by William Shakespeare in his 'Scottish play'. Originally the mormaer (a provincial ruler) of Moray, he seized the Scottish throne in 1040 after his predecessor Duncan I overreached himself by attacking Macbeth's Norse allies in Caithness. He was a generally popular ruler, respected for his generosity, and in 1050 even went on a pilgrimage to Rome. Unfortunately for Macbeth, Duncan's son Malcolm had survived and in 1054 he returned, aided by the English king Edward the Confessor, who was only too happy to destabilise Scotland. Their armies met at Dunsinnan on 27 July 1054, although there is no record of a forest 'moving' from Birnam Wood as Shakespeare has it. Macbeth was defeated, but struggled on for another three years as Malcolm's forces steadily gained ground, finally ambushing and killing Macbeth at Lumphanan, west of Aberdeen, where he made a last stand at a stone circle known as the Peel Ring.

1

Graham's Dyke (actually the Antonine Wall). Spanning the 37-mile (59-km) gap between the Clyde and the Firth of Forth, the Antonine Wall was a turf earthwork that marked the furthest north fixed frontier of the Roman Empire. Built on the orders of Emperor Antoninus Pius around AD 142, its construction was implemented by Governor Lollius Urbicus (a native of Tiddis in Numidia, now Algeria). Studded with 16 forts and numerous fortlets, the Antonine Wall marked a leap northwards in formal Roman control from the old line of Hadrian's Wall and remained an impressive sight long after the Romans had left. In the fourteenth century the Scottish chronicler John of Fordun recounted the tale in his *Scotichronicon* that an ancient Scottish hero called Gryme (or Grim) had managed to break through its defences and invade the Roman province to its south. The name Gryme's Dyke (or Graham's Dyke) stuck and it was referred to as such well into the nineteenth century.

2

Tryst of Falkirk. The union of Scotland and England in 1707 led to a rise in demand for Scottish cattle in the English market and the establishment of a series of 'trysts' or fairs for trading the beasts, which were then driven south of the border. The first one, at Crieff, west of Perth, was too far north and in 1710 the Duke of Hamilton set up a new one on Reddingmuir, where for 62 years, in August, September and October, tens of thousands of cattle plodded through the tryst ground. The enclosure of common land in the area meant the fair then had to move, first to Roughcastle and then to Stenhousemuir, where it lasted 115 years, by when the advent of the railways had made it redundant.

3

Linlithgow. Although its name translated from Gaelic means the rather unpromising 'loch in a damp hollow', Linlithgow was nonetheless a royal residence from the time of David I (1124–53). Stronger fortifications were built by the English king Edward I in 1302, following his invasion of Scotland, and then in 1424 James I ordered the construction of a new palace. There, James V was born in April 1512, to become king aged just 17 months when his father James IV perished in battle against the English at Flodden Field. A battle, in turn, caused his demise, when he broke down after hearing of the Scots defeat at Solway Moss in November 1542 and died three weeks later. His daughter, Mary Queen of Scots, was a week old at the time, and her prolonged minority and the factions which arose as a consequence contributed greatly to the turbulence of her reign. The palace fell into disrepair after her son, James VI, went south to claim the throne of England in 1603 and it collapsed in 1607. Although James ordered its restoration in 1620, it was almost completely destroyed by a fire in 1746.

4

Dunfermline. The Royal Burgh of Dunfermline rose to prominence in the eleventh century when it became the seat of royal power and the de facto capital of the Scottish kingdom, a position cemented by the foundation in 1128 of a Benedictine Abbey (which became the royal mausoleum). In 1295 John Balliol of Scotland and Philip IV of France negotiated the first formal treaty between their two countries. Signed in Paris on 23 October, it was then ratified in Dunfermline in February 1296, setting a seal on the 'Auld Alliance', which would be renewed by all Scottish monarchs until 1560, when an Anglo-

Scottish treaty put it to an end. Even so, there was hope of reviving it in 1745 during the Jacobite uprising of 'Bonnie Prince Charlie'.

5

Aloa (today spelled Alloa). Alloa's most famous site is its tower, built around 1400 by the Erskine Earls of Mar, which remains one of the best preserved Scottish medieval tower houses. It became prosperous through the wool, brewing, whisky distilling and, in particular, coal industries, aided by its port on the Clyde. Among its most renowned residents were John Erskine, the 6th Earl of Mar, the principal leader of the 1715 Jacobite rebellion, and Sir Ralph Abercromby, who served with distinction in the Napoleonic Wars (helping to capture St Lucia and St Vincent in the Caribbean in 1796; land an invasion force in the French-occupied Netherlands in 1799; and, most notably, command the British expeditionary force that went ashore at Aboukir, near Alexandria, in 1801 and helped drive the French out of Egypt).

6

Stirling (one letter different from 'sterling'). With its strategic position at the lowest viable crossing point on the River Forth, Stirling was long seen as a key stronghold of the Scottish Crown and was made a royal burgh in 1124 by David I. It was a target of Edward I's invasion in 1296, when the English captured its castle and it changed hands four further times until Robert Bruce retook it in 1314 following his victory at Bannockburn. The inability of both the Earl of Mar in 1715 and 'Bonnie Prince Charlie' in 1745 to capture the castle contributed to the failure of their respective Jacobite uprisings. Stirling became one of Scotland's newer cities in 2002 when it was officially awarded the title (the 'youngest' recipient being Perth), bestowed during Queen Elizabeth II's Golden Jubilee.

7

Inverkeithing (anagram of 'neither Viking'). The roots of Inverkeithing, just north of Queensferry, are said to run deep; it was the site of a Roman encampment during Julius Agricola's invasion

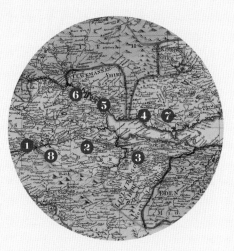

of Scotland in the AD 80s. Although this did not develop directly into today's town, by the fifth century there was a church there, founded by St Erat, a follower of St Ninian, who evangelised the Picts. The town received a circuit of stone walls with four stone 'ports' (or gates) in 1547, but by then its economic importance had begun to dwindle. It was the birthplace of Samuel Greig, a British naval officer, who was seconded to the Russian navy in the 1760s and won several notable naval victories for his adoptive country, including at Chesma in 1770 where he helped destroy a large Ottoman fleet, securing his promotion to admiral by Catherine the Great.

8

Bar Hill. Bar Hill fort was built by the Romans in the early AD 140s as part of the defensive works for the Antonine Wall. Its splendid view over the Kelvin Valley probably contributed to the decision to place it, not directly abutting the wall, as is the case for the other wall forts, but a little to its south so that it could sit atop the hill. Its garrison of 500 men came first from a unit of archers recruited near what is now Hamas in Syria, who were then replaced in the late 150s by a cohort from the Netherlands. Around AD 160 the Romans pulled their garrisons back to Hadrian's Wall and Bar Hill was demolished.

1

George Fridric Handel. One of the leading late Baroque composers, Brandenburg-born Handel became Kapellmeister to George, the Elector of Hanover, in 1710, but had already carved a reputation for himself in England even before his royal master ascended the throne there in 1714 on the death of Queen Anne. His operas, such as *Rinaldo* (1711), and oratorios, such as *Acis and Galatea* (1718), made him the darling of court and aristocracy, although royal commissions such as the *Water Music*, composed for a concert for George I on the Thames, and the *Coronation Anthems for George II* (1727) secured him even more valuable patronage. At his funeral on 20 April 1759, held in Westminster Abbey, the choirs of the Chapel Royal, St Paul's and the abbey itself joined together to pay tribute to the great composer in front of 3,000 mourners. Curiously, they did not sing a work of Handel's, but instead *The Funeral Sentences* by William Croft, which has been sung at every state funeral since (and for the Duke of Edinburgh's funeral in April 2021).

2

Richard II. Taking its name from Wilton House in Wiltshire, where it was hung between 1705 and 1929, the Wilton Diptych is a masterpiece of fourteenth-century art. Probably created around 1395, it is composed of two pieces of Baltic oak, painted front and back. On the interior, Richard II is depicted being presented by John the Baptist and two royal English saints (Edward the Confessor and St Edmund) to the Virgin Mary and a host of angels, set against a gorgeous, gilded backdrop. On the rear are shown the heraldic arms of Richard and a white hart, his personal badge. The work's artist is unknown – he is referred to simply as the 'Wilton Master' – and its

precise date is unclear, although it may have been associated with Richard's marriage to Isabelle of France in 1396.

3

Anthony van Dyck. A master of the Flemish Baroque, van Dyck began his artistic career when Rubens was still the pre-eminent artist in Antwerp, becoming his assistant by 1617. He first visited England the same year, but turned down an offer of becoming court artist for an annuity of £100, and instead split his time between Italy and Antwerp, where he painted wealthy aristocratic patrons. He returned to England in 1632, where Charles I made him 'principalle Paynter in ordinary of their Majesties', with an annual salary of £200. He made a number of notable portraits of the king (such as *Charles I at the Hunt*) and of Queen Henrietta Maria, as well as the royal children and a series of paintings of aristocrats, which provide an invaluable reference of how the upper echelons of English society liked to be seen (although he was later criticised for introducing a certain bland uniformity to British portraiture).

4

William Hogarth. Beginning his career as a humble engraver's apprentice, William Hogarth made his reputation from the 1720s with a series of brilliantly satirical engravings on political issues. In the 1730s he embarked on a series of more moralistic works, beginning with *A Harlot's Progress* in 1731. Its success was such that he followed it up with *A Rake's Progress* (1733-34), which follows the downward spiral into drink and depravity of a young country man who has come into an unexpected fortune. Replete with figures from the Georgian demi-monde, the series is a

Moll Hackabout arrives in London and encounters Elizabeth 'Mother' Needham, a notorious procuress, from 'A Harlot's Progress' by Hogarth, 1732.

masterful assault on the pretensions of the age, a theme that Hogarth pursued further a decade later in his *Marriage-á-la-Mode* series.

5

Thomas Gainsborough. A founder member of the Royal Academy, Gainsborough was one of the leading portrait painters of his day. Unlike his great rival Joshua Reynolds, he did not rely on Renaissance and Baroque Masters as his models, and favoured a naturalist approach, with his subjects shown in contemporary rather than antiquarian dress. Although he was born into a family of wool manufacturers, his artistic prowess brought him access to high society, and in 1759 he moved to Bath where he painted a long succession of aristocratic sitters, sometimes as many as five or six, who were keen to be immortalised by his brush. The portrait of Mr and Mrs Andrews, painted around 1750, is one of his masterpieces, and portrays the newly married couple Robert and Frances informally, if slightly stiffly, posed against an agricultural backdrop of their North Essex estate, which lay just a few miles from Gainsborough's own home in Sudbury, Suffolk.

6

J.M.W. Turner. Turner's mastery of light and colour has rightly made him one of the most renowned of English landscape painters. A barber's son, he nonetheless managed to gain entry into the Royal Academy Schools in 1789 and slowly built a following for his landscapes, including wonderfully nuanced watercolours. By 1807 he was established as the RA's Professor of Perspective and able to choose his subject matter, which ranged from the bucolic, such as *Mortlake Terrace* (1826), to those chronicling near-contemporary events (*The Fighting Temeraire*, 1839, showing the veteran of Trafalgar being towed up the Thames prior to its breaking-up). In *Rain, Steam and Speed* (1844) he turns his attention to one of the innovations of the age, showing a steam train crossing Maidenhead Railway Bridge, the blurriness of the summer rainstorm that enfolds the scene accentuating the sense of almost incorporeal speed of the train.

7

The Pre-Raphaelite Brotherhood. An initially secretive society of young artists, founded in 1848 to strip away the pretensions of the

'The Palace of Art' by Dante Gabriel Rossetti, 1857.

later Renaissance (typified by the works of Raphael) and return it to the purity of the late medieval and early Renaissance eras, the pre-Raphaelite Brotherhood featured among its leading members Dante Gabriel Rossetti, William Holman Hunt, John Everett Millais, James Collinson and Frederic George Stephens. Inspired by artists such as Giotto and van Eyck,

their treatment of biblical subjects and social issues was often regarded with suspicion by more conservative contemporaries, but works such as *Ophelia* by John Everett Millais secured their position as one of the most influential artistic movements of the nineteenth century.

8

Edward Elgar. With the first part of his career coinciding with a period of British imperial self-confidence, Elgar's works unsurprisingly combined a certain majesty with an infusion of late-nineteenth century Romanticism. Bold sweeping works such as the oratorios *Lux Christi* (1896) and *The Dream of Gerontius* (1900) contrast with the still-bold lyricism of *The Enigma Variations* (1899). The *Coronation Ode* (*Op. 44*) was written for the coronation of King Edward VII, planned for June 1902, but not used, as the ceremony was postponed for six weeks because of the king's sudden illness. The work's finale features the music of 'Land of Hope and Glory' (first employed by Elgar for his *Pomp and Circumstance March No. 1 in D Major* composed the year before), set to words composed by the poet Arthur Benson. It has been a regular feature of the Last Night of the Proms concert since the late 1920s.

The score for *The Enigma Variations*, by Edward Elgar, 1899.

9

Mr Kite. Pablo Fanque was born plain William Darby to an African father living in Norwich. He adopted his more flamboyant stage name after his circus career took off, performing vertiginous tricks on the trapeze and on horseback. By the 1840s, Fanque had his own circus touring widely in England and even performing before Queen Victoria. One otherwise unremarkable show in Rochdale in 1843 was advertised by a poster that declared it was 'For the Benefit of Mr Kite'. Almost exactly 125 years later, the Beatle John Lennon was browsing an antique shop in Sevenoaks, Kent, where he was shooting a music video for 'Strawberry Fields Forever', and he found the poster. He purchased it and was so taken with the words on the poster that he later used them to form the lyrics of the song 'For the Benefit of Mr Kite' on the *Sergeant Pepper's Lonely Hearts Club* album.

10

Gustav Holst. Cheltenham-born Holst came from a family of musicians (his great-grandfather had been a harp teacher at the tsarist court in St Petersburg in the 1780s) and he studied trombone at the Royal Academy. His grandfather Gustavus taught at Cheltenham Ladies' College in the 1850s, and Gustav followed in his footsteps when he became a music master at St Paul's Girls School in Hammersmith in 1905 (and, two years later, director of music at Morley College). It was while in the latter post that he composed his best-known work, *The Planets*, which received its premiere at the Queen's Hall in London on 29 September 1918 before an invited audience – it was said that the musicians only saw the score two days beforehand and the chorus for the *Neptune* movement had to be assembled hastily from the choir of St Paul's Girls School, where he still gave lessons.

11

Handel's *Music for the Royal Fireworks*. The Treaty of Aix-la-Chapelle, which ended the Austrian War of Succession in October 1748, was greeted with a general sense of relief, even though it failed to resolve many of the border questions between Habsburg Austria and the French and Prussians which had caused the war. In celebration, George Fridric Handel, by now the most recognised composer in Britain, was commissioned to write a piece of music to accompany a firework gala in celebration of the peace. The event took place on 27 April 1749 at Green Park, London, and the entertainment included a volley by 101 cannon as well as a breathtaking pyrotechnic display of fireworks. Sadly, these caused a wooden stand to catch fire and several bystanders were badly burned. Virtually the only thing to survive the evening unscathed was Handel's music, which has endured as one of the most-loved baroque pieces.

Genius Question

George Stubbs. Far better known as an equestrian painter, in 1762 Stubbs turned his hand to the painting of a more unusual – for Britain at least - four-footed animal. The zebra was sent by the governor of the infant British colony in South Africa as a rather unusual belated wedding present for Queen Charlotte (who had married to George III the previous year). The animal was female, its male companion having died aboard the HMS *Terpsichore* bringing them back to England, and was installed in the menageries at Buckingham Palace (along with an African elephant), where Stubbs painted it. The zebra created a sensation, attracting crowds of gawkers (being irreverently referred to as 'the Queen's Ass') and survived until its death in 1773.

1

The Don Pacifico incident. In 1847 the Athens house of David Pacifico, the former Portuguese consul-general in Greece, was burned down by an anti-Semitic mob. Don Pacifico, as he was known, had been born in Gibraltar and so was a British subject. He appealed to the British Foreign Secretary, Lord Palmerston, to force the Greek government to compensate him. In a classic example of 'gunboat diplomacy', in January 1850 Palmerston sent a naval squadron to blockade Athens and bully the Greeks into paying up. Despite objections from France and Russia, who shared with Britain a joint protectorate over Greece, Palmerston persisted and the Greeks agreed to pay Don Pacifico £4,000. In the event, owing to some lapses in paperwork, Pacifico only ever received £150 for his destroyed property.

2

Loughborough. In 1841, a former Baptist minister named Thomas Cook had a revolutionary idea on his way to a temperance meeting: what if the new railways could be used to transport members to such occasions? So, in July 1841 a group of 500 gathered to travel the 22 miles' (35km) round trip from Leicester to Loughborough, each paying a shilling and sixpence for a place on the train he had chartered from the Midland Railway Company. Cook expanded his operations to Liverpool in 1845, a first foreign trip took place to Switzerland in 1863, and before long Cook's Tours were a regular feature on the itineraries of Victorian travellers. The company continued to run them until its collapse in 2019.

3

Queen Victoria. In December 1861, Queen Victoria's beloved husband Albert died, capping a traumatic year in which she had already lost her mother. Although grieving for the dead was taken very seriously in the Victorian age, with rigidly defined periods of mourning for widows (for two years, in which wearing black was expected) and half-mourning (in which lavender, mauve and grey were permitted), Victoria took things a stage further, wearing black for the rest of her life. She secluded herself at Windsor, avoided official engagements and when she did begin to emerge it was largely to escape to other royal residences such as Osborne House on the Isle of Wight and Balmoral in Scotland. Her popularity plummeted, as republican sentiment rose and resentment festered against the 'Widow of Windsor'. There were even rumours of an affair or secret marriage with her manservant John Brown. Only in the 1870s did Victoria begin to throw off her mourning mantle, and by the time of her Golden Jubilee in 1887, she was once again the much-loved matriarch of the nation.

4

Isabella Bird. Travel was recommended to Isabella Bird by her doctor as a way of overcoming the after-effects of an operation on her spine when she was 19, and she barely stopped until her death in her 70s. A trip to Hawaii in 1872 was followed by a string of other extended expeditions, in the first of which, to the Rocky Mountains the next year, she was wooed by a one-eyed outlaw, almost went blind in a blizzard and drove cattle. Subsequent adventures saw her almost stoned to death by a mob in China and nearly drowned in India when her horse stumbled crossing a river. Her trip to Japan, which yielded *Unbeaten Tracks in Japan*, was sedate, but there, as throughout all her travels, she was a keen observer of local conditions and customs (including, in Hokkaido island, those of the indigenous Ainu people). The first female Fellow of the Royal Geographical Society, she fell ill after a final trip to Morocco in 1901, and died three years later.

5

Electoral Reform. Although the Great Reform Bill had extended the franchise in 1832, it was still very restricted, with only around a fifth of the adult male population of England and Wales eligible to vote, and demands grew for more radical change. In 1838 a series of petitions appeared, calling for universal suffrage, annual parliaments and voting by secret ballot. The movement to secure these reforms grew, and became known as Chartism, securing 1.3 million signatures for the first petition, and 3.3 million for a second in 1842. A third petition in 1848 was rumoured to have nearly six million signatories, but was found to have many forgeries (including multiple signatures by 'the Duke of Wellington'). National Chartist Conventions in 1840 and 1842 featured incendiary speeches, and pro-Chartist strikes broke out. The authorities, fearful of revolution, clamped down, arrested the leading Chartist organisers, and by 1848, when a great rally was organised on Kennington Common, the 170,000 special constables who had been sworn in far outnumbered the 20,000 Chartists who turned up. The movement fizzled out and only in 1884 did a new electoral reform bill triple the size of the electorate (although it still fell short of universal male suffrage and did not extend the franchise to women at all).

6

1846. The result of lobbying by large landowners who wanted to exclude cheap grain imports to preserve their profits, the Corn Laws were an early example of the use of trade tariffs to protect domestic industries. A sliding scale set by a first act in 1804 fixed a wheat tariff of 24 shillings per quarter if grain prices dipped below 63 shillings, and in 1815 a further measure forbade the importation of foreign grain at all if prices fell to below 80 shillings. Landowners profited, but the poor saw prices for bread soar,

as foreign grain could no longer make up for shortages at home. An Anti-Corn Law League was founded in Manchester in 1838, and led by Richard Cobden it mobilised industrial workers, who suffered most of all from the higher prices. With the Irish Famine from 1845 showing the devastation that food shortages could cause and the threat of uncontrollable agitation breaking out at home, in 1846 Prime Minister Robert Peel secured the repeal of the Corn Laws. It ended his political career, however, because the rift with the powerful landed lobby among the Conservatives tore the party apart and he was forced to resign four days after the repeal's final passage on 25 June 1846.

7

Isandlwana. In December 1878 the British High Commissioner in South Africa, Sir Bartle Frere, issued an ultimatum to the Zulu king Cetshwayo to dismantle his army, an effective and organised fighting body that threatened British ambitions in the region. A month after the Zulus refused three British columns entered Zululand to punish Cetshwayo. One column, under Lord Chelmsford, advanced towards the Zulu main *kraal* (headquarters) at Ulundi. A detachment of around 1,500 men was left at Isandlwana in an unfortified encampment. There, on 22 January, it was overwhelmed by a Zulu force around ten times its number. Defending too large a perimeter and struggling with ammunition shortages, two-thirds of the defenders were killed. It was one of the British Army's worst defeats, only partially masked by the heroic defence later that day of the nearby mission station of Rorke's Drift by around 150 British Army regulars against 20 times that number of Zulus.

8

The Salvation Army. In 1865 the Methodists William and Catherine Booth, appalled by the plight of the destitute in London's East End, decided that rather than wait for the impoverished to come to their meeting houses, they would engage in a mission in the poorest districts of London by setting up soup kitchens and refuges for abused women, preaching to those who came to them. In 1878 the name was changed from the Christian Mission to the Salvation Army, establishing it on a quasi-military basis with military-style titles and uniforms. Its brass band parades soon became a familiar sight in British towns and cities, and the Salvation Army spread its operations abroad, beginning with the United States and Australia in 1880. Today it operates in more than 120 countries.

9

Alice's Adventures in Wonderland. In 1862 the Reverend Charles Dodgson, a mathematics tutor at Christ Church Oxford took the Liddell sisters, daughters of a family friend, on a boat trip down the Isis River. As he did so he entertained them with the story of a girl named Alice (also the name of one of the sisters) who fell down a rabbit hole and experienced a series of magical

adventures. It was such a success that he wrote it down as 'Alice's Adventures Under Ground' and presented it as a Christmas present to Alice Liddell in 1863. When he showed the manuscript to further friends, they encouraged him to turn it into a book, and he expanded the work from 15,000 to 27,500 words, and added new scenes, such as the much-loved Mad Hatter's Tea Party. The result was finally published as *Alice's Adventures in Wonderland* in 1865.

10

1877. Much of India had come under direct British rule in 1858 after the removal of the East India Company's political powers following the Indian Mutiny. In 1876, Prime Minister Benjamin Disraeli decided to award the title empress to Queen Victoria, in part to bind India more closely into the empire, in part not to be outdone by Germany (which had introduced the title emperor in 1871), and also, no doubt, to win the queen's favour. The title was officially proclaimed on New Year's Day 1877 in a spectacular ceremony in Delhi presided over by the Viceroy Lord Lytton, who tactlessly remarked of the occasion that 'the further east you go, the greater becomes the importance of a bit of bunting'. Subsequent British monarchs retained the imperial title, with George VI being the last to hold it until India became independent in 1947.

11

The sealed-unit stove and Alexis Soyer. Alexis Soyer was Victorian England's answer to today's celebrity chefs. A French immigrant with a talent for cooking equalled only by his skill at self-promotion, he gained fame as the chef at the Reform Club, where he shook up its stuffy menu of overboiled meat and stale puddings. In 1851 he rose to the challenge of providing catering for the crowds expected at the Great Exhibition by purchasing nearby Gore House and turning it London's first really large restaurant, its 14 glass-

A handwritten page from the manuscript then called 'Alice's Adventures Under Ground' by Charles Dodgson (Lewis Carroll), 1862–64.

covered dining rooms each themed for a different culture. Modestly named 'Soyer's Gastronomic Symposium of All Nations', it featured a Chinese room adorned with silks inscribed with Confucian texts and an Arctic room equipped with stuffed arctic foxes and mirrors to create a sense of ice-bound vistas. For the adventurous there was an American cocktail bar, and for the more traditional the gas-powered ovens were so vast they could roast 600 joints of beef a day. Even so, he never forgot those of more modest means, inventing the first mobile soup kitchen and in 1855 *A Shilling Cookery Book for the People* was published. Always interested in technology – he used hot air balloons to scatter advertising leaflets for the symposium over London – Soyer's fertile mind also turned to the problem of outdoor cookery, devising a stove to solve the problem of inadequate nutrition among British troops fighting in the Crimea , where the open fires they used were hazardous, didn't work in damp conditions and required cumbersome preparation.

The answer was the 'Magic Stove', which could be fuelled by gas, coal, wood or even peat and was sealed, reducing fumes and heating the food more efficiently. One of his revolutionary devices could cook food for 50 troops in a single sitting. It made generations of British troops grateful, and was in use in the British Army as late as 1982.

Genius Question

Christina Rossetti. One of a set of extraordinarily gifted siblings whose father Gabriele had migrated to England in 1824, Christina was not outshone by her painter brother Dante Gabriel, but became one of the foremost poets of the age, penning collections including *The Goblin Market* (1862), its title poem a masterpiece of lyrical fantasy that secured her reputation, and *The Face of the Deep* (1882). Heavily influenced by the Anglo-Catholic movement, she wrote a number of devotional poems and works, including, in 1872, the words to 'In the Bleak Midwinter', for which the composer Gustav Holst composed a musical setting in 1906.

The Delhi Durbar to celebrate Queen Victoria taking the title Empress of India. 1 January 1877.

1

A disease that hit Tudor England, characterised by profuse sweating. Shortly after Henry VII defeated Richard III at Bosworth Field in 1485, people started dying in London of a mysterious affliction that caused severe pains in the neck and limbs, followed by heavy sweating, raging thirst, delirium and then – within 24 hours – death or recovery. England was struck again in 1502 – killing Prince Arthur, the heir to the throne, so paving the way for Henry VIII to succeed to the throne – and in 1507, 1517 and 1527, after which the 'sweating sickness' as contemporaries called it, disappeared. It is unclear what the disease, or its vector, was, although modern theories include a mosquito-transmitted infection such as dengue fever, a variety of plague or anthrax.

2

Papworth Hospital in Cambridge. The UK's very first heart transplant was carried out in 1968 at the National Heart Hospital in London, but the patient died 46 days later, after the anti-rejection drugs left him vulnerable to infection. The first really successful operation, following advances in preservation of donor hearts and post-operative care, was undertaken by Terence English at the Papworth on 18 August 1979. The patient, Keith Castle, survived the operation for more than five years (the average survival time is now 13 years, with the longest survivor being still alive 37 years after the operation, and even having received a second donor heart).

3

The dissection of corpses for medical purposes. Prior to the Act, the procurement of corpses for dissection for medical training was fraught with legal obstacles. The Murder Act of 1752 allowed it only in the case of executed criminals, but a drop in the number of executions meant that medics were reliant on the service of 'resurrection men' such as William Burke and William Hare. The pair supplied Edinburgh doctors through grave-robbing in the 1820s, but went one stage further by murdering victims to supplement the supply

Helen M'Dougal (Burke's wife), William Burke and William Hare, sketched by John Macnee during the trial, 1829. She was acquitted but later beaten to death by a group of women.

The Figure Explained:

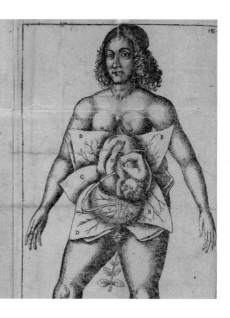

Being a Diſſection of the WOMB, with the uſual manner how the CHILD lies therein near the time of its Birth.

B B. The inner parts of the *Chorion* extended and branched out.

C. The *Amnios* extended.

D D. The Membrane of the Womb extended and branched.

E. The Fleſhy ſubſtance call'd the *Cake* or *Placenta*, which nouriſhes the Infant, it is full of Veſſels.

F. The Veſſels appointed for the Navel ſtring.

G. The Navel ſtring carrying nouriſhment from the *Placenta* to the Navel.

H H H. The manner how the Infant lieth in the Womb near the time of its Birth.

I. The Navel ſtring how it enters into the Navel.

From *The Midwives Book* by Jane Sharp, 1671.

of cadavers (for which Burke was hanged in 1829, with Hare escaping by turning King's evidence against his erstwhile partner).

4

It was the first British book about midwifery written by a woman. British medical practice regarding childbirth was clearly in need of a female perspective and before the seventeenth century there was a sharp divided between doctors (all male, but with little practical experience) and midwives (all female, but with no formal medical training). Deaths in childbirth were appallingly high. Obstetrical forceps were invented by the Chamberlens, a family of French Huguenot doctors in the 1560s, which might have improved matters had they not kept them a closely guarded secret for over 150 years. The leading midwifery manual *A Directory for Midwives*, written by the herbalist Nicholas Culpeper in 1651, suffered from the defect that he had never actually attended a birth. Sharp, in contrast, had been an active midwife for 30 years and was able to offer practical advice for easing childbirth and caring for the infant immediately post-partum.

5

Melcombe Regis. Characterised by the buboes (glandular swellings) that gave the disease its alternative name of bubonic plague, the Black Death is thought to have spread on Genoese galleys escaping an outbreak in the Crimea. It struck Italy in June 1347, from where it spread rapidly throughout most of Europe. Some time before the Feast of St John (24 June) in 1348, two ships came into harbour at Melcombe Regis in Dorset. It's not clear where they came from, but one at least of the sailors aboard carried the plague, which before long was sweeping through southern England, reaching London by September, and Scotland by year's end. Prayers, primitive attempts at quarantine and a variety of 'cures', such as eating crushed emeralds, achieved nothing, and by the time the plague burned itself out, between one-third and half of the population of the British Isles had died.

6

The 1854–55 cholera epidemic in London. Cholera first struck Europe in 1830, reaching London in 1832. It was widely believed that it was caused by 'miasma', toxic vapours in the air, which then entered the lungs. When, in 1854, a new epidemic broke out in London's Soho district, a local doctor,

'Death's Dispensary', sketched in August 1866.

John Snow, resolved to investigate its cause. He drew a map plotting cases of the disease clustered around a pump on Broad Street from which residents, having no directly piped supply, drew their water. He persuaded the local Parish Board commissioners to remove the pump's handle and almost immediately deaths began to drop off. The connection between infected water and cholera was thus proved, allowing the authorities to begin to take measures to control it.

7

The Crimean War. Born in Jamaica in 1806, Mary Seacole's mother was a traditional healer, from whom she learned many remedies, and Mary helped her to run a boarding house where many sick soldiers were treated. When Mary's husband died in 1844, she devoted herself full time to nursing, devising techniques such as mustard emetics to treat patients in an 1851 outbreak of cholera in Kingston that save many lives. When the Crimean War broke out, having heard that conditions in British military hospitals were very poor, she travelled to London and contacted the War Office, offering her services as a nurse, but

was rebuffed. She chose instead to fund her own travel to the Crimea, where she established the 'British Hotel' near Balaclava. Far from being a traditional hotel, it was a station for treating wounded and sick soldiers and a place they could stay while convalescing. She also went to the battlefields, treating soldiers soon after combat, unlike Florence Nightingale, whose hospital was situated at Scutari in Turkey, far from the front lines. Seacole was not paid for her services and suffered considerable financial hardship after the war, but in 1857 a huge fund-raising gala was held for her in London, which was attended by over 80,000 people; this and the proceeds from her autobiography *The Wonderful Adventures of Mrs Seacole in Many Lands*, allowed her to return to Jamaica. She returned to London in the 1870s, and died there in 1881.

8

Edward Jenner. Smallpox had been a scourge for centuries, often leaving those who survived it scarred for life. In the 1770s Gloucestershire physician Edward Jenner noticed that milkmaids contracted cowpox, a mild disease, from cows, but seemed immune to smallpox. In 1796 he injected his gardener's eight-year-old son James Phipps with serum from a milkmaid infected with cowpox, and then inoculated him with material taken from a smallpox sore. The boy did not develop smallpox and so became the first person to be 'vaccinated' (the word deriving from *vaccinia*, another term for cowpox).

9

Carbolic acid. Early nineteenth-century hospitals were unsanitary places, and post-operative infections killed many patients who had survived the surgical procedures themselves. Having read French physician Louis Pasteur's work on germ theory, James Lister, a surgeon at the Royal Infirmary in Glasgow, began experimenting to try to discover substances that might eliminate the 'germs' and save patients. He soon found that carbolic acid, which had been used to treat sewage, was effective at retarding gangrene if applied to wounds. He extended its use to cleaning surgical instruments and impregnating it into bandages. From its first use in 1865, carbolic acid, the first medical antiseptic, cut deaths from infected wounds at the Royal by two-thirds.

10

London's main sewer system. In 1858 the 'Great Stink' afflicted London, when an unseasonally hot summer combined with the copious quantities of human excrement and industrial effluent that seasoned the Thames to produce an odour so powerful that Parliament, overlooking the river, could barely function. Horrified MPs tasked the Metropolitan Board of Works (set up two years earlier) to resolve the issue. Its chief engineer, Joseph Bazalgette, devised a heroic (and expensive) scheme to connect all houses to a series of branch sewers, which then connected into one vast main sewer network. Hundreds of miles of pipe and copious quantities of concrete later, the system was largely complete by 1870. The great stink was abolished forever, and as a handy side-effect cholera was largely banished too, making Bazalgette one of the great heroes of metropolitan public health.

11

De Motu Cordis ('On the movement of the heart') by William Harvey. From ancient times medical writers had puzzled over exactly how blood was produced and how it moved around the body, their work largely stifled by the view of the second-century AD Roman doctor Galen

that it was generated by the liver. The English physician William Harvey (1578-1657) finally worked out that the blood was carried around the body by a dual circulatory system driven by the heart, which pumped it out through the arteries and then gathered it back through the veins. He confirmed his ideas with a series of dramatic experiments, which included making an incision into a live snake and then compressing the vein that led to its heart, causing it to empty of blood. He published his theory in *De Motu Cordis* in 1628, confirming his reputation as one of Britain's leading medical thinkers.

Genius Question

Scurvy. The disease, linked to Vitamin C deficiency, leads to general weakness, hair loss, bleeding and fatal infections, was recognised in pharaonic Egypt, but by the mid-eighteenth century had become the scourge of the Royal Navy. The diet aboard ship on a long voyage was deficient in vital nutrients, but no one truly understood this until Scottish physician James Lind conducted an experiment aboard HMS *Salisbury* in 1747. He divided the scurvy-afflicted sailors into six groups and gave each of them a supplement to test its efficacy. Those given vinegar, sea water, cider, garlic and mustard seeds, and (rather surprisingly) dilute sulphuric acid showed no improvement, while those fed lemons made a rapid recovery. The navy took a while to take notice, but by 1800 all sailors were given an extra ration of lemon juice, and levels of scurvy among crews fell dramatically.

A British Miscellany (*part three*)

1

A legal process by which Parliament declares someone guilty of a crime, Lord Edward Fitzgerald. Attainder was normally carried out through the passing of a bill, and is distinct from impeachment in that no actual trial (nor even any evidence) needed to be heard. English monarchs frequently resorted to it, including Henry VIII who had Parliament attaint Thomas Cromwell, his former chief minister, in 1540. The last bill of attainder was passed against Lord Edward Fitzgerald, one of the leaders of the United Irishmen's rebellion in 1798, although he died of wounds received during his arrest before he could be executed.

2

Benjamin Britten. The leading British composer of the mid-twentieth century, Britten remained close to his Suffolk roots (he was born in Lowestoft). A musical prodigy, by the age of 14 he had composed over 100 works and remained prolific throughout his adult career, which produced masterpieces such as *Peter Grimes* (1945) and *The Young Person's Guide to the Orchestra* (1945). In 1947 he established the English Opera Group, which gave rise to the Aldeburgh Festival, inaugurated in 1948 in the Suffolk coastal town Britten had made his home (and where he lived until his death in 1978). It has taken place each year since then, its centrepiece the Snape Maltings concert hall, which Britten had purpose built as a venue for the festival.

3

Queen Elizabeth (the mother of Queen Elizabeth II). Adolf Hitler had confidently expected that Britain would not oppose his expansionist plans in Europe (and might even support them). His

anger when the British government declared war on 1 September 1939 after the German invasion of Poland was extreme. Among those he particularly blamed for the British stance was the then queen, Elizabeth, whose popularity and refusal to be bowed he considered an obstacle to his ambitions. The woman he branded 'the most dangerous woman in Europe' was born Lady Elizabeth Bowes-Lyon in 1900, and even after her marriage to the Duke of York (the future George VI) in 1923, she can have had no inkling that she would become queen. Only the abdication of the duke's brother, Edward VIII, in 1936 propelled her husband to the throne and the difficult task of acting as a figurehead for the nation during World War Two. During the dark days of the Blitz, the queen refused to leave London, declaring: 'I will not leave unless the king does. And the king will not leave under any circumstances whatsoever.' After her husband's death in 1952, and the accession of her daughter Elizabeth II, she became 'the Queen Mother', and lived to see the twenty-first century, dying in 2002, aged 101.

4

Charles II, the King Charles Spaniel. Although a relatively new breed, being recognised by the Kennel Club only in 1945, it is a variety of the toy spaniel that was beloved of Stuart monarchs, and in particular Charles II, who had several of them. They are a frequent guest star in portraits painted by van Dyck and Gainsborough (such as van Dyck's c.1635 portrait *The Three Eldest Children of Charles I*), and it was in an effort to recreate the dogs shown in those paintings that the American businessman Roswell Eldridge set out to find examples of the by-then almost extinct breed. He put up a £25 prize at the 1926

Cruft's dog show for the dog and bitch closest to the seventeenth-century style and, when several were put forward, the King Charles breed was on the way to being born.

5

The A1. Running from Central Edinburgh to Central London, the A1 clocks in at 396 miles (637km). A system to classify – and a consistent approach to repairing – Britain's roads had become more urgent with the advent of the car. Work began on a classification scheme in 1913, but the report was delayed by World War One and the scheme was only made public in 1921, originally with T and L (for 'Trunk' and 'Link') rather than A and B roads. The system was blighted by all-too-frequent changes of numbering and the introduction in the 1950s of a 'super road' with an M classification. The first full-length motorway, the M1, opened in 1959.

6

John Locke. One of the most influential of English philosophers, Locke wrote seminal works on empiricism and the roots of democracy. Part of an intellectual circle that included the chemist Robert Boyle, he was elected an early Fellow of the Royal Society in 1668, and his connection with Lord Ashley, the Earl of Shaftesbury, brought him both political protection and danger, as his patron's fortunes waxed and waned. In 1682 Locke fled to the Netherlands, where he remained until the Glorious Revolution of 1688 brought the Dutch Stadtholder William of Orange to the English throne as William III. By then he had already written the *Two Treatises on Government*, which attacks the notion of the divine right of kings and maintains that the law of nature grants mankind certain innate rights, such as that to liberty and private property. The state of nature in which people originally lived, however, necessitated the partial giving up of some of these rights to a king but, unlike Hobbes, Locke maintains that should a king betray the social contract made with his subjects, they have the right to remove him.

7

1959 or 1966. The Notting Hill Carnival has twin roots. The first was an event organised by Claudia Jones in January 1959 at St Pancras Town Hall in an effort to soothe community relations after the eruption of race riots in Notting Hill and surrounding areas the previous August when mobs of white youths, many of them Teddy Boys, had attacked local Black residents. Her London Caribbean Carnival took place every year until her death in 1964. After its demise, Rhaune Laslett, a community leader, resolved to establish an event that would bring all the communities in Notting Hill together. The Notting Hill Fayre in 1966 had an eclectic group of participants, including Irish girl pipers and a Turkish-Cypriot band, while the Carnival Queen the next year was a Norwegian woman dressed as Marie Antoinette. Over time the event acquired a more firmly Caribbean flavour, influenced by Trinidadian carnival, with steel bands and extravagant carnival costumes. Although the 2020 event was virtual, the two-day event now attracts crowds of up to a million.

8

P.H. Newby. The inaugural Booker Prize was won in 1969 by veteran novelist P.H. Newby for *Something to Answer For*, his 17th novel, in which the main character Townrow returns to Egypt to investigate the murder of a friend's widow set against the backdrop of the Suez Crisis. The prize – known as the Man Booker from 2002 to 2019 – was initially £5,000 (but by 2021 had reached ten times that amount) for the best English-language novel published in the UK or Ireland by a Commonwealth citizen. In 2014 it was opened up to all English-language writers and has been won since its inception by novelists including V.S.Naipaul, Iris Murdoch, Salman Rushdie, Thomas Keneally, Kazuo Ishiguro, Ian McEwan, Hilary Mantel and Margaret Atwood.

9

It never has. The Isle of Man has a very particular constitutional relationship with the United Kingdom, born of a complex history. It, like Jersey and Guernsey, is a self-governing dependency of the British Crown, but not part of the United Kingdom. It has its own parliament (the Tynwald, with two houses, the Legislative Council and the House of Keys) and its own laws, with only its foreign relations delegated to the UK government. The island was occupied by Norse Vikings at some point in the eleventh century and remained under the rule of the Scandinavian kings of Dublin and Earls of Orkney until another Norseman, Godfred Crovan, established an independent Kingdom of the Isles in 1079. After the defeat of the last major Scandinavian expedition to Britain in 1263, the Isle of Man see-sawed between English and Scottish control, until it definitively fell to England in 1346. It was then ruled by a variety of English 'Lords of Man' with sovereign power, although recognising the authority of the Crown in London. In 1765 the incumbent Charlotte, Duchess of Atholl, sold the suzerainty of the island back to the British Crown for £70,000. After this revestment, the Isle of Man was ruled directly from London, but then in 1866 a measure of self-government was granted and the current constitutional arrangements established (with the appointment in 1986, for the first time, of a Chief Minister).

10

Dadhabai Naraoji. Born near Mumbai in 1825, Naraoji was a professor of mathematics at the city's prestigious Elphinstone College and promoted girls' education before moving in 1856 to London. There he became Professor of Gujarati at University College London. As well as founding the London Zoroastrian Association, the East India Association and the London Indian Society, he lobbied vigorously to promote Indian rights, arguing that colonialism caused wealth to drain from colonies and disadvantaged their progress, a case he powerfully argued in his *Poverty and Un-British Rule in India* (1901). By the time of its publication he was already an MP, having tried unsuccessfully to win election in 1886 for the seat of Holborn, but then in 1892 winning for the Liberals at Finsbury with a wafer-thin majority of five votes. He argued for Irish home rule, women's suffrage and, above all, for an alleviation

of the colonial regime in India. Defeated in the 1895 election, he moved back to Mumbai and was elected president of the Indian National Congress in 1906. He was also Britain's first Zoroastrian MP and was allowed to take his oath on the *Khordeh Avesta,* a Zoroastrian sacred text, rather than on the Bible.

11

The first 'test tube' baby. Born at Oldham General Hospital on 25 July 1978, Louise Brown was the first child ever born after the 'in vitro' fertilisation of an embryo (this was done in a large glass jar, but the press, on getting hold of the story, dubbed it a 'test tube'). The fertility pioneers Robert Edwards and Patrick Steptoe had tried implanting in vitro fertilised embryos in 282 women before their success with Louise's mother Lesley Brown, and her birth caused a media storm (and some concerns over whether the procedure was ethical). Since Louise's birth, the procedure has become widespread and over eight million babies have been born worldwide using the technique, with over 300,000 in Britain alone.

Genius Question

Aspirin. The ancient Greeks knew the pain-relieving properties of the bark of the willow tree, but by the eighteenth century this had been largely forgotten. Then in the early 1750s, clergyman Edward Stone remarked on the bitter taste of a piece of willow bark that he had been chewing while walking near his home at Chipping Norton in Oxfordshire and wondered if it might have medicinal qualities. He dried the bark of *Salix alba* (white willow), ground it up and administered the powder to 50 patients suffering from fever and found it had remarkable success in easing their pain. He wrote of his discovery in a letter to the Royal Society in April 1763. Aspirin, one of the ubiquitous drugs of the modern era, was born.

Dadhabai Naoraoji, from the *The Mirror of British Merchandise and Hindustani Pictorial News,* 1892.

Mr. D. Naoroji.

مسٽر ڊي نوروزجي *

1

1928. Although women had first received
the right to vote in general elections in 1918
after a long struggle by the suffragettes and in
recognition of their contribution to Britain's
war effort during World War One, that right
was confined to women aged over 30 who
met a property qualification. That gave 8.5
million women the vote, but still left a third of
the adult female population disenfranchised.
It took further lobbying by organisations such
as the National Union of Societies for Equal
Suffrage, the example of a cohort of female MPS
elected in 1924 (such as the former actress Ellen
Wilkinson) and the overcoming of the opposition
of traditionalists, such as Winston Churchill (who
argued it was better to raise the voting age of men
to 30, than reduce that of women to 21), to get
the Equal Franchise Act passed in 1928, which
equalised the voting age of men and women at 21.

2

Letchworth Garden City. The squalor of mid-
Victorian cities, which had required heroic efforts
on the parts of social reformers to improve, led
some to think that the future of urban society
lay in the establishment of entirely new cities,
which would be planned in such a way as to
provide adequate facilities, including housing
and education, for all, and not just for the rich.
In 1902 Ebenezer Howard published *Garden
Cities of To-morrow* in which he laid down a
blueprint for a city to be built according to these
ideals. Three years earlier, the Garden Cities
Association, which Howard had founded, bought
land at Letchworth in Hertfordshire on which,
from 1903, a community for 32,000 people was
built according to a plan devised by the architect
Raymond Unwin, using Howard's principles.

A further garden city followed at Welwyn in
1920, while after World War Two a series of
'New Towns' were established, including Hemel
Hempstead, Harlow, Basildon, Milton Keynes,
Runcorn, Cumbernauld and Cwmbran.

3

The establishment of the Commonwealth. As
the British Empire matured and demands grew
for independence, or at least autonomy, the
greatest concessions in that direction were made
to those colonies, such as Canada, Australia and
New Zealand, which had received a large number
of British settlers. The establishment of the
Dominion of Canada in 1867 and the Federation
of Australia in 1901 brought with them the
expectation of autonomous government, albeit
with continued links to the 'mother country'. A
series of imperial conferences tried to address
the issue further, that of 1926 declaring that the
Dominions (as the 'settler colonies' had become
known) should be 'united by a common allegiance
to the Crown, and freely associated as members
of the British Commonwealth of Nations'. In
1931 the Statue of Westminster enshrined in law
the principle that the Dominions had legislative
independence, with certain exceptions regarding
the succession to the throne. It laid the basis for
the modern Commonwealth, which began to
emerge once the bulk of British colonies in Africa
and Asia achieved their independence from the
late 1950s onwards.

4

The Waste Land. One of the most influential
poems of the twentieth century, T.S. Eliot's
434-line *The Waste Land* was published in 1922.
Replete with quotations from and references
to classical literature, Arthurian legend and

the works of a wide range of authors, such as Homer, Virgil, Dante Alighieri, Chaucer, Shakespeare, Milton and Baudelaire, its dense network of allusions and complex interweaving of monologues was found so forbidding by some that Eliot himself provided copious notes to help readers navigate them.

5

Neville Chamberlain (anagram of 'enliven herbal claim'). Steeped in British political tradition – his father Joseph has been Secretary for the Colonies in the 1890s – Neville Chamberlain rose steadily through the ranks of Conservative governments in the 1920s, becoming the Chancellor of the Exchequer in 1931 and then the prime minister in 1937. Faced with the task of confronting Germany's increasingly aggressive political and military stance, he sought compromise, a policy that came to be called 'appeasement' – supported by those British Conservatives and nationalists who either had some sympathy with Germany or wished to steer clear of continental entanglements. Chamberlain travelled to Germany three times in 1938 in a bid to avoid war over Hitler's demands that Czechoslovakia cede its German-speaking Sudetenland region

to the German Reich. On 30 September 1938 Chamberlain made the Munich Agreement with Hitler, and, thinking he had secured peace, he returned to Heston Aerodrome wielding a piece of paper, which he said symbolised the desire of 'our two peoples never to go to war with one another again'. He later characterised it as 'peace for our time', but he had put far too much trust in Hitler's good faith: less than a year later war broke out with Germany and in April 1940 Chamberlain resigned.

6

The pipeline built to provide fuel supplies for the D-Day landings. D-Day, the largest military amphibious landing ever undertaken, required planning on a heroic scale in all aspects of its operations to deliver over 150,000 troops onto the Normandy beaches on the first day of the attack. Part of the logistical challenge was the need to supply hundreds of thousands of gallons of fuel each day to the advancing Allied forces. Planning for PLUTO (the Pipe Line Under The Ocean) began in 1942, using the expertise of the Anglo-Iranian Oil Corporation to design pipes with a hardened lead core reinforced by galvanised steel wire. Trial pipelines were built over the rivers Medway and Clyde and across the Bristol

'Peace for our time', from the
Daily Sketch, 1 October 1938.

Channel, and huge pumping stations constructed at Sandown on the Isle of Wight and Dungeness in Kent. Two pipelines were laid: one, codenamed Bambi, ran to Cherbourg but never became fully operational; the other, nicknamed Dumbo, led to Boulogne (and then to Calais), which began pumping on 26 October 1944. The rapid Allied advance, which had captured the port of Antwerp the previous month, rendered PLUTO partly redundant, but Dumbo still pumped over 380,000 tons of fuel to the Allied forces.

7

Warfield. Born Bessie Wallis Warfield in 1896 in Maryland, Wallis married the US Navy officer Win Spencer in 1916, but the marriage ended in divorce in 1927. The following year she married the British shipbroker Ernest Simpson, before becoming involved with Edward, then Prince of Wales, in early 1934. The relationship became an open secret, and the couple holidayed together in Europe, although the reticence of the British press to publish any scurrilous details about the royal family kept it confined. When George VI died on 20 January 1936, the prospect of a king, the head of the Church of England, being married to a double divorcée proved too much for the establishment and, under intense pressure, on 10 December Edward abdicated. The couple were married in June 1937 and received the titles Duke and Duchess of Windsor, but relations with the rest of the royal family remained frosty right up until the duchess's death in 1986.

8

He came first in the Marathon, but was disqualified. On 24 July 1908 a crowd of 100,000 at London's White City Stadium awaited the first runner in the Olympic Marathon to enter the stadium. The man who did was a surprise: Dorando Pietri, a sweet-shop worker from Capri, had not been rated, but had overtaken the runaway leader, South African Charles Hefferon, who had rashly accepted a glass of champagne from a well-wisher two miles from the finish and had been struck with cramps shortly after. Pietri himself began to suffer extreme dehydration and when he entered the final straight, he was wobbling visibly and stumbled and fell five times. Each time the race umpires helped him up and he finally made it over the line at an agonising crawl. The American Johnny Hayes came second, and his team lodged an official complaint about the assistance Pietri had received. As a result, the Italian was disqualified. Hefferon, who had managed to resume the race, came in third, but because of Pietri's disqualification he ended up with the silver medal. Pietri won the hearts of the British crowd for his effort and was awarded a consolation silver cup by Queen Alexandra.

Finishing the Marathon, from *Illustrated Sporting & Dramatic News*, 1 August 1908.

9

It was the first arrest facilitated by the use of the telegraph. Dr Hawley Crippen, an American homeopath who moved to London in 1897, conducted a tangled love life in which his involvement with his typist Ethel Le Neve led him to poison his wife, Cora, at a dinner party at his home in Holloway and bury the corpse in the basement. Suspicions were aroused when Ethel was seen wearing Cora's jewellery and the dismembered torso was found after a police search. By then Crippen and Le Neve had already fled, taking passage on the *SS Montrose* steamer from Antwerp to Canada. The captain, who became suspicious of the couple, used the new Marconi telegraph aboard to telegraph Scotland Yard and alert Inspector Dew, who was handling the case, on 22 July. The policeman managed to catch a faster steamer, the *SS Laurentic*, from Liverpool to Quebec, and boarded the *Montrose* disguised as a pilot as it sailed up the St Lawrence River. Once aboard he arrested Crippen and Le Neve, and escorted them back to Britain. Crippen was tried for murder, found guilty on 22 October and was hanged at Pentonville Prison a month later. Le Neve was tried on a lesser charge of being an accessory after the fact and was acquitted.

10

A scandal involving a shortage of artillery shells. As the initial fluid phase of World War One on the Western Front stabilised into the trench lines that would characterise it for the next four years, so a problem emerged for the contending armies. Advances in artillery technology and the now-static nature of the front meant they were expending far more shells than expected. By March 1915 it was clear that the shortage was becoming critical and fingers were pointed at Lord Kitchener, the Secretary for War. After an abortive assault on Aubers Ridge in May 1915, which was blamed on a lack of high explosive shells, *The Times* ran an article headlined: 'Need for shells. British attacks checked. Limited supply the cause.' The pressure on the Liberal prime minister, Herbert Asquith, became so intense that he was forced to dismiss several ministers and form a coalition government with the Conservatives (and including one Labour minister). It was the end of the last purely Liberal government in British political history.

11

Butlin's, Skegness – the first British holiday camp. With their low prices and regimented entertainment marshalled by jovial 'redcoats', holiday camps were a boon for many hard-pressed families. They began with Billy Butlin's first camp in Skegness, opened in April 1936. Butlin, who had worked in travelling fairs in the 1920s, managed to secure the services of Amy Johnson, the first woman to fly solo from Britain to Australia, for the opening day. Requisitioned by the military during World War Two, Butlin's camps (of which there were ten by the 1960s, with numerous small holiday parks and hotels) bounced back after the war with heated swimming pools. The advent of overseas package holidays in the 1970s hit the business hard, but it survived in a slimmed-down form and Skegness, with the Skyline Pavilion, a domed structure to protect twenty-first-century holidaymakers from the British weather, still welcomes over 400,000 visitors a year.

Genius Question

HMS *Royal Oak*. At the outbreak of war in September 1939, much of the main British battlefleet was at Scapa Flow in the Orkneys, a harbour that was believed near impregnable with booms and blockships that prevented access by submarines. On 14 October the German U-boat *U-47*, captained by Gunther Prien, managed to evade the blockships and enter Scapa Flow, where 18 British warships were moored. At around 1am his lookout located the *Royal Oak* and the submarine fired three salvoes of torpedoes, the third of which struck amidships – and within a quarter of an hour she had sunk. Although around 400 survivors were pulled from the waters, 833 men perished in Britain's first naval loss of the war. It was a terrible blow at a time known as the 'Phoney War', which had lulled many into a false sense of security because no land fighting had taken place involving British troops.

1

St Valentine's Day. Far better known for his *Canterbury Tales* and *Troilus and Criseyde*, Geoffrey Chaucer wrote *The Parlement of Foules* (or 'Parliament of Fowls') around 1380, possibly on the occasion of the marriage of Richard II and Anne of Bohemia. In it, the narrator falls into a deep sleep and dreams that the Roman general Scipio Africanus leads him to a garden where he witnesses a parliament of birds debating how to choose the best mate and with the figure of Nature having determined the winner, they all sing in praise of St Valentine.

2

Currer Bell. Brought up like her sisters Anne and Emily in Haworth on the Yorkshire Moors, in the north of England, Charlotte was aware that, as a woman, her literary endeavours might easily be overlooked. She and her sisters resolved to use the pseudonyms Currer (Charlotte), Ellis (Emily) and Acton (Anne) Bell in submitting work to the London publisher George Smith. Although a first novel, *The Professor*, was not published, Smith took on *Jane Eyre* from Charlotte, which issued in October 1847 to great acclaim, with *Wuthering Heights* by Emily and *Agnes Grey* by Anne coming out later in the year. In July the following year, the sisters went to see their publisher in person to quash rumours that the Bells were one person, at which point Smith discovered for the first time that his star novelists were all in fact women.

3

It was the first book published in English by an Indian. Its author, Sake Dean Mahomet, led a highly colourful life. Born in 1759 in Patna, Bengal, already then under British rule, he served as a trainee surgeon in the English East India Company's army and then in 1784 accompanied his superior officer, Captain Godfrey Baker, to Ireland. In Cork he married an Irishwoman (against the wishes of her family, not because he was Indian, but because he was a Muslim). While in Ireland Mahomet published *The Travels of Dean Mahomet*, outlining his life to that date, but providing invaluable information about the people, customs and topography of Bengal as well as the courses of the conflicts in which he had served. Mahomet and his wife moved to London and in 1810 opened Britain's first Indian restaurant, the Hindoostanee Coffee House, in Marylebone. He also worked in a nearby bathhouse, where he introduced the practice of shampooing to Britain (in the form of *champi*, a steam bath of herbs and oils). In 1814, when the restaurant failed, Mahomet and his wife moved to Brighton where he established his own steam bathhouse specialising in shampooing and in 1822 was even appointed royal 'shampooing surgeon' by George IV.

4

Charles Dickens (anagram of 'cracked his lens'). One of the most prolific and best-loved of British novelists, Dickens based some of his poignant portraits of London's lower orders on his own experience, sent to work in a blacking factory aged 12, when his father was incarcerated in Marshalsea debtors' prison. His literary success began with the serialisation of what would become *The Pickwick Papers* in 1836. *Great Expectations* was one of his later works, published in 1861, and tells of the good fortune of the orphan Philip Pirrip (Pip) at the hands of his secret benefactor, the convict Magwitch. Its early scenes are set on the North Kent coast, not far from Gad's Hill Place in Gravesend, Dickens's final home.

5

Aphra Behn. Born in 1640, Behn led a colourful life at a time when there were few career options open for a respectable woman. She gained employment as a royalist spy in the Netherlands in 1665, tasked to report on and subvert English exiles plotting against Charles II. The debts she racked up there and her husband's death forced her back to London, where she began to write poetry, plays and novels, becoming the first Englishwoman to earn a living from the pen. Her most famous novel, *Oroonoko,* is based on a journey she is said to undertaken to Surinam as a young woman and the friendship she made with an enslaved African prince there.

6

C.S. Lewis. Lewis's *Narnia* series, which began with *The Lion, the Witch and the Wardrobe,* is replete with Christian imagery (the killing of the mighty lion Aslan on the stone table by the White Witch is a scarcely concealed reference to the crucifixion). It seemed something of a surprise, therefore, when he published *The Screwtape Letters* in 1942, a series of epistles from Screwtape, a demon and high official in the Infernal Civil Service, to his nephew Wormwood who was busily trying to lead a young Christian man into damnation. Tolkien, who was a fellow Oxford don, was horrified at the dedication and profoundly disliked the book, which he thought was shallow and ill-considered in its discussion of demonic arts. In the end, though, Screwtape lost, because his target saw through him and escaped his clutches.

7

Thomas Hardy. Hardy was born near Dorchester in 1840, the son of a master mason and his novels are steeped in the life and lore of the West Country at a time when a centuries-old way of rural life was ebbing away. Although the settings of his Wessex novels are on the face of it imaginary, they bear a strong resemblance to the real Devon, Dorset, Wiltshire, Somerset and Hampshire. Casterbridge, the setting of *The Mayor of Casterbridge,* is based on Dorchester;

Aphra Behn (1640–89).

Alfredston in *Jude the Obscure* (1895) is a version of Wantage; while scores of other locations have real-world analogues.

8

H.G. Wells. A visionary writer of science fiction, his novels included *The Time Machine* (1895), in which the protagonists travels to a distant future where a cataclysm has divided mankind into the surface-dwelling Eloi who are preyed on by the troglodytic Morlocks, and *The War of the Worlds* (1898), in which invaders from Mars almost destroy humanity with their fearsome fighting machines only to be laid low by a 'flu virus. He died aged 79 at his home on Hanover Terrace overlooking London's Regents Park. Unaware that he was seriously ill, he simply told his carer to leave him alone shortly before he expired.

9

Winnie the Pooh. The much-loved tales of the misadventures of the bear Winnie the Pooh and his companions Tigger the tiger and the donkey Eeyore were not A.A. Milne's first literary venture. His 1917 play *Wurzel-Flummery* tells the story of Anthony Clifton who leaves £50,000 in his will to two men, one an MP, on the condition that they take the ridiculous name Wurzel-Flummery, all as a means to prove people will do anything for money. *Winnie-the-Pooh*, first published in 1926, was based on the adventures of his son Christopher Robin's toys and in its Latin translation *Winnie ille Pu* became in 1960 the only book in Latin ever to appear on *The New York Times*' best-seller list.

10

William Shakespeare. Although he made his career in London, after his death in 1616, Shakespeare was buried in the chancel of Holy Trinity Church in his home town of Stratford-upon-Avon. His gravestone bears the inscription: 'Good friend for Jesus sake forbeare, To dig the dust enclosed here. Blessed be the man that spares these stones, And cursed be he that moves my bones' – an epitaph (and curse) the great playwright was said to have composed himself.

11

Both at one point worked for the government. Geoffrey Chaucer had already come to the attention of the English court by the 1370s, when he served on two diplomatic missions to Italy. In 1374 he was also appointed controller of customs at the port of London, overseeing tariffs and subsidies on imports of wool and tanned hides. In 1382 he additionally received responsibility for wine duties, but was then transferred to become a Justice of the Peace in Kent, and served as an MP in the parliament of 1386. Although he struggled with debts and navigating the difficult political climate during the reign of King Richard II, he still secured further office as Clerk of the King's Works.

Somewhere in between his bureaucratic responsibilities, he found time to write *The Canterbury Tales*.

Trollope, most famous as author of the *Chronicles of Barsetshire* cycle of novels, spent most of his career as a Post Office official, beginning with a junior clerkship in 1834, basing *The Three Clerks*, published in 1857, on his experiences in the lower rungs of the civil service. Towards the end of his Post Office days he introduced the postal pillar box, and in 1866 overhauled the system of London postcodes, abolishing the NE code, which was found to account for too little mail. He failed to follow in Chaucer's footsteps into parliament, standing for the Liberals in the Yorkshire seat of Beverley in 1868, but finishing last of the four candidates.

Genius Question

Winston Churchill. Better known for his career as a politician, whose highlights included 63 years service as an MP and two stints as prime minister (1940-45 and 1951-55), Churchill won the Nobel Prize for Literature in 1953 'for his mastery of historical and biographical description as well as for brilliant oratory in defending exalted human values'. The works which won him the coveted award were *The World Crisis*, his history of World War One, and a similar multi-volume work, *The Second World War*, which uniquely benefitted from his role at the very centre of the political action. Far less well known is *Savrola*, published in 1900, which was Churchill's only full-length novel. It tells of the struggles of Savrola to defend the freedom of Laurentia against its dictator, President Molara, who has tinkered with the electoral list to ensure his permanent election, prefiguring many of the problems faced by modern democracies.

1

Marconi's radio studio 2LO on the Strand in 1922. Early radio broadcasting in Britain was a chaos of amateur transmissions, to which professionalism was brought by an organisation such as Marconi, which established its 2LO station at 335 Strand in May 1922. It operated independently until later that year, when the main radio broadcasters in the United Kingdom got together to establish the British Broadcasting Company (the forerunner of the Corporation), of which 2LO became a part on 14 November 1922. The building, Marconi House, only remained a BBC studio until the following year, when broadcasting shifted to nearby Savoy Hill, and is now a luxury block of flats.

2

The King's Hall Picture Palace in Tooting, London, 1909. Although the first 'cinematographic' exhibition was held in London in 1896 when the Lumière brothers showed a film in the theatre of the London Polytechnic on Regent Street (later to become the Regent Street Cinema), it wasn't a purpose-built cinema venue. That first goes to the King's Hall Picture Palace on Tooting High Street, which opened on 30 January 1909 and operated until 1946, when it became a confectionary store, then a car sales showroom before it was demolished in 2013.

3

The St Martin's Theatre. Based on a short story by Agatha Christie and originally called *Three Blind Mice* (but which had to have its name changed because there had been a pre-war stage production with that name), *The Mousetrap* opened at the Ambassador Theatre on West Street on 25 November 1952. It transferred to the next-door St Martin's Theatre, which had a larger

capacity, in March 1974. The longest-running play in the world, it showed without a break, reaching its 27,500th performance in 2018, only finally being forced to pause its run in March 2020 because of restrictions caused by the COVID-19 pandemic.

4

A cannon shot during a production of *Henry VIII*. Elizabethan theatres clustered south of the river in Southwark, outside the legal reach of the authorities of the City of London. From 1599, William Shakespeare, already well established, was based at the Globe Theatre on Bankside (in a building moved bodily from Blackfriars, after its owners, the Burbages, quarrelled with their landlord). Around 15

The Globe, detail from Wenceslaus Hollar, 1647.

Shakespeare plays premiered at the Globe. In late June 1613, Shakespeare's latest play, *Henry VIII*, was in its first week of production when, as part of the performance, a cannonade was fired to mark the entrance of the king to a masked ball. Sparks reached the thatched roof, which set light, reducing the theatre to ruins in less than an hour. A second Globe was built in 1614, which operated until 1642 when all London's theatres were closed by Parliament, and the name remained in abeyance until a modern reconstruction, built as closely as possible to the original and near its site, opened in 1997.

5

George Arliss for *Disraeli* in 1929–30. Directed by Alfred Green (who had his greatest success in 1946 with *The Jolson Story*), *Disraeli* centred around the British Prime Minister Benjamin Disraeli's efforts to buy out the Suez Canal after the Khedive of Egypt (who owned a large share) had run up an impossible debt to British bankers. Its British-born star George Arliss, who played the title role, had lived in the United States since 1901, and had a film career that spanned almost

30 years (until his final appearance in *Cardinal Richelieu* in 1939). Although he was nominated the year after his *Disraeli* success, for *The Green Goddess*, he never won another Oscar.

6

1963. The BBC's landmark science fiction series about a time-traveller from the planet Gallifrey first starred William Hartnell from the broadcast of Doctor Who's first adventure 'The Unearthly Child' on 23 November 1963 until 1966. The show ran with his six successors battling Daleks, cybermen and a host of sundry other alien villains until it was cancelled in 1989. Since its revival in 2005, the tally of doctors has passed a dozen, who have appeared in over 860 episodes.

7

David Garrick. Hereford-born Garrick was destined for the law, being enrolled at Lincoln's Inn before his father's death in 1737 gave him a legacy that allowed him the freedom to enter first into the wine trade, and then in April 1740 into theatrical production, when he put on a show of *Lethe: or Esop in the Shades* at London's Drury Lane Theatre. By early next year he was acting, at first taking on a role anonymously when the original actor fell ill on the night, and then, after a smash hit as Richard II, publicly. His naturalistic style was a tonic to audiences used to a rather rigid acting method, and the poet Alexander Pope remarked of him: 'That young man never had his equal an actor, and he will never have a rival.' Garrick's career went from strength to strength, until in 1747 he raised £8,000 that enabled him to buy the Drury Lane Theatre. He ran it successfully, being able to choose the plays (and putting on more-or-less original versions of Shakespeare, which other theatre-owners had 'improved'), although he had to weather several audience riots when he tried to abolish cut-price tickets for those who entered past halfway through a play. Garrick retired from acting in 1765.

David Garrick, from *Dramatic Characters*, 1773.

Mr GARRICK in the Character of HAMLET
Act I. Scene 4.th

8

Allan Ramsay's theatre on Carrubber's Close, Edinburgh. The Lanarkshire poet and playwright

Allan Ramsay began his career as a wigmaker, but the publication of several volumes of poems had established his literary reputation by the 1720s. On 8 November 1736 he opened his own theatre on Carrubber's Close in Edinburgh, in the face of fierce opposition from the city's Presbyterian establishment. In the tussle of wills, the Kirk won, and the theatre, Scotland's first public theatrical venue, closed within a month and it was not until 1767 that the English actor David Ross received permission to open another playhouse, beginning Edinburgh's long association with the theatrical world.

9

1951. Much loved by generations of British radio listeners, *The Archers* began its long run on 1 January 1951. A saga of rural life set in the fictional village of Ambridge, in the equally fictional count of Borsetshire somewhere in the Midlands, it was originally conceived as a way of providing public service education for farmers at a time of rapid modernisation. Some of the characters have appeared in the show for decades (Ted Kelsey played Joe Grundy for 34 years), and with over 19,000 episodes having aired, the show is in little danger of losing its title as the longest-running radio serial of all time.

10

Shirley Bassey. The gallery of stars who have performed Bond themes is a glittering one. The 24 films up to *No Time to Die* in 2020 have featured numbers by artists such as Louis Armstrong, Tom Jones, Lulu, Paul McCartney, Tina Turner, Madonna and Billie Eilish. But only one singer has got the Bond invite more than once. Shirley Bassey has sung a title theme three times: for *Goldfinger* (1964), *Diamonds are Forever* (1971) and *Moonraker* (1979). Cardiff-born Bassey left school at 14 and, already notable for her singing talent, toured in theatrical reviews before landing a West End part aged 18, and her first record contract a year later. Her single 'As I Love You' was the first by a Welsh artist to reach No. 1 in the charts, in January 1959, and a string of hits followed in the 1960s and early 1970s.

When her final album *I Owe it To You All* was released in 2020, she became the first ever artist to have had a top 40 album in seven consecutive decades.

11

The actors playing them are brother and sister. Sarah Siddons became one of the most celebrated actresses of Georgian England, famed for her powerful portrayals of Lady Macbeth. Her early career, though, was patchy. Coming from a family of travelling actors, from 1774 she played in regional venues to some acclaim, but her London debut at David Garrick's Drury Lane Theatre was a flop and she went back to touring. In October 1778, she undertook the daring experiment of appearing in a lead male role at Liverpool's Theatre Royal. This time it was a huge success; her Hamlet, played opposite her brother's Laertes, helped restore her reputation and a return to the London stage at Drury Lane in 1782, where she was a much-loved fixture for the next 20 years. Her brother Philip, who abandoned vocational training as a priest to become an actor, finally got to play the lead role in *Hamlet* in 1783 and spent much of his career playing alongside his more famous sister.

Genius Question

Burgundy. One of the most successful of the comedies made by the Ealing Studios in the late 1940s and 1950s, *Passport to Pimlico* tells the tale of the efforts of the London district of Pimlico to escape the rigours of post-war rationing when documents discovered in a bombed-out cellar reveal that the area had been ceded by King Edward IV to Charles VII, the last Duke of Burgundy, and his heirs. A descendent is found, a committee of councillors appointed, and Pimlico declares itself part of Burgundy and exempt from the jurisdiction of the British government. Chaos ensues as black-marketeers flood in and the British government declares a blockade. As their attempt to take control veers wildly out of control, the people of Pimlico finally negotiate a return to British rule.

1

Five. Anthony Eden (1955–57), Harold Macmillan (1957–63), Alec Douglas-Home (1963–64), David Cameron (2010–16) and Boris Johnson (since 2019) all attended Eton College, perhaps Britain's best-known private school. They joined a further 15 pre-World War Two colleagues, making 20 Old Etonian prime ministers in all (of whom no fewer than nine also went on to study at Christ Church, Oxford).

2

Port of Tilbury, London. After World War Two, Britain sought to fill gaps in its labour market

A BBC Caribbean Service pamphlet, 1959.

Going to Britain?

Foreword by
Sir Grantley Adams C.M.G., Q.C.

Prime Minister
of The West Indies

in growing areas such as public transport and the new National Health Service by attracting workers from British colonies, in particular the Caribbean. Although the HMT *Windrush* was not the first vessel to carry Caribbean migrants, it brought the first large group, of 1,027 passengers (800 of them West Indians, who embarked at Kingston, Jamaica, in April 1948) for the two-month journey to London via Mexico. The migrants paid from £28 for a deck class ticket and, after their arrival at Tilbury on 21 June, formed the first substantial West Indian community in London, the foundation of the 'Windrush Generation', whose struggles against the discrimination they encountered when trying to find housing and employment belied the promises made to them before they sailed.

3

Neil Taylor for Wales. Born to an Indian mother whose roots lay in Kolkata in Bengal, Neil Taylor's career began with Wrexham in 2007, and he was then signed for Swansea in 2010, where he made 179 appearances before his transfer to Aston Villa in 2017. Already a Welsh junior and U21 player, he made his debut for the first team in May 2010 in a friendly against Croatia, so becoming the first player of Asian origin to play for Wales (and the only one to play for one of the four British international sides). He was also picked for the 2012 British Olympic football team, appearing four times before Great Britain was knocked out in the quarter-finals. He was named Asian Footballer of the Year in 2013 and 2015.

4

1967. Although Winston Churchill had been encouraging other European countries to form a larger economic bloc to ensure post-war stability and stave off a collapse that might spread Soviet hegemony still further, he, and his immediate successors, chose to stand aside when the 1951 Treaty of Paris was signed to create a common regime for the iron and steel industries of six countries. The same nations – France, Luxembourg, Belgium, the Netherlands, Germany and Italy – then agreed the Treaty of Rome in 1957 to work towards a common market in goods and services. Again, Britain kept apart. By 1961, however, it was clear, after a series of currency crises and the beginning of Britain's decolonisation process, that the country would struggle to stand alone and Prime Minister Harold Macmillan put in a first application to the EEC for British membership. Fearing what he saw as Britain's pro-American inclinations and that Britain might subvert the Common Agricultural Policy mechanism for subsidising farmers, the French President Charles de Gaulle vetoed the application in July 1963. A second application by Harold Wilson in November 1967 suffered the same fate, and it was only after de Gaulle relinquished the French presidency in 1969 that the negotiations that ultimately led to British membership in 1973 came to fruition.

5

A tower at the Festival of Britain. In a bid to provide some much-needed cheer after the privations of World War Two, and to revive memories of the Great Exhibition of 1851 at the height of the nation's imperial pomp, the government in 1943 began to plan for a Festival of Britain that would lift a people 'half crushed by austerity and gloom'. In 1950 a series of pavilions and more substantial buildings began to go up, including a Dome of Discovery on the South Bank at which they could enjoy edifying exhibitions about 'The Land' and 'The People of Britain', and a Festival Pleasure Garden in Battersea Park. More than eight million people ultimately visited the main event at the Festival of Britain, but the majority of them seem to have been most taken with the Skylon, a futuristic cigar-shaped needle-like structure suspended around 50 feet (15m) from the ground by a series of cables. Despite its enormous popularity, the iconic structure was demolished in 1952 when the festival ended, because it was deemed too expensive to dismantle and relocate. Much of its metal structure was sold to a scrap metal dealer, who then turned it into commemorative paper knives.

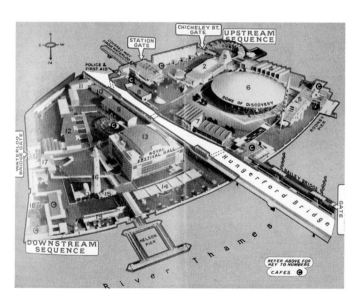

'All in One' souvenir map guide to the Festival of Britain, 1951.

6

Harold Macmillan. By the late 1950s, pressure for independence was mounting in many of Britain's colonies, seeking to follow the example set by India and Pakistan in 1947. Ghana (formerly the British colony of the Gold Coast) was the first of Britain's African possessions to achieve its freedom, in 1957, and others pushed for an accelerated timetable. On 3 February 1960, during a visit to South Africa, Harold Macmillan delivered a historic speech to the parliament in Cape Town. During it, he acknowledged that: 'The wind of change is blowing through this continent. Whether we like it or not, this growth of national consciousness is a political fact.' It was an indication that Britain would not block African nationalist aspirations and roused a fury of opposition from members of his own party. In October that year, Nigeria won its independence, followed by Sierra Leone and Tanganyika in 1961. By 1968, with the independence of Swaziland, only Rhodesia (now Zimbabwe) remained under a breakaway white settler government that finally relinquished power to a majority African nationalist regime in 1980.

7

Margaret Thatcher. Britain's first female prime minister, Margaret Thatcher's route to power was far from traditional. The daughter of a grocer in Grantham, Lincolnshire, she attended grammar school and studied Chemistry at Oxford (studying X-ray crystallography under Dorothy Hodgkin, one of the pioneers of the discovery of the structure of DNA). With a strong belief in self-reliance and a conviction that traditional consensus politics had not served Britain well, she rose in the ranks of the male-dominated Conservative Party to become Education Minister in 1970, and when Edward Heath resigned as party leader following the loss of the 1974 general elections she emerged, to the surprise of many, as leader of the Opposition. As Britain's economy stagnated and industrial strife spread, she struck a chord with the electorate, winning a convincing general election victory in 1979, and further terms in

office in 1983 and 1987. Her promise then that 'where there is discord, may we bring harmony' conflicted with political realities and her radical restructuring of economic policy, which led to mass unemployment, the dismantling of much of Britain's industrial infrastructure, large-scale and bitter industrial disputes, particularly with the miners, and the privatisation of key industries left a conflicted and often bitter legacy. Her reputation as the 'Iron Lady' won her as many political enemies as friends, but she was without doubt one of the most influential British politicians of the twentieth century.

8

1970. First formed in the late 1950s as the Quarrymen, The Beatles – who, after an initially fluid early membership, settled down to the quartet of the 'Fab Four' (Paul McCartney, John Lennon, George Harrison and Ringo Starr) – became the best known of the wave of British pop bands in the 1960s, their popularity transferring even to the notoriously unreceptive United States market. Testing their mettle initially at Liverpool's Cavern Club and in Hamburg, their tie up with manager Brian Epstein in 1961 and hit singles such as 'Please Please Me', which topped the UK charts for 30 straight weeks, propelled them to megastar status. A sell-out tour to the United States in 1964 confirmed the phenomenon of Beatlemania, but increasing friction between band members in the late 1960s meant their final album was *Let It Be*, released in May 1970, a month after the band announced their break-up.

9

Betty Boothroyd. Yorkshire-born Boothroyd, the daughter of textile workers, studied Art and wanted to pursue a career as a dancer before a foot injury led her to turn to politics. After serving as a Labour local councillor in Hammersmith, London, she was elected as MP for West Bromwich in a by-election in 1973. She served as a government whip, on the House of Commons Select Committee on Foreign Affairs and on the Labour Party's National Executive Committee, then as Deputy Speaker from 1987 to 1992, before being elected Speaker in 1992, the first female holder of the office in a long line that stretches back to Peter de la Mare in 1376. A believer in modernising an office sometimes seen as an archaic anachronism, she chose not to wear the wig sported by previous Speakers, and her sometimes irreverent style won her many admirers in her five years in office.

10

1998. 'The Troubles', which broke out in Northern Ireland in 1969 between the contending Protestant and Catholic communities, claimed over 3,500 lives among the security forces, civilian victims and the various paramilitary organisations committed either to bringing about a united Ireland or securing Northern Ireland's position within the United Kingdom. Successive attempts at a political solution had all foundered until back-channel negotiations brought about a ceasefire in 1994, and then the beginning of multi-party talks in June 1996. These finally produced an agreement that laid down a road map for paramilitaries to disarm and cease violence, for enhanced cross-border co-operation, the strengthening of safeguards for the Catholic community in the province and the creation of a devolved Northern Ireland Assembly. Approved by voters on both sides of the border in twin referenda in May 1998, the Belfast or Good Friday Agreement (GFA), as it became known for the day of its signature, brought together formerly violent rivals to work within the same political framework to effect change through consensual politics rather than violence. Despite sporadic violence from extreme rejectionists, the GFA has held ever since, although it was brought under huge strain during the process of the United Kingdom's withdrawal from the European Union, which raised questions about erecting a hard customs border across the island of Ireland.

11

The first Black woman to be elected to Parliament. Although there were Black or mixed-race male MPs already in the nineteenth century (with Henry Galgacus Yorke, who served as MP for York from 1841 to 1848, being possibly the first), it took until 1987 for the first Black woman, Diane Abbott, to be elected to Parliament for the constituency of Hackney & Stoke Newington. Her previous career included stints at the Home Office, the National Council for Civil Liberties and as a television researcher, before becoming a Westminster City Councillor in 1982. Positioned politically on the left of the Labour Party, she has been an outspoken advocate on issues such as race relations and Palestine, leaving her at times at odds with the party leadership. She has served as Shadow minister for Public Health, International Development and as Shadow Home Secretary.

Genius Question

Glasgow in 1990. The European Capitals of Culture initiative, which seeks to highlight the richness and diversity of European cultures, as well as regenerating cities and providing a boost to tourism, began with the selection of Athens in 1985 as the first cultural capital. Glasgow was chosen as Capital of Culture for 1990, and its year of incumbency is credited with instilling a new sense of confidence in the city's arts scene, as it hosted blockbuster exhibitions, such as one on Van Gogh at the Burrell Collection, and concerts by Pavarotti and the Rolling Stones. The only other British city to have been selected as a European Capital of Culture was Liverpool in 2008. Another was due to be picked from a shortlist of five for 2023, but the United Kingdom's withdrawal from the European Union in 2020 caused the invitation to be cancelled.

Invention & Technology

1

Traffic lights. Even in 1868 London had a traffic problem, with the junction at the northeast corner of Parliament Square proving particularly hazardous, as horse-drawn carriages hurtled pell-mell through it. When two MPs were injured crossing the road, Parliament resolved on action and a new system designed by railway signals engineer John Peake Knight was installed. A gas-operated lamp indicated green for 'go' and red for 'stop', although it had to be manually operated by a policeman, and the lamps proved hard to see, so semaphore arms were later added. This, the world's first set of traffic lights, brought some order, but most drivers simply did not understand what the new-fangled contraption was supposed to indicate, and the lights kept breaking down. Finally, in January 1869 a gas leak caused them to explode, badly injuring the policeman on duty. Shortly after they were removed and traffic lights did not return to the capital until 1926. By then they had three colours (red, amber and green) and electric traffic lights finally arrived in Britain in 1927 after a trial in Wolverhampton.

2

Ada, Countess of Lovelace. The daughter of the poet Lord Byron, Ada was a mathematical prodigy at a time when such endeavours were unusual, and almost always discouraged, among

Ada Lovelace's algorithm paper, 1843.

Diagram for the computation by the Engine of the Numbers of Bernoulli. See Note G. (page 722 et seq.)

women. Her mother, Anne, Lady Byron, was also a talented mathematician, and this and her family's social connections in London brought her into contact with scientists such as Michael Faraday and, more importantly, Charles Babbage, who had spent decades designing the Difference Engine and Analytical Engine, early forms of computer (the latter of which was too technically complex to be fully built at the time, but which used punched cards designed for a weaving loom to automate processes). Ada became close to Babbage and carried out a long correspondence with him. In 1843 she wrote a paper commenting on an Italian translation of a lecture by Babbage in which she added notes setting out how the Analytical Engine might be used to calculate Bernoulli numbers (a mathematical sequence of rational numbers). In effect, she had devised the first algorithm.

3

Television. Attempts to transmit moving pictures electrically over a distance had been underway since the late nineteenth century, but none had been successful. In the early 1920s Glaswegian John Logie Baird began work refining a system using a large spinning disk and a photocell originally devised by the German Paul Nipkow in 1884. A series of disasters – the disc span too quickly, sending shards flying everywhere – did not dishearten him, and by early 1925 he had succeeded in producing a blurry silhouette five lines wide, which he showed in Selfridges. Later that year he had fine-tuned his invention, so that a human face was almost recognisable. Then, in his attic laboratory at 22 Frith Street in Soho, he gave a full public demonstration on 26 January 1926 with a scan rate of 12.5 pictures per second. The 50 scientists Logie Baird had invited were suitably impressed, and the television age was born.

4

Finding longitude at sea. Although it was comparatively easy for mariners to find their latitude at sea using a sextant and observations of the sun, calculating longitude needed some complex trigonometry, which required precise measurements of time to be made. Unfortunately, the motion of ships at sea threw all mechanical clocks out of kilter, and even a slight aberration rendered them useless. The Admiralty in London promoted the passing of the Longitude Act in 1714, which offered a prize of £20,000 for anyone who could devise a means of measuring longitude accurate to within half a degree. Yorkshire-born clockmaker John Harrison spent 30 years working on the problem and in 1762 came up with the H4, a clock whose complex mechanism defied the roll-and-pitch of the Atlantic to measure the longitude of Kingston, Jamaica, to a level that far exceeded the Admiralty's parameters. Despite his success, it took years of legal argument and the intervention of King George III in 1773 for Harrison to receive a payment of £8,750 in addition to the £10,000 advance the Admiralty had paid him for H4. He never did officially receive the prize under the Longitude Act that was his rightful due.

5

Tarmac. Scottish civil engineer McAdam was concerned with the lamentable quality of contemporary road surfaces and conducted a series of experiments using a sequence of large rocks, overlaid with smaller stones and then fine gravel. His appointment as Surveyor General of Roads for Bristol in 1815 allowed him to lay a large quantity of the new surfaces, with the process being named 'macadamisation' in his honour. The 'tar' was added in 1902 when the Welsh inventor Edgar Hooley mixed tar in as a grout to the macadam surface to stop it rutting. He called this new mixture 'Tar Macadam', which when shortened became 'tarmac'.

6

Providing light safely in a mine. Making available light sources in nineteenth-century mines was hazardous because any naked flame was likely to ignite the coal gas and other flammable substances in which mines abounded. Although others had proposed solutions, the first successful design was devised by the chemist Sir Humphry Davy (also famous for being the first to isolate the elements potassium, sodium, calcium, strontium, barium, magnesium and boron). In 1815 he presented the lamp, which worked by using an iron mesh to stop the methane it burned from escaping into the outside air. The flame on Davy's lamp also burned with a blue hue if flammable gases were present, giving miners an early warning signal. Although effective, the lamps were easily damaged, only provided light that was very dim and also enabled the working of previously unsafe seams. As a result, the lamp's impact on mining safety was far less than Davy had hoped for.

7

Owen Maclaren. Maclaren was a retired aeronautical engineer who had also been a test

Hunphry Davy's miner's safety lamp, 1817.

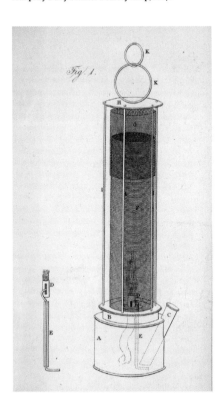

pilot, flying, among other aircraft, the Spitfire. In 1965 he noticed his daughter's struggle with the unwieldy prams of the era and resolved to help. Using his knowledge of the aluminium retractable landing gear of the Spitfire, he created a lightweight baby buggy whose frame could be folded in on itself with ease. The design was so successful that in 1967 he began to produce this first model, the BO1, commercially and within ten years was manufacturing 600,000 buggies a year. His insight has been a boon to generations of parents and his company's buggies and their imitators are now available worldwide.

8

Sir Tim Berners Lee. Although an internet of sorts had existed since the late 1960s, originally pioneered by the US Advanced Research Projects Agency (ARPA), its main use became linking university departments to each other and the pages that existed on it were isolated entities, not easily linked together. Tim Berners Lee's insight was to envisage hypertext, a way of linking internet pages into each other to form an information web, in which users could easily jump from one page to another. He put forward the proposal in a paper in March 1989, although his boss was sceptical at first, writing as his comment: 'Vague, but exciting.' Berners-Lee persisted, and by 1991 had built the world's first website. By 1993 he had created HTML, the hypertext language driving what by now was described as the World Wide Web. Today there are an estimated 1.7 billion websites, all in existence thanks to Berners Lee and his determination to overcome indifferent initial feedback.

9

The Higgs Boson. Throughout much of the twentieth century, theoretical physicists struggled to explain the increasingly complex world of subatomic particles and how forces such as magnetism and gravity might be combined into one single overarching grand unified theory. One particularly vexing problem was why particles have mass at all, and in 1964 Edinburgh researcher Peter Higgs came up with the idea of a particle (which came to be named the Higgs Boson) that bestowed mass on other particles. Although it all worked in theory, the Higgs Boson proved elusive and, despite concerted efforts, not one could be detected. That was until 2012, when an experiment at the Large Hadron Collider (LHC) in Switzerland, which accelerates particles to near the speed of light and causes them to collide to observe their interactions, succeeded in identifying a Higgs Boson (and measurements the following year confirmed it). After a 48-year wait, it seemed that Peter Higgs had been proved right.

10

George Cawardine. The Anglepoise lamp, a fixture now found in millions of homes and offices, owes its existence to a bankruptcy. When Horstmann, the car company for which automotive engineer George Cawardine worked, got into difficulties he turned his expertise in vehicle suspension systems to creating a lamp whose light could be easily focused in different directions. Using a system of springs and levers, he came up with an iconic design, which also had a stable heavy base and a shade that reduced both glare and the amount of electricity that the lamp consumed. Cawardine initially wanted to call his lamp the Equipoise, but the Trade Marks Registry told him he couldn't trademark the name because it was an already existing word, so he opted for Anglepoise instead.

11

Because it is Isaac Newton's first reflecting telescope. Reflecting telescopes use a series of curved mirrors to reflect light and produce an image, which is then visible in the viewing lens.

They were devised to overcome the problem of chromatic distortion, which causes the various wavelengths of light to disperse and blur the image in a refracting telescope (the type invented by Hans Lippershey in the Netherlands in 1608). Newton first succeeded in building a small reflecting telescope with a concave mirror in 1668 and then constructed a larger one, which he demonstrated to the Royal Society in 1671. Although Newton was able to use his to observe the four Galilean moons of Jupiter, reflecting telescopes only really came into their own in the eighteenth century when it became possible to build them with larger apertures and today the largest is the Gran Telescopio Canarias on La Palma, completed in 2009, which has an aperture of 410in (10.4m).

Genius Question

The equals sign. Welshman Robert Recorde studied Medicine at Oxford University in the 1520s, which he practised throughout his career. Although he secured a position as court physician to King Edward VI and Queen Mary, a failed venture in a silver mine in Wexford in Ireland and a rash libel suit involving the Earl of Pembroke left him struggling financially. His real love seems to have been mathematics, and he wrote a series of instructional works, introducing algebra to an English-speaking audience. In *The Whetstone of Witte* he introduced the modern equals sign, justifying his use of two parallel lines on the grounds that 'no two things can be more equal'. Although it took a century for the new symbol really to catch on, now Recorde's invention is among the most ubiquitous of mathematical signs.

1

At the Theatre Royal, Drury Lane, London, in September 1745. England was in need of a stiff dose of patriotism in September 1745 because the Jacobite armies of Charles Edward Stuart, the Young Pretender, had just delivered a stinging defeat to George I's redcoats at Prestonpans, just east of Edinburgh. The way south for the Jacobites to England now seemed clear, and in the fevered atmosphere expressions of English national pride, intended to boost morale, abounded. The words to 'God Save the King' had been in circulation for some years, but in the aftermath of Prestonpans the composer Thomas Arne set them to music and the composition was sung at the Theatre Royal just days after the battle. In the end, though, it was arms and not anthems that bested the Jacobites, whose defeat at Culloden in April the following year spelled the end of the dreams 'Bonnie Prince Charlie' had of becoming Charles III.

2

The ship whose wreck in 1120 killed 300 people, including Henry I's heir William Adelin. In the interconnected world of twelfth-century Europe, Henry I's only legitimate son William Adelin went to France in autumn 1120 to pay homage to King Louis VI in order to accede to the Duchy of Normandy. The return voyage, from Barfleur, seemed to go well, but the elated passengers, including much of the young nobility of England as well as William, took to drinking and carousing. In a fit of bravado, the crew, also somewhat inebriated, tried to push their vessel, the *White Ship*, ahead of the other ship that had accompanied the mission. The *White Ship* struck a rock and began to sink. William got away in a boat but turned back to save his half-sister

Matilda and was drowned along with 300 others. The sole survivor was a butcher from Rouen. The loss of his son grieved Henry greatly and led to the ruinous civil war known as the Anarchy, which broke out after his death in 1135 between the partisans of his nephew Stephen, whom he had named as heir, and his legitimate daughter, also named Matilda, who had married the Holy Roman Emperor Henry V in 1114. In June 2021 remains believed to be the wreck of the *White Ship* were found by divers off Barfleur.

3

ENSA. The Entertainments National Service Association (ENSA) was established in 1939 as war loomed. Its first big concert was a broadcast in October 1939 featuring the popular conductor Mantovani and a rendering of 'We're Going to Hang out the Washing on the Siegfried Line'. As the war went on, entertainers such as Gracie Fields, Arthur Askey, George Formby and, above all, Vera Lynne – who earned the accolade 'the Forces' Sweetheart' – travelled to the theatres of war to boost the troops' morale. Not everyone appreciated the shows, saying the acronym stood for 'Every Night Something Awful', but it helped launch many stars' careers, such as Peter Sellers, whose performances for ENSA, culminating in *Jack and the Beanstalk* at a Paris theatre in 1946, helped propel him to post-war success.

4

Blue Streak. Britain's post-war political strategy centred on its determination to remain a great military power (although always in alliance with the United States) and a key component of this was an independent nuclear deterrent, with the first British test of an atomic bomb in October 1952. At first the deterrent was to be delivered by a fleet of V-bombers, armed with Blue Steel air-to-surface missiles. Concern about the vulnerability of the bombers while on the ground led to the development of a ballistic missile system, known as Blue Streak, which was commissioned in 1955. Severe cost overruns and technical difficulties plagued the project and inflated the initial estimates from £50 million to £300 million in 1959, with a possible final cost of £1.3 billion, which led to its cancellation in April 1960 before the system was ever put into service. As a result, Britain bought the American Polaris system, which entered service in 1968, and then the Trident missile system, commissioned in 1994.

5

The Times did not print news on its front page. Although it began publication in 1785, *The Times* did not print news on its front page until 1966, instead filling the space with advertisements and court circulars. As a result, great events such as the Battle of Waterloo, the Charge of the Light Brigade, the Indian Mutiny, the Relief of Mafeking, the Battle of the Somme and D-Day were all relegated to the inside pages. *The Times* published its account of Waterloo on page 3, four days after the battle, which had taken place on 18 June 1815, the delay being due to the vagaries of communication at the time, as the bearer of Wellington's initial despatch was held up in the Netherlands and had to cross the English Channel in a rowing boat. Only when he finally made it to London, late on 21 June, did anyone in Britain have official confirmation that Napoleon had been defeated (or even that the battle had taken place).

6

Håkon IV the Old. Having asserted Norwegian dominance over Iceland in the early 1260s, Håkon decided to enforce Norway's long-standing claims over Orkney, Shetland and the Hebrides. In response, the Scottish king Alexander III began raiding the Hebrides in a bid to prevent Håkon gaining a foothold in Scotland that might prove troublesome to dislodge. Håkon countered by launching a fleet of his own, which began coastal raiding in a revival of the high Viking style. Then,

on 2 October 1263, a storm forced Håkon and his men ashore near Largs in Ayrshire, where they ran in to a Scottish force led by Andrew of Dundonald, the High Steward. In the skirmish that ensued, the Norwegians were forced back to their ships and Håkon retreated back to the comparative safety of Orkney. There he caught a chill and died, his last days enlivened by the reading of the Norse sagas at his deathbed. His successor Magnus VI effectively signed away the Hebrides by the Treaty of Perth three years later and no more Viking fleets were seen off Britain's coasts.

7

It still is. The Act of Settlement, which was passed in 1701 when it was clear that Queen Anne, after 17 pregnancies had resulted in stillbirths or short-lived infants, would bear no heir, was intended to exclude the Catholic descendants of the deposed James II from the throne. Instead, the crown was to pass to the Protestant Sophia, Electress of Hanover (although she in fact predeceased Anne by two months in June 1714). Since 1701 Catholics, as well as those converting to Catholicism, have been barred from succeeding to the throne, as well as, until the Succession to the Crown Act of 2013, anyone who married a Catholic.

8

Thomas Tallis (anagram of 'llamas shot it'). One of England's leading Renaissance composers, who introduced Continental European notions of polyphony into English choral music, Tallis's early career was as an organist at a succession of priories, an avenue that closed off with Henry VIII's Dissolution of the Monasteries. He was instead forced to turn to royal patronage, joining the Chapel Royal in 1543 and serving there under the various changes in the religious regimes of Henry VIII, Edward VI, Mary and Elizabeth I. He gained financial security when Queen Elizabeth I granted him, together with his rival Robert Byrd, a monopoly over the printing of sheet music in 1575. One of the first English composers to set the liturgy to music, among his most famous compositions are the 40-part *Spem in alium*, the *Magnificat* and the *Lamentations of Jeremiah*.

Rudyard Kipling. Considered one of the great writers and observers of Britain's imperial age, Mumbai-born Kipling was awarded the Nobel Prize for Literature in 1907 'in consideration of the power of observation, originality of imagination, virility of ideas and remarkable talent for narration which characterize the creations of this world-famous author'. He made his reputation with *Plain Tales from the Hills* (1888), which relied strongly on the Indian setting of its short stories, and by the time he returned to England in 1889 he was lionised as a literary genius with a popular touch. Today he is best remembered for *Kim* (1901), about an Irish orphan in India, the children's tales in *The Jungle Book* (1894) and, above all, for the poem *If*, first published in 1910.

10

Each begins with 'san'. Sandringham House and its extensive estate in Norfolk were bought by Queen Victoria for her eldest son (the future Edward VII) in 1862 in the hope of providing a refuge from the temptations of his rather colourful social life in London. It is owned today by Queen Elizabeth II as her private home, rather than in her capacity as head of state.

The Royal Military Academy Sandhurst in Berkshire was the site of the Military Academy for the training of officers for the British and Indian Army from 1812. In 1947 it merged with the Royal Military Academy in Woolwich (for the Engineers and Artillery) and since 1984, when women's officer training was relocated there, it has been the sole initial training school for officers in the British Army.

The sandwich, a British lunchtime snack, is named after Edward Montagu, the 4th Earl of Sandwich, who asked his cook to come up with a form of food he could eat without getting up from the card table. As a result, in 1762 the 'sandwich', with meat stuffed between bread was born.

11

Annie Besant. Married at 19 to a severe Anglican preacher, Besant defied convention by separating from him and becoming involved in radical politics, adopting anti-religious views, joining the National Secular Society and becoming a leading light in the early Fabian socialist movement. As joint editor of *The National Reformer,* she promoted universal education, women's suffrage and birth control. In 1888, she became a vocal advocate of the Bryant & May match girls who were protesting about poor conditions in the factory (where 14-hour days were the norm, fines were levied for talking or going to the toilet, and the phosphorous used in the manufacturing process caused bone cancer). She supported their successful strike, which achieved some improvement in working practices and led to the establishment of a female workers' union. Later, she became involved in the Theosophical Society, a movement that melded spiritualism with Hindu mysticism, and became active in the Indian independence movement, joining the Indian National Congress, and helping establish the All India Home Rule League.

Genius Question

The War of Jenkins' Ear. The colourfully named war constituted the first stage of Britain's involvement in the War of the Austrian Succession and came about through an incident in 1731 when a Captain Robert Jenkins had his ear sliced off during a confrontation in the Caribbean with Spanish coastguards, who suspected him of carrying contraband (trading with the Spanish Americas being at the time largely restricted to Spanish vessels). In 1738 he appeared before a House of Commons Committee and made an emotional appeal for compensation at a time when tensions with Spain were mounting. Proponents of action against Spain, which had increased its seizure of British ships, seized on Jenkins's case to push for war and in July 1739 a fleet was despatched to the Caribbean. The war, which merged into the general conflict with Spain, saw several British assaults on Spanish ports, but it ended with few gains for Britain as Spain remained in possession of its Caribbean territories and control over its trade while Jenkins remained in possession of only one ear.

42 Anagrams & Enigmas

1

130 (39 plus 1,001 divided by eight). *The 39 Steps*, released in 1935, helped propel Alfred Hitchcock to the front ranks of great film directors. Very loosely based on a 1915 spy novel by John Buchan with the same title, it tells the story of Richard Hannay (played by Robert Donat) following a chance encounter with a woman (shortly after to be murdered) who reveals an espionage organisation called 'The Thirty Nine Steps' intent on stealing British military secrets. Despite the best efforts of the spy ring and an innocent bystander named Pamela, who becomes suspicious of Hannay, he eventually unmasks the group after a series of adventures tautly and humorously plotted by Hitchcock in what Orson Welles later described as a masterpiece.

The Thousand and One Nights, a traditional Arabic collection of folktales dating back to at least the ninth century tells the story of King Shahriyar, who marries and kills a new wife each evening but is thwarted by the beautiful and talented Shahrazad. She tells him a new story each day, but leaves it on a cliffhanger last thing each evening, so that the king, wishing to know the ending, spares her life (and after 1,001 nights he has so fallen in love with her that he spares her life). It includes tales such as 'Aladdin' and 'Ali Babi and the Thieves', which have become well known internationally. The best-known English translation was that published in 1885 by Richard Francis Burton, who spent three years exploring the Arabian Peninsula between 1853 and 1855 (including a pilgrimage to Mecca conducted in disguise) and became the first European to see Lake Tanganyika in 1858.

Although there were several Anglo-Saxon kings called Edward (notably Edward the Confessor from 1042 to 1066), the first post-conquest king of that name was Edward I, who came to the throne in 1272, and the last was Edward VIII, who abdicated in 1936 after a reign of just under 11 months. Between them, Edwards have ruled England (and then Britain) for 143 years.

2

Because 'his father's son' was also his brother Arthur. Both Henry VIII and his elder brother Arthur share the position of being their father's son. Arthur had been married to Catherine of Aragon before his early death in 1502. When Henry wanted to divorce Catherine of Aragon in order to marry Anne Boleyn, he and his legal advisers tried to cite a verse in the Book of Leviticus (20:21) that seems to forbid a man from marrying his brother's wife, but Catherine's advisers preferred one in Deuteronomy (25:5) that actually enjoined him to do so. The pope took Catherine's side, which finally resulted in Henry's split with the Roman Catholic Church and the proclamation of himself as head of the Church in England in 1534.

3

52 (101 Dalmatians plus *Three Men in Boat* divided by *A Tale of Two Cities*). Originally entitled *The Great Dog Robbery*, Dodie Smith's children's novel *The Hundred and One Dalmatians* was published in 1956 and relates the misadventures of two Dalmatian puppies, Pongo and Missis, after they are kidnapped. Born near Bury in Lancashire in 1896, Smith moved from a career in acting into writing and achieved lasting critical acclaim with *I Capture the Castle* in 1948. Smith kept Dalmatians as pets, and used the name of the first of them, Pongo, in the novel, which was adapted as an

animated film by Disney as *101 Dalmatians* in 1961 (and then as a live action film in 1996 and as *Cruella* in 2021).

Jerome Klapka Jerome (his middle name was after a famed nineteenth-century Hungarian nationalist general) won a wide following for his gently humorous, resolutely unpretentious style, first exhibited in *The Idle Thoughts of an Idle Fellow* (1886), but which reached the peak of its success with *Three Men in a Boat*, published in 1889, which centres on the comic adventures of three friends and their dog, Montmorency, as they make their way on a leisurely boat journey up the Thames.

One of Charles Dickens only two historical novels (the other being Barnaby Rudge, set during the Gordon Riots of 1780), *A Tale of Two Cities*, published in 1859, is set in revolutionary France and deals with the adventures of Dr Manette, a French doctor imprisoned in the Bastille before the revolution; Sydney Carton, an Englishman who falls in love with Manette's daughter; and Charles Darnay, a French émigré sentenced to the guillotine by a revolutionary tribunal. Not everyone appreciated the novel, and the critic Fitzjames Stephens savaged it in a review as 'puppy pie and stewed cat': 'No popularity can disguise the fact that this is the very lowest of low styles of art.'

4

139 (1314 from 1513 [is 199], then take away *Waverley; or 'Tis Sixty Years Since*). Robert Bruce's stunning victory against the English army of Edward II in June 1314, in which the English knights failed to dislodge the Scottish infantry schiltrons and foundered in the anti-cavalry ditches dug by the Scot in the boggy ground, secured Scotland's independence. Flodden Field in September 1513 was an altogether gloomier affair for Scotland, in which James IV's impetuous invasion of northern England in support of his French allies ended in a disastrous defeat that left 10,000 Scots, including the king himself, dead on the battlefield. Walter Scott's compendious series of 'Waverley novels', written over a 17-year period, covering over seven centuries of Scottish

history, numbered over 25 titles, including *Rob Roy* and *Ivanhoe*. It began with the eponymous *Waverley; or 'Tis Sixty Years Since* and deals with the dilemmas of Edmund Waverley, an English gentleman, as he is alternately pushed and pulled to and from support for the Jacobites in the run-up to the 1745 uprising.

5

Roland Butcher (anagram of 'decathlon burr'). Barbados-born Roland Butcher played county cricket for Middlesex from 1974 before making history as the first Black player to represent England at Test Match level. He made his debut on 13 March 1981 in his hometown of Bridgetown in the Third Test against the West Indies, which led the local newspaper to run the headline 'Our Boy, Their Bat'. Butcher made 17 and 2 against a ferocious West Indian attack that crushed England, winning the Test by 298 runs. He played two further tests on the tour, but was then dropped. A serious eye injury almost ended his career completely in 1983, but he recovered and continued to play first-class cricket until 1990 when he retired to go into coaching.

6

Agatha Christie (anagram of 'gatecrash Haiti'). The queen of detective fiction, Agatha Christie's 66 novels have been translated into over 100 languages and sold more than two billion copies, making her the best-selling English-language novelist of all time. She introduced one of her best-loved characters, the eccentric Belgian detective Hercule Poirot, in her first novel, *The Mysterious Affair at Styles* (1920), with the amateur sleuth Miss Marple making her debut in a full-length novel, *The Murder at the Vicarage* (1930). In a real-life drama, in 1926 after her husband asked for a divorce, Christie disappeared, leaving her abandoned car near a quarry. Despite an extensive search conducted by over 1,000 policemen (and featuring a séance organised by Sir Arthur Conan Doyle), she was not found for ten days, when she reappeared at a Harrogate hotel. Where she had been in the meantime remained a mystery.

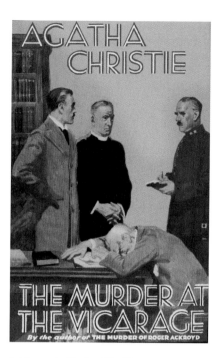

Front cover to *Murder at the Vicarage*.

7

The change to the Gregorian calendar in England in 1752. The Julian calendar instituted by Julius Caesar in 46 BC had not quite resolved the awkwardness that while the calendar has 365 days, the Earth goes around the sun in just less than 365.25 days, meaning the addition of a 'leap day' every four years. By the late sixteenth century the calendar was around nine days adrift and so, after long debate, Pope Gregory XIII decreed a reform by which nine days were dropped to bring everything back into harmony. Unfortunately, this reform, promoted by the head of the Catholic Church was not accepted in many Protestant or Orthodox Christian countries. Britain had to wait until 1752 for a similar reform to take effect. By then the calendar was 11 days out of line with the seasons and so Parliament legislated that Wednesday 2 September would be followed by Thursday 14 September. Understandably, many people

were bewildered and some protested that their lifespan was being shortened by 11 days or that the consequential movement of saint's days, Christmas and Easter was sacrilegious. However, there is no evidence, as once was claimed, that people actually rioted under the slogan 'Give us our Eleven Days', a myth that may have arisen from William Hogarth's satirical engraving *An Election Entertainment*, which deals with the 1754 election campaign, in which the handling of the calendar reform was an issue, and which portrays a banner bearing the slogan.

8

Osborne House (anagram of 'oboe unhorses'). Bought by Queen Victoria and Prince Albert in 1845 for £28,000, Osborne House, near Cowes on the Isle of Wight, offered the perfect escape for the royal couple from the pressures of life in London and Windsor. The old house that had sat at the centre of the estate was demolished and a new residence built between 1845 and 1851, with later additions, such as the Swiss Cottage, built for the royal children in 1853, and extensive remodelling of the gardens. Victoria and Albert spent several months each year at Osborne until the prince's death in 1861. The house offered a comforting retreat during Victoria's period of mourning and she continued to visit it until she died there on 22 January 1901. Edward VII then gave the house to the nation, and, although part of it acted as a college for naval cadets until 1921, since 1954 it has been fully open to the public.

9

Galleons ('galleons town' is an anagram of 'wllngtns', the consonants in Wellington's, plus 'aoeo', the vowels in Napoleon). Although Britain joined in several coalitions against Napoleon, and Wellington sparred with French armies in Spain during the Peninsular War from 1807 to 1814, the two great generals never actually met on the battlefield until Waterloo, the climactic battle that followed the French emperor's escape from exile on Elba on 26 February 1815. With the aid of loyalist generals he reassumed power and invaded Belgium where, around 12 miles (20km) south of

Brussels on 18 June, he met his nemesis. Having failed to stop the Prussian army led by Blücher uniting with the British forces under Wellington, Napoleon's army, was crushed in a vice, and despite spirited fighting even the veterans of the Imperial Old Guard, who by repute had never lost a fight, were forced into retreat. Even so, Wellington, after the battle proclaimed it 'the nearest run thing you ever saw in your life'.

Genius Question

Alan Turing (the letters are his name expressed as the place in the alphabet of each one). Mathematical genius Alan Turing was a pioneer of cryptanalysis and contributed to the early development of understanding of artificial intelligence. He devised the Church-Turing thesis that any calculation of process of logical reasoning that can be carried out by humans could also be performed by a mechanical computer. He turned these techniques to cracking the German Enigma code when British Intelligence recruited him during World War Two, and by spring 1940 had devised the Bombe, a machine that mechanised the code-breaking process to cut massively the time needed to decrypt German military ciphers. In the post-war period he devised the 'Turing Test' as a criterion for an artificial intelligence machine: such a machine is intelligent if a human interacting with it cannot distinguish between it and a real human interlocutor. Despite being awarded an OBE for his services and elected a fellow of the Royal Society in 1951, he was harassed for his homosexuality and in 1952 was convicted of gross indecency and forced to undergo chemical hormone treatment. As a result, he lost his government security clearance and had to stop work. Two years later he died from cyanide poisoning and many suspect that his treatment by the authorities caused him to commit suicide.

Picture Credits

All illustrations from the collections of the British Library unless otherwise stated.
Key - (t) top, (b) bottom, (c) centre, (l) left, (r) right

Endpapers William Stukeley, *Verolanium Antiquum*, 1721. Maps K.Top.15.47; **Page 2** *Punch*, 19 June, 1897. P.P.5270; **5** Lewis Carroll, *Alice's Adventures in Wonderland*, 1866. C.59.g.11; **7** The Queen Mary Psalter, 1310-20. Royal MS 2 B vii, f.259; **9** Trade card for Cadbury's Cocoa, c.1885. Evan.4283; **10-11** *Spooner's pictorial map of England & Wales: arranged as an amusing and instructive game for youth*, 1844. Maps C.44.b.60; **12** Claude Flammarion, *L'Atmosphère...*, 1887. 8755.k.13; **13** The View of the Frost Fair, 1739. Maps K. Top.27.411; **14** Inigo Jones, *The Most Notable Antiquity of Great Britain, vulgarly called Stone-hen, on Salisbury Plain*, 1655. 454.f.1; **15** William Stukeley, Altar stone found at Mickelgate, York, 1747. Maps K.Top.45.11.c; **16** *The bloody prince, or a declaration of the most cruell practices of Prince Rupert and the rest of the cavaliers in fighting against God...*, 1643. E.99.(14); **18** The Guild book of the Barber Surgeons of York. Egerton MS 2572, ff.18 & 20; **20** John Sinclair, *Scenes and Stories of the North of Scotland*, 1890. 010370.f.11; **21** Richard Ayton, *A Voyage round Great Britain undertaken in the summer of the year 1813*, 1814-25. G.7045; **22(t)** Richard Ayton, *A Voyage round Great Britain undertaken in the summer of the year 1813*, 1814-25. G.7043; **22(c)** Conwy Castle, 1811. Map K.Top.46.46.k; **22(b)** Slate Quarries: A View of Harlech Castle, 1798. Maps K.Top.47.62.f; **24** Hartmann Schedel, *Liber chronicarum mundi*, 1493. 187.h.1; **25** Fanny Duberly, Camp before Sebastopol, 15 April 1855. Photograph by Roger Fenton. Add MS 47218A, f.147; **26(t)** British Library; **26(bl)** South West View of Lincoln Cathedral, 1810. Maps K.Top.19.30.p; **26(br)** South West view of the cathedral church of Salisbury, 1813. Maps K.Top.43.39.o; **27(t)** The Cast Iron Bridge near Coalbrookdale, 1782. Maps K.Top.36.26.g; **27(b)** West Front of the Royal Palace at Hampton Court, 1786. Maps K.Top.29.14.l.1; **28(t)** Shutterstock; **28(b)** *The Graphic*, 5 August 1882; **29** Egerton MS 3028, f.30; **30** *Dublin and the Sinn Féin Rising*, 1916. 9508.f.10; **32** *Illustrated Sporting and Dramatic News*, 28 November 1896; **33** *Illustrated Sporting and Dramatic News*, 7 April 1883; **35** John Lydgate, *The Lives of SS. Edmund and Fremund*, c.1450-60. Harley MS 4826, f.4r; **37** Evert

A. Duyckinck, *Portrait Gallery of Eminent Men and Women of Europe and America*, 1872-74. 10604.g.10; **38** *The Motorist and Traveller*, 8 February 1906; **40(tl)** A view of the Horse Guards after T.H. Shepherd, 1816. Maps K.Top.25.4.b; **40(tr)** W. Finden, *The ports, harbours, watering-placeas and coast scenery of Great Britain*, 1842. 1502/320; **40(b)** Gilbert White, *The Natural History and Antiquities of Selborne*, 1789. G.2432; **41** Philip H. Delamotte, *Photographic Views of the Progress of the Crystal Palace, Sydenham*, 1855. Tab.442.a.5; **42(tl)** Sir Thomas Malory, *Le Morte d'Arthur*, c.1471-83. Add MS 59678, f.35; **42(tr)** Daniel Defoe, *A Journal of the Plague Year*, 1722. 1167.e.3; **42(b)** Christopher Marlowe, *The Tragicall History of the Life and Death of Doctor Faustus*, 1620. C.39.c.26; **43(tl)** Aylett Sammes, *Britannia Antiqua Illustrata*, 1676. C.83.k.2; **43(tr)** Wellesley Albums, 1798-1805. NHD 32, f.42; **43(b)** Map of Venice, c.1720. Maps *22670.(5); **44** 'Totius Britannaie Tabula Chorographica', c.1400. Harley MS 1808, f.9v; **47(t)** Glasgow, 1810. Maps K.Top.50.53a; **47(c)** View of the Port and Town of Newcastle upon Tyne, from the Rope Walk, Gateshead, 1819. Maps K.Top.32.66.i; **47(b)** View of Manchester Exchange, 1810. Maps K.Top.18.81.e; **48** John Stuart Mill by Spy. *Vanity Fair*, 29 March 1873. P.P.5274.ha; **51(t)** Charlotte Bronte, *Shirley*, 1859. 12602.k.8; **51(bl)** James Edward Austen-Leigh, *A memoir of Jane Austen*, 1870. 10855.e.8; **51(br)** Mrs Julian Marshall, *The life and letters of Mary Wollstonecraft Shelley*, 1889. 2408.d.3; **52** G.W. Thornbury, *Old and New London*, 1863. X.802/203; **53** Cyril Hall, *Motor and Plane*, 1932. 012803.l.38; **54(t)** Lock & Whitfield, *Men of Mark*, 1876-83. P.P.1931.pch; **54(bl)** John Forster, *The life of Charles Dickens*, 1872-74. Dex 316; **54(br)** Photograph c.1860. Add MS 47458, f.31; **56** George Carleton, *A Thankfull Remembrance of Gods Mercy*, 1624. G.5117; **57** *Warhafftige ... Beschreibung der ... Verrätherey so jemals erhört worden, wieder die Königliche Maiestat, derselben Gemahl unnd junge Printzen, sampt dem gantzen Parlament zu Londen in Engeland fürgenommen ... Alles mit schönen Kupfferstück geziert unnd dem Leser für Augen gestellet*, 1606. G.6103; **59(tl; tr; c; bl)** Peter of Langtoft, *Chronicle of England*, c.1307-27. Royal Ms 20 A ii, ff.8v-10r; **59(br)** John Lydgate, *Verses on the Kings of England to Henry VI*, late 15th century. Cotton MS Julius E iv, f. 7; **60(t)** North West View of the Cathedral Church of Durham, 1809. Map K. Top12.34.p; **60(c)** South West View of the Collegiate Church of Saint Wilfred, 1809. Maps K.Top.44.46.f; **60(b)** South Prospect of the Metropolitan Church of St. Peter, 1742. Maps K.Top.45.7.l; **62(tl)** *Punch*, 14 July 1909; **62(tr)** Trustees of the British Museum; **62(b)** Library of Congress, Washington, DC; **63(t)** *Les sanglots pitoyables de l'affigée Reyne d'Angleterre*, 1649. 9512.c.2(5); **63(bl)** *Les Grand chroniques de France*, 1332-50. Royal MS 16 G vi, f.343v; **63(br)** *The Sketch*, Wedding number, 19 July

1893; **64** Mary Evans Picture Library/AllStars; **65** Getty Images; **66** Christopher Saxton, Gloucestershire, *The Burghley Atlas*, 1574-92. Royal MS 18 D iii, f.97r; **68** George W.M. Reynolds, *Grace Darling or the Heroine of the Fern Islands*, 1839. 12655.i.8; **69** The South Pole, 18 January 1912. Photograph by Henry Robertson Bowers. Add MS 51042, f.3; **70** John Thompson, *Street Incidents*, 1881. RB.23.b.6198; **73** *The Chronicles of Crime; or, the New Newgate Calendar*, 1841. 1131.d.1,2; **74** Felix Leigh, *London Town*, 1883. 12805.s.9; **75** Southwark Cathedral by Wenceslaus Holler, 1647. Maps C.18.d.6 (110); **76** Engraving after Sir Godfrey Kneller. Library of Congress, Washington, DC; **78** James Dorret, *A General Map of Scotland and Islands thereto belonging ...*,1750. Maps K.Top.48.26.8 Tab.End; **80** George Bickham, *An Easy Introduction to Dancing*, 1738. K.2.d.20.; **81** *A Night View of the Public Fireworks order'd to be exhibited on occasion of the General Peace*, 1749. Maps C.18.d.6; **83** G.A.S. [G.A. Sala], *The House that Paxton built*, 1851. 012331.de.83; **85** William Harvey, *Exercitatio anatomica de motu cordis et sanguinis in animalibus*, 1647. 783.f.4; **86** *Caribbean Carnival Souvenir*, 1960. Andrew Salkey Archive Dep 10310; **87** *Evening News*, London, 17 July 1978; **88** *London Opinion*, 5 September 1914; **89** Photograph by David Noble. © The John Hinde Archive/Mary Evans; **90** Edward Lear, *Nonsense Botany, and Nonsense Alphabets, etc.*, 1889. Cup.400.a.42; **91(l)** Lock & Whitfield, *Men of Mark*, 1876-83. P.P.1931.pch; **91(r)** *Life of Chaucer*, sixteenth century. Add. MS 5141, f.1; **92** Theatre Royal, Liverpool, Friday 2 October 1778. Playbills 225 (1); **94** Marc Tielemans/Alamy Stock Photo; **95** Mary Evans/Allstar/David Gadd; **96** *Lessons from Noble Lives*, 1875. 10602.aaaa.14; **97** David Brewster, *Memoirs of the life, writings and discoveries of Sir Isaac Newton*, 1855. W57/5485; **98** Library of Congress, Washington, DC; **101** Public domain/CIA; 102-103 Selection of poems by Charles d'Orleans, c.1500. Royal MS 16 F ii, f.73; **105** View of Dunkeld on the River Tay, 1813. Maps K.Top.50.75b; **106** Yoshio Markino, *The Colour of London*, 1907. 10349. pp.4; **109** North-west view of Porchester Castle by Samuel Buck, 1733. Maps K.Top.14.64.b; **111** *The History of his Sacred Majesties most Wonderfull Preservation, after the Battle of Worcester*, 1660. C.55.f.6; **113** Plan of the Battle of Culloden, 1746. Maps K.Top.48.22; **115** Peter of Langtoft, *Chronicle of England*, c.1307-27. Royal Ms 20 A ii, f.6; **117** Christopher Saxton, *An Atlas of England and Wales*, 1579. Maps C.3.bb.5; **118** *Political sketches of H.B.* [i.e. John Doyle], 1829-43. Tab.435.a.1-8; **121** David Livingstone, *Missionary Travels and Researches in South Africa*, 1857. C.194.b.103; **123** The Cathedral Church of Bangor by Johannes Kip, 1708. Maps K.Top.46.44.e; **126** Arms of the East India Company. Foster 589; **127** Execution of Charles I, 1649. Crach.1.Tab.4.c.1.(18.); **128** Photograph by H.D. Girdwood, 1915. Photo 24/(29); **129** *Statua Nova*, 1488-89. Hargrave

MS 274, f.204v; **130** Letters patent of James I, 1610. Add MS 36932; **131** Magna Carta. Cotton MS Augustus II.106; **132** A View of the Cast Iron Bridge over the Severn at Coalbrook Dale in Shropshire, 1782. Maps K.Top.36.26.d; **134** 'The Dorchester Unionists imploring Mercy !!! of their king.' HS.74/1630; **135** James Gillray, 'True Reform of Parliament,-i.e.-Patriots lighting a revolutionary bonfire in New Palace Yard, 1809.' Maps C.18.d.5, (174); **138** *The Illustrated Sporting and Dramatic News*, 19 December 1896; **142** Egerton MS 3028, f.55r; **144** Cotton MS Tiberius B v, f.40v; **146** *Encomium Emmae reginae*, eleventh century. Add MS 33241, f.1v; **147** Braun and Hogenberg, *Civitates orbis terrarum*, 1600–23. Maps C.29.e.1 (3); **149** W. & D. Downey, *The Cabinet Portrait Gallery*, 1890–94. 10803.h.9; **152** *The Caricatures of Gillray*, 1818. 745.a.6; **154** *Dickinson's Comprehensive Pictures of the Great Exhibition of 1851, from the originals painted for ... Prince Albert, by Messrs. Nash, Haghe and Roberts*, 1854. Cup.652.c.33; **157** *see* **44**; **159** William Stukeley, *Verolanium Antiquum*, 1721. Maps K. Top.15.47; **161** Belfast, c.1770–1800. Maps K.Top.51.41.a; **163** Thomas Hobbes, *Leviathan; or the Matter, Form and Power of A Common Wealth Ecclesiastical and Civil*, 1651. 31.k.14; **164** Philosophical works and fragments mostly by Roger Bacon, late thirteenth century. Royal MS 7 F viii, f.129r; **166** Christopher Kelly, *History of the French Revolution, and of the Wars Produced by that Terrible Event...*, 1820–22. 9525.f.1; **167** John Thompson, *Street Incidents*, 1881. RB.23.b.6198; **171** Department of Transport, *The Highway Code*, 1968. PP/37/25a; **172** *The Tatler*, 17 December 1919. ZC.9.d.561; **174** 'East India Stocks', 1788. P1769; **177** *Annales monasterii sancti Albani*, late fifteenth century. Cotton MS Claudius D i, f.73; **180** The Sheares Bible, 1701–31. Add.62708, f.289v; **181** *The Booke of common praier, and administration of the Sacramentes, and other rites and Ceremonies in the Churche of Englande*, 1559. C.25.m.7; **185** Paul Cohen-Portheim, *The Spirit of London*, 1935. 010349.cc.39; **187** John Nash, *The Royal Pavilion at Brighton*, 1827. 557*.h.19; **190** *The Sketch*, Wedding number, 19 July 1893; **193** *see* **66**; **195** Ernest Shackleton, *The Antarctic Book*, 1909. C.118.g.6; **196** Olaudah Equiano, *The Interesting Narrative of the Life of Olaudah Equiano, or Gustavus Vassa, the African*, 1789. 1489.g.50; **197** Robert Southey, *The Life of Nelson*, 1884. 10818.b.2; **199** Mrs Rundell, *Modern Domestic Cookery*, 1851. 7950.b.42; **201** *The Women's Petition Against Coffee*, 1674. 1038.i.47.(1.); **203** James Gillray, 'Impeachment Ticket for the Trial of W-rr-n H-st-ngs Esqr', 1788. P3335; **206** View near Richmond, 1811. Maps K.Top.41.17.k; **207** G.W. Thornbury, *Old and New London*, 1863. X.802/203; **208** Mary Somerville, *Physical Geography*, 1858. 10002.bb.12; **209** *A Plan of the harbour and parts adjacent on the Isthmus of Darien where the Scotch Company settled*, 1743. Maps K.Top.124.24.2; **210** Seal of Robert II of Scotland, 1386.

Seal XLVII.52; **213** *see* **78**; **215** Joseph Gay, *The Lure of Venus: or a Harlot's progress.... Founded upon Mr Hogarth's six paintings*, 1733. 11661.b.27; **216(t)** Alfred Tennyson, *Poems*, 1857. 11647.e.59; **216(b)** Edward Elgar, *Enigma Variations*, 1899. Add MS 58004; **220** Lewis Carroll, 'Alice's Adventures Under Ground', 1862–64. Add MS 46700, f.88; **221** James Tolboys Wheeler, *The history of the imperial assemblage at Delhi, held on the 1st January, 1877, to celebrate the assumption of the title of Empress of India by Her Majesty the Queen*, 1877. 9057.i.1; **222** *Trial of William Burke and Helen M'Dougal, before the High Court of Justiciary, at Edinburgh ... December 24. 1828, for the murder of Margery Campbell, or Docherty....*, 1829. 1245.c.29; **223** Jane Sharp, *The Midwives Book, or the whole art of midwifry discovered*, 1671. 1177.b.19; **224** *Fun*, 18 August 1866. PP.5273.c; **229** *The Mirror of British Merchandise and Hindustani Pictorial News*, c.1892. 14119.f.37; **231** *Daily Sketch*, 1 October 1938; **232** *Illustrated Sporting & Dramatic News*, 1 August 1908; **235** Aphra Benn, *Poems upon Several Occasions*, 1687. 11626.bb.5; **237** Wenceslaus Hollar, Panorama of London, 1647. Maps 162.h.4; **238** *Dramatic characters or Different portraits of the English stage*, 1773. 11795.ee.41; **240** BBC Caribbean Service, *Going to Britain?*, 1959. 8296.bb.36; **241** *Geographia* 'All in One' Map Guide, 1951. 010349.n.71; **244** Luigi Federico Menabrea, *Sketch of the Analytical Engine invented by Charles Babbage ...*, 1843. C.T.192.(5.); **246** George Stephenson, *A Description of the Safety Lamp*, 1817. RB.23.a.29768; **253** Agatha Christie, *Murder at the Vicarage*, 1930. NN.17328.

Acknowledgements

Assembling a puzzle book such as this poses almost as many conundrums for the author as there are questions contained within it. I would like to thank all those who have assisted at the various stages of the book's production: in particular John Lee at the British Library, who commissioned the title and whose suggestions have been invaluable. I am also most grateful to Christopher Westhorp, the Project Editor, without whose careful editing and planning the book could never have come to completion, Sally Nicholls for her amazing work in sifting through the capacious archives of the British Library's collections to select images to illustrate the question-and-answer rounds, and Allan Somerville for his elegant design that so beautifully frames the questions. And finally to my family who patiently endured months of my trying out questions on them.

St Julian Ptochotrophium
fundatum a Galfrido Abbate
circa 1126.

Ecclesia St Stephani
ab Ulsino Abbate ædi-
ficata circa 930.

Via Romana

Porta Urbis Ciliqui.

Ecclesia Cœnobij ac Offa
Rege fundata fuit circa
793 è ruinis Verolamij.

Fons Sacr
Holywell

Ruderia
Cœnobij

Burgus
St Albani ubi
olim Sylva.

Helenshurst,
Anglorum Proto
martyris sub
Dioclesiano
morte clara

Porta Cœnobij

Ecclesia Cœnobij

Rome
land

Crux Memoriæ Eleonoræ
Reginæ uxoris Edwardi I positra

Campanil

Horti

Horti

Ne Censeretur Verolamium penitus
abolendum Vestigia Romanorum hic
ubique quondam a deterrimo quoq; illius
rudereibus fieri potest adumbrata, ædit.
Ioannis Vitæ, Ecclesiophani Societati
Antiquariæ Londinensi communicanti
ex tempore posuit   Wm Stukeley
1721.